Every man has room in his face
for all his ancestors.

Emerson

OLD GLORY

a pictorial report on the Grass Roots History Movement

and

The First Hometown History Primer

an America the Beautiful Fund book published in association with

 WARNER PAPERBACK LIBRARY

WARNER PAPERBACK LIBRARY EDITION
First printing: October 1973

Copyright © 1973 by The America the Beautiful Fund

All rights reserved.

This Warner Paperback Library Edition is published by
arrangement with The Amazing Life Games Company.

Warner Paperback Library is a division of Warner Books, Inc.,
315 Park Avenue South, New York, New York 10010.

 A Warner Communications Company

CONTENTS PART 1

They Live Neighbors

A sense of identity springs from knowing where you come from. It feels good to walk down the same streets your grandfather did, especially if there's something about those streets that still looks like it did back then. That's part of the reason people have taken to the streets, armed with paint scrapers, plumb bobs, old blueprints and memories: to rediscover their own town's origins.

I'll See You There

Do you remember cloakrooms, double desks, pot-bellied stoves, and the schoolteacher who cooked hot meals for her students? Can you recall the days when the railroad station was a town's door to the future and the entrance to the outside world? Have you forgotten that your ancestors built their theaters, opera houses and churches with their own hands? Townspeople who haven't forgotten are resurrecting these community meeting places in the same spirit of cooperation with which they were built. And they are using them to bring communities of individuals together.

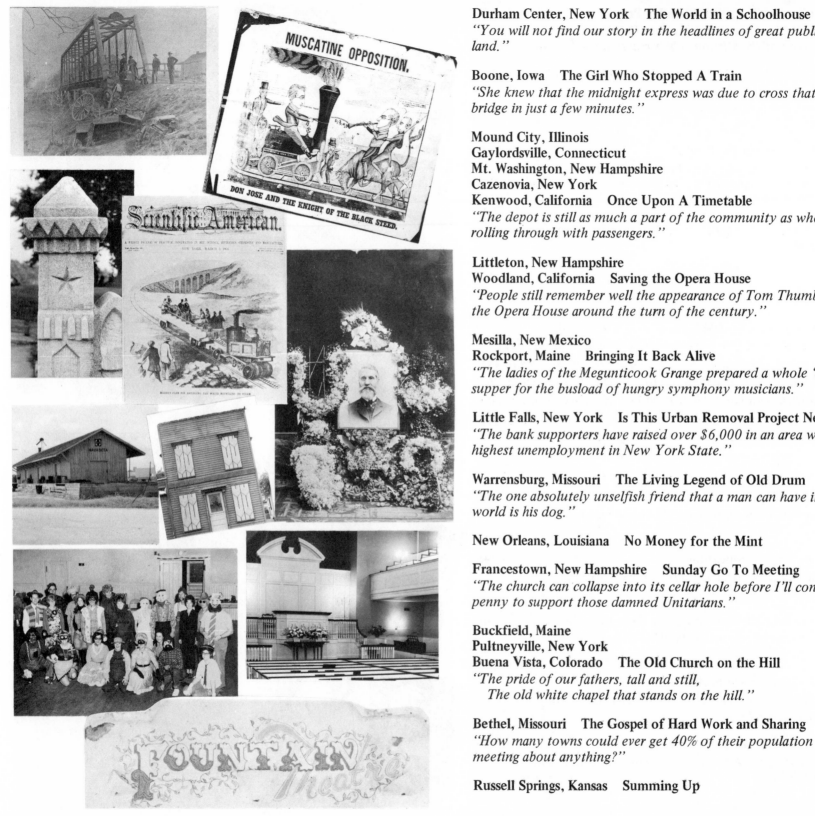

The Quiet Fields of my Fathers

Tilling the soil, building shelters, raising livestock; working with just two hands or with tools or with simple machines, alone or with neighbors; growing, harvesting, preparing, storing food. The farm has been home for millions of Americans, and farming has been, in general, a good life. Many people still feel close to the earth, and don't want to see the old life slip away.

The Home Fires Burning

Any house that's held the baby-crying, birthday-partying, banquet-feasting, affection-showering, grief-sharing and grandchild-spoiling of several generations of one family shouldn't have to face an old age empty of people. Old houses offer useful and attractive spaces for public activities, and they come already equipped with the spirit of people living and working together in harmony. Be it one room or a hundred, there's no place like a historic home.

Hands To Work

There was a time, not too long ago, when making things was a matter of life and death — instead of a leisure time activity. You only possessed what you could make with your hands, unless you were very rich or citified. There are some places where people are still making things, simply because they never stopped. In other places, people are re-learning traditional crafts from people whose own youngsters weren't interested — or they are digging craft items out of attics (or out of the earth) and re-inventing the techniques which once produced these tools and treasures of day-to-day life.

CONTENTS PART 2

1776 ☉ 1973

We Give You Time Capsules . . .

the History of the United States as seen through the eyes of a local history buff. Starting on page 15, and running at random intervals through this book, are 98 little boxes like this one, each containing history headlines and images representative of a two year period. Why? Well, for one thing, it's a way to pay our dues to History with a capital H. More importantly, it's good exercise once in a while to see history as it happened (in bits and pieces and at random) rather than all laid out like they do in books. For those of you who like your history straight, we recommend a non-stop reading.

The America the Beautiful Fund

is a non-profit foundation which is supported by public contributions for the purpose of encouraging grass roots heritage and environmental activities like the ones in this book. Through the Fund's *Rediscover America Program*, citizen groups all over the country are given technical assistance, and in some instances, "seed" grants for local history projects, once they can demonstrate a capacity to make effective use of assistance. For more information about how you can help the Fund (or vice versa), see page 191.

Paul Bruce Dowling   *executive director*
Nanine Bilski   *projects director*
Lesley Sudders   *administrative assistant*
Susanne Wellford   *administrative assistant*

Old Glory Staff

James Robertson   *editor*

Carolyn Robertson
Peder Jones
Queenie Taylor
James Bagnall   *associate editors*

Alden Robertson   *photographer*

Sadako McInerney
Gay Reineck
Jack Reineck
Jean Robertson
Jamie Jobb
Jane Davis
Sandra Bagnall

Photographs provided by other sources are listed with Acknowledgments on page 187.

MASON,
THE TIN MAN,
will be in BONAPARTE until
JULY 3d.
with a large stock of
Stamped and Hand-Made Ware.
DON'T FAIL
TO
Call and Get Prices.

Will be at the store of WIL-
LIAM WILLIAMS where there
can be found a well selected stock
of Family Groceries.

N. B. In case of the absence of
Harry Mason or Mr. Williams, we
have made arrangements so that
our customers can shove their
money under the door.

The town hall had never looked finer. The platform at the end of it was backed by a shouly draping of flags. At intervals along the walls were festoons of flags. The gallery fronts were clothed in flags. The supporting columns were swathed in flags.

W. HERRICK AV. ANY SATURDAY. 1900-1910

A chewing gum party will be given at high noon at Nunnally's.

Our dinner was a success, but that is not to be wondered at. Every woman for miles around contributed.

There is much to be learned in a country store. *(P.T. Barnum)*

We say the cows laid out Boston.
Well, there are worse surveyors.
(Ralph Waldo Emerson)

WHAT CHESTER MAKES MAKES CHESTER. *(Sign outside Chester, Pennsylvania)*

THEY LIVE NEIGHBORS

A patch of flowers in a new country signifies kind people, clean beds and good bread. *(Henry Ward Beecher, 1887)*

America is a nation of home towns.

Neighbors, you stand related unto one another; and you should be full of devices, that all the neighbours may have cause to be glad of your being in the neighbourhood. (Cotton Mather, Essay to the Good)

Cuero: Where America Talks Turkey.

★ Cuero, Texas
The Town That Remembered ★

Does your town have municipal amnesia? The ailment is common to small towns, neighborhoods — anywhere people take their past, their surroundings (and themselves) for granted. Cuero, Texas, had it, but they found a cure.

"The Cuero Turkey Trot is one of the world's unique celebrations. About the turn of the century, practically everyone in the Cuero area kept a flock of turkeys. With an ever-expanding market developing for these large birds, Cuero's first poultry processing plant was established in 1908.

"At that time, everyone drove the turkeys to market, much like the cattle drives. Soon individual farmers began to buy the fowls produced by their neighbors, and they would drive the flocks to market en masse. They came by the hundreds and soon the thousands.

"Word of mouth spread the fame of these drives and each year saw more and more out-of-towners coming to Cuero, Turkey Capital of the World.

"In 1912, the name 'Turkey Trot' was selected to commemorate this spectacle, and a fair and king-size parade and celebration began."

Cuero itself wasn't much to look at. In the space under the awnings over the main street, it was pretty much the same as any other small Texas town. The windows had the usual crowded displays. Most of the storefronts were veneers —

early post-war modern — plastic and aluminum laid up over the original stone and brick. And most people didn't pay too much attention — they hardly noticed the changes.

But Sharon Steen looked up. Above the awnings and plastic signs she discovered what Cuero used to look like. She saw the tops of the storefronts. The wonderful stone and brick buildings of the eighties and nineties. And she asked herself: "Why are such good buildings so covered up with junk?" That did it.

What followed was a Texas tornado in the form of Sharon Steen and anyone she could entice or bully into helping her. During most of 1972 they worked to restore the Main Street for the town's 100th anniversary and the new and improved Turkey Trot.

Though they started with Main Street, what happened in Cuero went much deeper than painting storefronts. Because everyone was invited to become a part of it, the Cuero project has given the whole town a new lease on life. The people who live there are seeing their town in a new way, and are placing new value on things they had taken for granted.

At the very beginning, Sharon Steen and her friends did two things that turned out to be absolutely right. First: Reverend Rogers McLane, an amateur photographer, began prowling attics looking for old photos of Cuero. What he found amazed townfolk. He carefully copied all the old pictures he could find onto slides and put them together with music and a narration. The resulting show got the whole town talking about what it used to be like in Cuero. That was important.

Here are two "after" pictures. Above is one of the town's barbers standing in front of his shop, the very first one to be completed. The chair is from his own collection. Down the street a bit, is another completed storefront (left) in front of which stands Sharon Steen with her husband Lias. If Sharon looks pleased with herself, she has every right to be.

More Than Skin Deep

Once the search for Cuero's past was underway, townspeople began to look at things a little differently. Behind modern cosmetic facades they found store interiors that looked almost as old as the buildings. Soon, merchants who had stubbornly resisted modernizing were finding their "old-timey" looks paying off.

Second: Sharon Steen put together committees. She didn't ask for volunteers. A meeting was called. "After the meeting I got up and said, 'all right now, the artists committee is . . . ' and I just read off the names. And do you know, not one of them let me down."

The following announcement was circulated to merchants in town:

To: Tenants & Building Owners of Down Town Cuero

From: Restoration Committee

Exciting things are being planned for down town Cuero. As any 100 year old lady would, she needs a face lift - and the Chamber of Commerce's Down Town Restoration Committee is formulating a master plan for just this purpose.

Briefly, for those of you who have not heard about this project, let's touch on the why's, what's, when's, who's, etc.

Why? _____ In the past few years there has been an awakening of interest in old buildings. Many cities are spending vast sums of money to build what we have here. We could attract tourists state wide to our town, but more important this area has become run down with more empty buildings appearing all the time. Take a close look at this area and you will find some appalling sights. If something isn't done it will become impossible to attract new tenants or owners in the future.

Who? _____ This committee is composed of some 30 interested citizens of Cuero (some tenants & owners among them) who have talked of a coordinated plan for years, and are willing to give their time and talents for this effort. One town that hired a firm to do this for them spent $9,000 for the service.

What _____ do we mean by restoration? The proposals do not call for expensive remodeling work. Most of the goal will be achieved by cleaning, painting, and restoring trim to show off the architectural highlights of the buildings. Much of the unattractiveness is caused now by paint colors that do not blend, sagging awnings, and unattractive signs that add nothing to the natural beauty of the buildings and do little to help promote business.

How? _____ Local artists are preparing sketches of each building minus unattractive signs, dirty junky windows, peeling paint, etc.; the color committee will coordinate colors to paint trim, suggest sandblasting & repairs where needed; materials committee is preparing estimates on material & labor; and landscaping, signs, streets, & alleys, are being gone over carefully. Don't be surprised if you see people peering in all your windows:

When? _____ As this is Centennial and Turkey Trot year we hope as much as possible can be done by then but this project is for posterity not just October, 1972.

Much of this you may have already heard or read about and wondered why you haven't been contacted sooner. The committee felt that you would want to see the completed coordinated plan before you made up your minds to participate. We plan in the very near future to hold a general presentation for you. We hope you will make every effort to attend this meeting or send us a representative. I think you'll be very pleased and surprised with what we have to show you. As alot of hard work has gone into this project, We ask that you give us a chance to show it to you.

One owner, Joe Reuss, because of his civic pride, as well as hoping to rent his old drug store building asked for a sketch the week this committee was formed, and has already started work on it. Ten others have indicated they are ready to go to work on their buildings.

We know you too are proud of our "grand old lady, Cuero" and want to be a part of her fresh look.

Sincerely,
Sharon Steen
Chairman- Restoration Committee

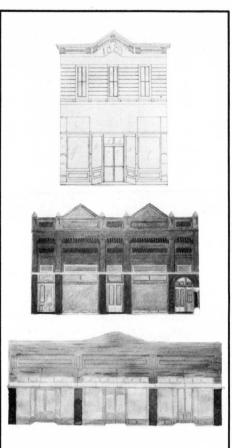

Art for Cuero's Sake

The artists committee was made up of anyone in Cuero who wanted to help by making renderings of what the downtown buildings would look like after renovation. Volunteers ranged from grammar school students to high school drafting students to an eighty year old great-grandmother water-colorist.

The Cuero Youth Corps
"The high school coaches were anxious to have something for their boys to do after school to keep them in shape, so one coach organized the Youth Corps. These boys are doing all the hardest work, like scraping old paint. The owners pay them $1.75 an hour and the coach who supervises them gets $2 an hour. We feel this is our answer to Job Corps. We are providing work for the youth of our community who at 15 and 16 years old can't get jobs. They get some money and a chance to do a service for the community, as well as keeping busy and fit."

Her committee of volunteer artists made colored drawings of what each building would look like when restored to its original condition. Her committee of estimators were responsible for getting information on costs. (They tried to make the changes as simple and inexpensive as possible — sometimes only a matter of painting to accentuate the building design.)

Originally Mrs Steen and her friends had planned to hold a big meeting and present their plans to all the merchants and building owners at once. But that never happened. As is often the case with volunteer efforts, it didn't all get done in time. Instead, individuals were assigned to take their work around to each owner. Sharon thinks they got better results that way, because committee members were assigned to merchants they knew best.

Sharon and her workers used a "take-me-or-shoot-me" approach with owners. They walked into each place of business prepared to take nothing but yes for an answer. They had done their homework. The merchants were impressed by the work that had been done and the enthusiasm of the volunteers. If a merchant didn't like the colors suggested, he was urged to choose his own. Often the committee was delighted to find owners willing to go even further than the recommendations. Those who couldn't afford much expense were encouraged to use the Cuero Youth Corps who provided a work force organized just for the purpose.

On October 20-23, 1972, the annual Turkey Trot and Centennial took place in the "new Cuero." Sharon Steen described it in a letter:

" . . . Turkey Trot and Centennial was a rousing success even though the weather went from hot (85 degrees) to cold (50 degrees) to rainy (3 inches in one day!). Even had a small tornado that blew the pageant stage down the day of the big show. But as you've learned, small town people are something else and we all banded together and put it up again in 2 hours.

"All of the downtown stores had displays of old items in their windows — from farm tools to fine furniture. And I'm so pleased to tell you that by October 20th we had 29 buildings fixed up in the downtown area. It is so pretty and I'm so proud of our town. We are going on to get the rest of the owners to do their buildings and to develop our city park, new 'old fashion' light standards, etc., as we plan to stage the mall idea downtown every year. It was a

Part way along in the Cuero project, a local sign painter turned up two old sign painter's style-books and asked the Restoration Committee if they thought he should approach merchants to do painted signs to replace the neon and plastic that was coming down. This is one of many instances in which the imagination of town residents contributed to the Cuero project's success.

big success with food booths, street dances (om-pah-pah and western), gun fighters, turkey races, dress contests, beard contest, etc. The brass band performed like champs and even the leader (barber) said, 'they did wery vell!!' I couldn't write about all this without saying that the parade was the best! Of course everyone has bands, floats, etc., but we are the only place in the world that 'trots turkeys' down the street. The 1500 range turkeys raised just for this event did beautifully.

"... It made me feel real good to know that I'm part of a vast and growing brotherhood of people who are trying in our own small way to preserve the good and meaningful things of our country. I spent a week in Houston last week and I truly feel sorry for people who must live there all the time. At a cocktail party some old high school friends said, 'how can you stand living in a hick town?' I just laughed and said, 'well — let's see — how can I stand being able to see the stars and moon at night and sun at day; or knowing my children can walk to town safely; or smile and speak to everyone you pass; or hear piano music from a barber shop; or 25-cent beer in a quaint old bar — Man — I can stand it fine!!' "

Sincerely,

Sharon Steen

If a town is essentially the sum of what its people care for and believe in, Cuero, Texas, won't have to worry about its next 100 years. The people of Cuero have discovered that it isn't what color the paint is that counts — it's whether you care enough to pick up a brush in the first place.

Sharon Steen likes to tell about the town she visited that hired an architect to tell them what should be done and had to pay $9000 for the advice. Then she smiles and tells you that her budget was $35 and there was a little left over.

The Boys in the Band. These gents stopped what they were doing one sweltering morning and gave up a lunch break so this picture could be taken. Bennie Prause, left, is the director of the Cuero Municipal Band. The members are Harold Dreyer and Ed Davidson — clarinet; Bill Martin and Charles Stone — trumpet; Jimmy Prause — snare drum; A. E. Marquis — tuba; Ray Voelkel — bass drum; and Walter Brown McClung — Sousaphone.

Two Cuero Institutions: Bandstand and Band
The Plaque next to the bandstand reads: "This bandstand, successor to earlier ones in Cuero, is a replica of the first one erected in this park used for concerts, picnics, bazaars, ice cream socials and political rallies. Cuero musicians won renown as the official band for the internationally famous Turkey Trot founded in 1912 and opened that year with a parade led by Governor Colquitt."
Someone in town found an old photograph of the original town band and now there is talk about having town seamstresses use that picture to remake the original uniforms for the gentlemen you see here.

What does your town's name mean?

Lester Giese says: " 'Cuero' is a Spanish word meaning rawhide or leather. When they were moving cattle across the country, many were drowned in the quicksand near the present site of Cuero and the only thing they could save off the drowned cattle was the hide. It became a place where a lot of skinning and tanning was done."

Fort Benton, Montana

The Birthplace of Montana Holds Its Own

People in Fort Benton, Montana, call their city *The Birthplace of Montana*, **and they have a seventeen year old Community Improvement Association that considers keeping the city's heritage alive to be permanent top-priority. They think their town was maybe the greatest freighting center in the whole Northwestern United States during the 1860's and 1870's — the pioneer years. And when you're number one, isn't it smarter to hold on to what you've got than throw it away and start over again?**

Fort Benton has had a habit over the years of re-using old buildings. (The 1883 Firehouse is the Jaycees meeting hall, the 1882 Murphy Neel building is a restaurant, the 1883 Davidson-Moffat Factory building now houses the town newspaper — the *River Press* — and structures such as the 1884 river ferry station have become private residences.) What the Community Improvement Association does is parcel out money for renovation work — and direct volunteer labor — so enterprises can afford to stay in these great structures. Joel Overholser, who is a long-time Association member (also the *River Press* editor and a prolific history writer), describes the first CIA projects:

"Bill Johnstone, Fort Benton native and superintendent of schools, currently vice president for administration at Montana State University in Bozeman, was prime mover in the organization of the Fort Benton CIA in 1956. Bill had a Fort Benton museum as a primary goal. CIA raised $4,216 in 1957, enough to finance a 20 x 70 concrete block building. With virtually all labor donated, FFA boys did the footing and cement floor work, local men roofing and finishing, the Fort Benton museum came into existence in time to open in 1958.

A museum committee of five, again headed by Bill Johnstone, planned the layout of twenty displays of Fort Benton's colorful history.

"For the interior, several dormant funds, including a $4,500 Centennial fund dating to 1946, were raised, about $5,500 in all. Local school teachers provided art work, an electrician the wiring, a school class a diorama, dozens of local men and women with various talents contributed time and labor, among them Johnstone as chief carpenter. CIA, as sponsor, has since underwritten the small deficits annually. The museum drew 21,290 visitors in 1972. It is open in warm weather months. An addition in 1964 doubled its size."

The CIA tries to attend to all community needs, and they have a new development plan that would be ambitious for a city fifty times the size of Fort Benton. Jon West and current CIA President Ken Smith are talking up a recreational and historical park complex to occupy six blocks near the river — featuring the blockhouse from the original military Fort Benton (1850) which still stands, a refabrication of other Fort buildings, a community swimming pool, tennis courts, a restaurant on a floating riverboat, renovation of a dozen "steamboat-days buildings" and more. Sounds a bit crazy, maybe, but in a town that gets ready for tomorrow by thinking about yesterday, you can never tell.

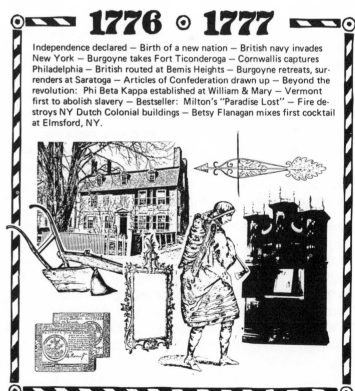

1776 ⊙ 1777

Independence declared — Birth of a new nation — British navy invades New York — Burgoyne takes Fort Ticonderoga — Cornwallis captures Philadelphia — British routed at Bemis Heights — Burgoyne retreats, surrenders at Saratoga — Articles of Confederation drawn up — Beyond the revolution: Phi Beta Kappa established at William & Mary — Vermont first to abolish slavery — Bestseller: Milton's "Paradise Lost" — Fire destroys NY Dutch Colonial buildings — Betsy Flanagan mixes first cocktail at Elmsford, NY.

Bonaparte, Iowa, doesn't have municipal amnesia. The people in this small river town know their town hasn't changed much since the turn of the century. Only a few of the old brick buildings have gotten covered up because the post-War trend to modernize America missed Bonaparte completely.

The trouble is that not everyone in Bonaparte is sure they *want* an old town. Instead of a fresh coat of paint, some residents would rather give their town a new suit of tin, or knock it down and start over.

Fortunately, Bonaparte is in Van Buren County, an area with strong feelings for history. And those feelings are what saved one of Bonaparte's oldest buildings. Mary Warner, Dorothy Kerr, Charles Easter and other townspeople formed the Bonaparte Historical Association when they heard that the Aunty Green Hotel was scheduled for demolition. Evidently a lot of other people had good feelings about the hotel — and about a group that would work to save it — because now over 180 of Bonaparte's 500 residents are members of the Association — Bonaparte's small army of volunteers.

And the future for Bonaparte? It's uncertain. Two forces are pushing for opposite kinds of change here as in many small towns. Some want to modernize, others to restore. Right now, things seem weighted in favor of the restorers: the local historical society is large and has made a good start. It might be that this small army of volunteers will be able to hold onto every remaining bit of the town that their great-great grandfathers built for them.

Aunty Green Slept Here

There were fancier hotels in town. But this was where workingmen stayed in the late 1850's. That was when the railroad came to Bonaparte. Before that it was a family residence, built around 1844 by John Green for his wife, known later as Aunty Green. After it was converted to a hotel, salesmen used to put up there. There was a big hoist on the upstairs porch, and a trapdoor that made it easy to get the trunks of samples up and down. Aunty Green died in 1891 and is buried up on the hill. In 1971, the owner of the property was going to tear it down. He thought it was an eyesore. Mary Warner and her friends convinced him to give it to the county historical society, and he did. The Bonaparte Historical Association has been given the responsibility for restoration and re-use. Aside from a seed grant from the America the Beautiful Fund, it is all being done with local money and volunteer labor.

1778 ● 1779

Washington at Valley Forge — Treaty of Alliance: France recognizes "United States" — British evacuate Philadelphia — Tories-Indians massacre Pennsylvanians — Americans abandon Rhode Island — British take Savannah, Brier Creek — Spain enters war against British — Congress draws up peace terms — Famous last words: "I have not yet begun to fight" John Paul Jones in Bonhomme Richard-HMS Serapis battle — In vogue: "Quarter racing" horses sprint in Virginia.

"They ought to tear all them old buildings right down to the ground."
— a Bonaparte resident

Ben Hendricks is crazy to save the last remaining lock on the Des Moines River. For him, it is a symbol of the days when big boats with names like "Globe," "Julia Dean," "Time and Tide," "Colonel Morgan," and "Lovilla" passed along next to the town's main street. Hendricks has put together a slide show of old time Bonaparte photographs. He serves up this bit of history along with meals in his restaurant.

Meek Bros.' Pants Factory.

The above picture was taken last summer at the time we acquired the County Green building.

We put on a new roof, replaced the windows, replaced brick on the west wall which were blown out during a storm, also repaired a bulge in the upper half of the east wall.

We removed the island with the light post & have done extensive clean up work to the building & the grounds.

We plan to remove the cement block building on the west this summer.

Most pictures taken in Bonaparte, 1973, look just like Bonaparte, 1893. In 1893, the big building (right) housed the Meek Brothers Pants factory. Now it's occupied by the Fairfield Glove Company.

STREET FAIR

MEEK BROTHERS PROPRIETORS OF Bonaparte Woolen Mills AND PANTS FACTORY.
ESTABLISHED 1837
Bonaparte, Iowa.

Oberlin Chautauqua 1909.

Anyone over thirty who grew up on a farm must have memories of going to town — talking, visiting, in no particular hurry to conclude business matters — or of those special times, when every farm family from all around came into town, for a wedding or a revival meeting or a traveling festival, and everybody was busy socializing.

People in Oberlin couldn't stand to see their town fade away with the passing of family farms. Rather than sit around being wistful about how good living in Oberlin used to be, some of the people who still live there have gone to work to make Oberlin that much fun again.

The Sappa Valley Arts League, under the leadership of Mrs Neva Aase, has people busy working on history-oriented painting and literature projects all year 'round. The Arts League shares quarters with Oberlin's "Last Indian Raid Museum"; if one of the Arts League members is painting a harvest scene from memory, and can't quite picture what the old bailing machines looked like, the museum has photographs — and Mrs Kathleen Claar, the curator, probably knows who in the area still has one sitting out back.

And everybody comes into town for the Mini-Sapa Jubilee. The Sappa Valley Arts League hooks a good portion of the county into helping with preparations. The Jubilee gives folks an opportunity to show off skills from pioneer days — or learn them, if their generation missed out — like sod-house building.

You don't have to preserve original buildings in order to keep the history of a town alive. In fact, in Oberlin, you couldn't do that, because the original buildings were all made of sod, and washed into the prairie long ago. But you can preserve the spirit and traditions which built Oberlin in the first place — which may be the best part of living in Oberlin.

★★★★★★★★★★★★★★★★★★★★★★★★

Oberlin, Kansas
That Old Pioneer Spirit

★★★★★★★★★★★★★★★★★★★★★★★★

DECATUR CO. KANSAS

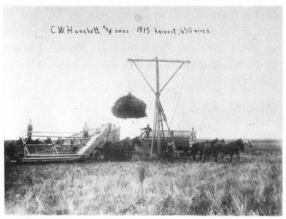

C.W. Hanchett & sons 1915 harvest, 650 acres.

COWCHIPS

Dad would harness up the horses
To the wagon large and strong
Then call to all of us children
Who had to go along.

We always seemed quite ready
And never tried to shirk
For Father said it did kids good
To do a little work.

Now to find the pasture
Where the chips by millions lay
We would toss them in the wagon
To save for winters day.

"Look out, Elsie, that's a wet one,
Better leave it lay
And we will come and get it
On another sunny day."

Well, soon we took our trophies home
And stacked them firm and neat
Assured that this would be enough
To supply our winters heat.

We used them in the cook stove
And they made the heater glow
Oh, those cowchips did a lot of good
When cash and fuel were low.

The Sappa Valley Arts League encourages a mixture of history and the arts. The poem to the right is both earthy and straight-forward — dealing with the historic problem of how to keep the home fires burning on a treeless plain. It is from a collection by Mrs Frances Knitig entitled **Short Grass Saga.** *Below, sculptor Pete Felten produced his "pioneer family" in place on Main Street while the whole town watched. Arts League instructor Darrell Elliott assists an elderly resident with a painting from childhood memory.*

"The small town is fighting for survival. There is some of the old pioneer spirit being revived here because people are beginning to think their town may die. They care now. . . . Nobody can survive on one tract and 200 acres of wheat." — *Mrs Duane Aase, president, Sappa Valley Arts League*

Good (John Simonsson) triumphs over evil (Dr Phil Lauber) while Little Nell (Karen Aten) looks on — in a production of "He Ain't Done Right by Nell." Capacity audiences loved it and demanded more — just as their grandparents did in earlier days. One of the many traditional attractions which make up the Mini-Sapa Jubilee held in Oberlin at the end of September. Other activities include antique shows, old-time band music, an art show, and sod house-building.

How To Build A Sod House

Just as all stage coaches and covered wagons were not made after one pattern, neither were sod houses. However, this is an effort to tell, step by step, how the old Soddies were built. While this deals with the early day soddies, the same methods would be used today, substituting new materials for floors, roofs and door and window casings. The advantages of sod houses were that the material was at hand (it was the only thing available) and they were warm in winter and cool in summer. Added to this, they were fire-proof.

The first step in the building of a sod house would naturally be to locate the desired spot, determine the size of the house and roughly estimate the needed supply of sod. Next would be to locate a tract of virgin Blue stem grass or second choice would be buffalo grass. It is the matted roots which act as binders and hold the sod together. To prevent crumbling, the sod should be neither too dry nor too wet to handle.

The sod cutting plow would be set to the desired depth, which is three to four inches. The sod was cut with a regular sod turning plow or by a home-made sod cutter. The strips of sod were cut from one to two feet in width, depending upon the desired thickness of the walls. Using sharp spades or sod cutting knives, the strips of sod were then cut into convenient lengths to be handled, usually two to three feet in length.

While these bricks of sod were curing, other needed material was hauled to the building site. For the ridge pole, a tree or pole the length of the house was needed; however, if there were a dividing wall and it was impossible to find a pole long enough, two might be used. Besides the ridge pole, shorter poles and smaller in girth were used. These were placed two to three feet apart, from the walls to the ridge pole.

Next the building was outlined with a layer of sod, grass down, making sure the corners were true. A three foot space was left for the door. As each layer of sod was placed brick fashion, the joints of each layer midway to that of the previous layer, remembering to place the grass side down, the walls were built to about four feet. It is important to keep the walls straight and true and this end was accomplished by using a plumb line, which in the early days was usually a heavy bolt attached to a string.

As the walls went up, the sod was carefully checked for loose soil or weeds with shallow roots and this soil, along with that shaved from the interior of the walls, was used to fill in the cracks between the sod brick ends. If clay soil was available, this made for a more water tight seal.

Now it was time to consider the windows. Split saplings from five to seven inches in thickness were used, flat side out for both the door and window lintels, usually five to six feet in length. This was for added strength. Holes were bored in the saplings and wooden pegs, ten to twelve inches long were driven into the sod walls. Saplings were also used for the window casings and sills. The windows were set well to the outside of the wall, resulting in deep windows which were ideal places for house plants when completed. For the most part, one sash windows were used.

The sod walls were built to approximately seven and a half feet and the gables at each end were raised two feet above the walls, giving the desired roof fall. The tops of the gables were notched to hold the ridge pole. The shorter and smaller poles or saplings were then fitted into notches in the walls and secured to the ridge pole. When lumber was not available, and it seldom was, fine willows, prairie hay, sunflower or corn stalks, whatever material was at hand, was placed across these smaller poles or rafters, woven together any way, a layer of sod, cut the same depth as the walls, was placed on top of this. Again remembering to place it grass down. Whenever possible, clay dirt was sprinkled over the roof, making for a tighter seal. Native plants such as cacti, which thrives in dry weather, were encouraged to grow on the roofs, preventing washing away of the soil when the rains came. Also saplings were placed at the outer edge of the roof, both ends and sides to hold the sod in place. If lumber and tar paper were available, these made for a longer lasting and much more satisfactory roof.

One problem to the housewife when lumber was not available for the roof, not only did the dirt sift down but occasionally spiders, worms and other insects, even mud when it rained. To prevent this happening, housewives tacked sheets or blankets above the most vulnerable places, like the table and the beds. This worked so well that as soon as possible, entire ceilings were covered with muslin. The drawback here was that it would become so soiled that it had to be taken down once a year or perhaps more often, lengths ripped apart, washed, sewed back together and put back upon the ceilings. One advantage, those early day citizens could always take their ceilings with them if they moved.

Chimneys were merely holes cut in the roof, with the stove pipe sticking out and a piece of tin fitted around it to prevent leaking and also to prevent a fire hazard. For the floors a sharp spade was used to remove all grass down to the bare soil. Occasionally coarse table or stock salt was scattered over the floor and the whole kept damp. In a short time the floors became hard and smooth, almost like cement. For those who could afford hand loomed carpet, it was laid wall to wall, over a fat layer of clean straw. This like the muslin ceilings had to be taken up each year, taken apart at the seams, labourishly washed in a tub, resewed and laid over a fresh layer of straw.

A sod house should stand at least six months before plastering the inside walls. This allows for settling of the sod walls and prevents future cracks in the plaster. When the time came to plaster the walls, they were smoothed down with a sharp spade, then dampened well to prevent the dry sod from absorbing the moisture from the plaster. The plaster consisted of native clay soil mixed with a little sand. Walls were then given a final finish of white wash made from native lime and water. Some used milk which was more effective than water. This could be tinted in various ways and colors but for the most part, it was left white. If the builder could accumulate enough old newspapers, the walls were often papered with these, which made for good reading for the family, but also for faulty posture, since the newspapers were put on every which way.

This is back-tracking a bit but before the walls were plastered, the deep window recesses were rounded off which not only made them easier to plaster but more attractive. Curtains for sod houses were usually fashioned from newspapers or wrapping paper from the grocery stores, cut in attractive designs.

A well built sod house, given a minimum of care, would last for many a year and they could always have an added wing. Nature provided the insulating material needed. If good sod could still be found, no doubt people would still be building sod houses. Possibly the nicest thing about the sod house era, they seldom had a mortgage placed upon them.

This is Kathleen Claar who reigns over The Last Indian Raid in Kansas Museum, which is both a mouthful and a fine community museum. She also wrote the article on this page, and the poem below. All the old photographs on this and the previous two pages are from her collections.

There wasn't any architect,
No banker made a loan,
To solve their housing problem
They were strictly on their own
They didn't sign a mortgage
And they didn't own a lot;
They stopped their covered wagon
At a likely looking spot.

Only sod to build their houses,
Hard packed earth their floors.
Windows few and far between
And hand made were their doors.
No timber trees, no lumber mills
Not even native stone;
But when at last they had them done
A home to call their own.

No mansion, but a sturdy house
Their own strong hands had made
It stood on fertile acres
That had never been surveyed.
No warranty, no abstract fee
No red tape legal fuss;
They just came out and built the west
And left all that to us.

"I feel like I've lost my best friend somehow," said the circuit court judge when the Court House burned. His offices had been inside. Everyone in Fincastle knew what he meant, because a lot of what Fincastle meant to its residents was symbolized in the beautiful building.

Fincastle is a small Virginia town with but four hundred residents — but what Fincastle lacks in numbers, it makes up for in energy and determination. The flagstone-lined streets pass an incredible variety of one and two century old buildings: no less than fifty log houses, several Gothic churches (one built in 1771), many attractive antebellum mansions, an old brick blacksmith's shop and an imposing Court House built in 1818 in a Jefferson "provincial Greek Revival" design. The spire and belfry of the Court House tower over Fincastle's venerable downtown area. Fincastle's four hundred have taken it upon themselves to save their whole town as a living link with Colonial America.

Historic Fincastle, Inc., the local society dedicated to preserving the architectural heritage of the town, has seen its share of difficulties. In 1970, just when a town-wide preservation push was beginning to happen, the old Court House burned, leaving a burnt-out shell haunting Main Street. From 1970 to 1972, the town looked like the Yankees or the Tories had just marched through. Historic Fincastle — led by Mrs Hellen Caldwell — convinced nay-sayers to let the town raise the money for rebuilding the landmark, instead of sweeping it away in favor of a parking lot. The fund raising was successful, and now the Court House stands as tall as ever.

Its imposing presence is a constant inspiration to the little town as residents work diligently to save it all — even the intricate flagstone paths — from falling into disrepair. In Fincastle, little details and great landmarks are both considered important to preserving life as it used to be; and the result is a floor-to-ceiling approach that is working.

Steeples are symbolic of Fincastle, Virginia, since from any vantage point, in the vicinity of the village, the steeples of the churches and Court House rise majestically above all other buildings, and in 1770 when land was set aside for the Court House, land was also set aside for the Church.

HISTORIC FINCASTLE, INC.

1780 ⊙ 1781

Charleston falls — New Jersey invaded — Mutiny at Washington's winter camp — Benedict Arnold found guilty — British beaten at King's Mountain, Cowpens — Standoff at Guilford Court House — Cornwallis returns to Virginia — Washington, Lafayette surround Yorktown — Cornwallis surrenders — Revolution virtually over — Beyond the war: Pennsylvania abolishes slavery — Articles become first federal constitution — Bank of North America established — First town clock ticks in New York — Estimated US population: 2,781,000.

What happens when the traditions of a small town are threatened by the increasing urbanization moving in from a neighboring city? In Social Circle, Georgia, that threat was successfully overcome by a festival which celebrated the town's unique character. "A Day in Social Circle" sparked renewed interest in the town's past and inspired a plan for the renovation of its downtown — a safeguard of its future.

College professor Glenn Pelham, his designer wife Susan, and their neighbors Larry Farmer, Louise Trotter, Roy Malcolm and a few others organized the "Day in Social Circle," and everybody in town prepared for it by initiating a massive cleanup campaign. They were so pleased with the response that they decided to continue the civic enterprise. Glenn and Susan went to work on the crest of this community interest, and about a month after the festival they came up with Project One.

Glenn says: "You have to educate people to the fact that what they have grown up with can be of terrific value. 'A Day in Social Circle' helped to do that, and Project One will continue the effort. It is a comprehensive plan for the restoration of Social Circle. It starts by forming an Identification Society, appointing a landscape commission to try to accent the beauty we have, by identifying older residences and buildings, by putting a parkway down the middle of the main street, by planting memorial trees along the sidewalk, running back the old gas lights that used to be here. We've already gotten a good response. The president of the bank said it shall be done to a 'T'. The powers that be liked it, and so did the community.

"Social Circle has a population of less than two thousand. 'A Day in Social Circle' was the first festival in our history that helped townspeople realize what a great place it is to live and how important it is to preserve its identity. We were becoming a bedroom for Atlanta. That won't do. We need a community effort to enlist the help of the entire town." Something has already happened in Social Circle in this direction, and there is more to come. Social Circle is on its way.

"How odd it seemed that five or six generations of a family could live and die within the radius of a few miles. It was a pleasure that everywhere you went in Social Circle people knew who you were and who your mother and grandmother were and remembered exactly how each one looked coming down the aisle on her wedding day."

The legend of Social Circle goes like this. "A group of men, meeting at the crossroads between four different commercial centers, were sitting around the well having their usual drink. Some claim it was a Saturday night and a bonfire was nearby. A stranger approached, was greatly surprised at such hospitality, and exclaimed, 'This is surely a social circle.' From that time until the present, the name of the village has remained Social Circle."

NORTH   EAST ELEVATION   SCALE 1/8" = 1'-0"

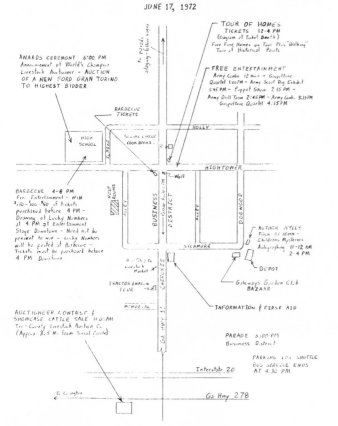

WELCOME TO
A DAY IN SOCIAL CIRCLE
JUNE 17, 1972

"But one of the most interesting things to us has been perhaps the subtlest of all things and that is, people have never known the ages of their houses. And yet when the report book (for Project One) was first published, a lot of the older people in town were just beseiged, we understand, by other people who said, 'tell me what you know about the beginning of the houses'."

"Social Circle isn't a place you stay away from for long. So every summer we went back . . . to get a good watermelon daddy would say. You can tell by the way it thumps if it's a Georgia melon . . . and to get a fresh peach mother would say. She could just taste those peaches all the way from Miami to Social Circle. She could just taste them."

What started as a community-wide cleanup for the town's open house (above) has turned into a home-grown plan for the preservation of Social Circle's old-time southern character. The street elevations (below) are taken from Project One which the town's history buffs drew up to keep Social Circle from being gobbled up by nearby Atlanta.

NOTE: BUILDING SIZES APPROXIMATED

WEST ELEVATION   SCALE 1/8" = 1'-0"   NORTH

**What happens to a town when its one industry
closes down? Empty streets, creaking doors and
wind whistling down forgotten alleys? Not in
Pocahontas. People there have an idea that may
bring enough visitors into town to keep it alive.
They're not doing anything new — in fact,
Historic Pocahontas, Inc., is doing everything old.
They've discovered that the town's most valuable
natural resource just might be its gaudy coal
mining past.**

Pocahontas grew around Jordan Nelson's coal patch — a
mine that proved to have the largest seam of high-quality
bituminous coal the world has ever seen. From 1874 until
1952, it provided 44 million tons of premium Original
Pocahontas coal for a growing industrial nation.

After the mine closed down, the town began to die. There
was no work, and people drifted away. The vacated
buildings deteriorated. Nobody saw much hope, either,
because Pocahontas — in an isolated mountain valley —
seemed unsuited for anything but coal mining.

Around 1970 the slow death met some opposition. Old-
time residents like Mrs Edna Drosick and her husband (a
retired coal miner), and a newcomer, Carol Perfin, wife of
a high school teacher, decided that the town wasn't so
poor that it had to let itself fall to pieces; and they and
some neighbors formed Historic Pocahontas, Incorporated.

It didn't take much talking to get other residents to think
about history: everybody in town played a part in
Pocahontas' big coal mine. And nobody had to look very
hard to see how much of yesterday was still there: except
for one cinderblock laundromat and two quonset huts, the
town is pretty much unspoiled nineteenth century.

Pocahontas was a hard drinking town. Estimates put the number of saloons between 23 and 65, and they all did a land-office trade. Legend has it that men used to come to Pocahontas from surrounding dry counties by the trainload and sop up so much of the spirits that saloon-keepers used to rake the money into bushel baskets. In the photo below, women and children campaign for a politician who evidently promised to dry out the town.

In the photo to the left, Edna Drosick walks past one of the storefronts she hopes Historic Pocahontas, Inc., will get a crack at. Prices are in their favor: most small houses are priced under $10,000; cabins like the one above can be bought for $200. The picture above Mrs Drosick is the inside of the opera house which is to be refurbished, and that's Carol Perfin, the lady who helped get it all going.

You might ask, "why restore old buildings in a depressed no-industry town?" The answer is that there is too much town and too much history to let die. The people in Pocahontas believe that by restoring their town, they will attract both visitors and new residents. They might be right. And if they are, they will have created a future for Pocahontas . . . out of its past.

Visitors to Pocahontas will find, in addition to a townful of period buildings, a demonstration coal mine — which they can drive (if in a hurry) or walk through. If they want to know something about coal mining, they can ask practically anybody in town, and get an authoritative answer. (That's what Pocahontas High School students have been busy doing — interviewing their elders to gather fact and legend about the mines.)

Mrs Drosick and Mrs Perfin know the town like the backs of their hands, and they know at least one story for every building in town. Through their efforts, a fine old town hall/opera house will get a new lease on life, as will several storefronts and a pretty little company house on the top of a ridge above town. They will restore some buildings to be rented to businesses, others to provide guest accommodations for visitors. They also plan to knock down a brace of almost-collapsed garages in order to make room for what will be Pocahontas' only park.

It just might be that there's life in the old town yet.

1782 ⊙ 1783

British evacuate Wilmington, Savannah & Charleston — House of Commons votes to make peace — Talks begin in Paris — Preliminary articles signed — Florida ceded to Spain — Congress ratifies treaty, disbands army — Last Loyalists leave NY — Beyond the war: Harvard medical school opens — Noah Webster published first speller — Robert Aitken prints first US Bible — Mass. outlaws slavery — Travel time: 5 days on Philadelphia-Baltimore stage.

This is the story of how the keeper of the oldest inn in America and an architect have teamed up to help a little Hudson River town hang on to its old-time downtown, and the business that keeps it alive.

Charles La Forge says: "What started the whole thing was the citizens uniting to keep business in town in the face of a new shopping center on the outskirts. The local bank hosted a dinner for businessmen and the facts were laid out. People began to realize we were losing the attractiveness of our village, and our pride along with it."

Rehabilitation of the town's old commercial buildings got underway. About that time, La Forge bought a retired fire house right around the corner from his hotel. "I converted it to a gift shop. It helped people see what could actually be done. Now more people are thinking about the potential in this town."

La Forge's collaborator and friend is Richard Crowley, an architect who has contributed his time and talent to helping with rehabilitation work. His energy is matched by his passion for history. One of his pastimes is to pore over old maps of the Rhinebeck area to see which old homes are still standing. His research has begun to make townspeople curious about the area's past — a prerequisite to a community-wide effort.

If La Forge, Crowley and the others in Rhinebeck have their way, the center of this village will be around for another century or so, unaffected by anything as temporary as a shopping center.

Left: This building was erected in 1870, and it's still in use today in the center of town, as are the buildings on either side of it. Rhinebeck's buildings have withstood time and weather remarkably well, so the restoration efforts have a head start.

Below: Vincent Astor owned this fine automobile, the first car in Rhinebeck. But his driving skills didn't match his car, and local roads were designed to accommodate the horse. There was one bend that Mr Astor just couldn't navigate; he kept going off the road. Finally he just bought the whole section and straightened out the bend for himself.

A local craftsman is making oldstyle handcarved shop signs like the tobacconer's Indian (left). Initial efforts tended to be cosmetic, but more complex restoration work is evolving from such beginnings.

The Beekman Arms Hotel is said to be the oldest hotel in America. In 1954, it was almost torn down to make way for a gas station, but a group of citizens rescued it. They managed to keep it open, but it was not until La Forge stepped in that it became a commercial success. "It is just a small country inn," he says.

La Forge jokingly admits that from time to time he has help from one of the former owners of the Beekman Arms. "A French sea captain who used to own the hotel is buried in the cemetery right across the street. Whenever I feel the need of a little inspiration, I go over there and sit on his grave for a while." Judging by the success of La Forge's efforts in Rhinebeck, the old captain must know what he's talking about.

Two of the oldest and best-preserved textile mills in America stand near the Winnepesaukee River in Laconia, New Hampshire. The only reason they are still there is that a small group of local citizens — the Save the Mills Society — has been fighting City Hall for the past four years to keep the mills from being torn down.

The battle to save the mills has gone from living room to court room, from shopping paper to national magazine; it has caused city government changes, inspired poetry, brought experts in from Washington, D. C., and incited individuals to attempt arson. The Save the Mills Society has been faced time after time with final, negative decisions. If the leaders — Richard Davis, Lawrence Baldi, Norman Weeks, Peter Karagianis and others — had given up, Laconia would have another parking lot now instead of two sturdy and useful brick buildings.

Laconia started a downtown redevelopment project in the mid-1960's. The South Beacon Street property where the two mills are located was right in the middle of the redevelopment area. Laconia City Councils of 1961 and 1965 had pledged the city to preserve the mill buildings.

So the city government was given responsibility by the Laconia Housing and Redevelopment Authority (which was in charge of the redevelopment project) to restore the mills "if feasible." Because of this agreement, the city was also obligated to purchase the land on which the mills are located.

But the City Council sitting in 1969 had a majority which felt that the mills were financial liabilities and ugly reminders of unpleasant, low-paying work, and they didn't want to spend any tax dollars on the mills except to tear them down. Mayor Tabor, Councilmen Gove, Lakeman, and Cellupica, and City Solicitor Norberg all wanted the South Beacon Street Property to be used for a new and modern City Hall, and a big parking lot. They began proceedings to have the idle mills razed.

Many Laconians agreed with the prior councils' opinion that the mills were far too valuable to be destroyed, and tried to convince the then-current city government to reconsider. They found, though, that the anti-mill faction was firm in its resolve. On January 23, 1970, sixty area residents met and elected Richard Davis as President of the Save the Mills Society. The battle was on.

Peter Karagianis, Priscilla Shannon, Beth Ide and Paul Mirski are four of the Laconians who fought City Hall for four years. They are standing inside the Belknap Mill, which after renovation will serve the town as a senior citizens center, arts loft, museum, film workshop and general gathering place.

Below is what they fought so hard to save: The Belknap-Sulloway Mill on the left was built in 1828. Its bell was cast by an apprentice of Paul Revere. On the right is the recently renovated Seeburg-Busiel Mill, built in 1853.

**Laconia, New Hampshire
Fighting City Hall**

29

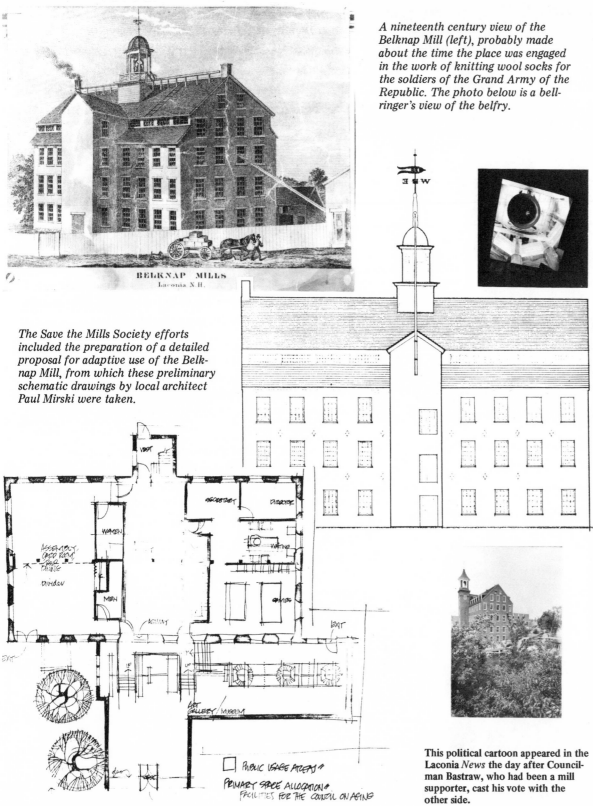

A nineteenth century view of the Belknap Mill (left), probably made about the time the place was engaged in the work of knitting wool socks for the soldiers of the Grand Army of the Republic. The photo below is a bell-ringer's view of the belfry.

BELKNAP MILLS
Laconia N.H.

The Save the Mills Society efforts included the preparation of a detailed proposal for adaptive use of the Belknap Mill, from which these preliminary schematic drawings by local architect Paul Mirski were taken.

□ PUBLIC USAGE AREAS
PRIMARY SPACE ALLOCATION &
FACILITIES FOR THE COUNCIL ON AGING

This political cartoon appeared in the **Laconia** *News* the day after Councilman Bastraw, who had been a mill supporter, cast his vote with the other side.

Not everybody wants to save landmarks. Economics, aesthetics, even bad memories can provide a rationale for knocking things down and starting over again. And most citizens in a town can be persuaded that such destruction is necessary — even beneficial — if nobody speaks to the contrary. The Save the Mills Society succeeded because its members spoke to the people, and gained public support for the mills — and then kept their supporters active over the long months of the struggle. As a result, Laconia *still* has two of the oldest and best-preserved textile mills in America. It also has several thousand citizens who are personally involved in saving their own history.

As graphic demonstration of the grit of Laconia's Save the Mills Society members, we reprint on the opposite page a scenario of the battle, as excerpted from several pounds of Priscilla Shannon's newspaper clippings on the subject.

THE GRAVEDIGGERS !

Scenario of the Battle
(exerpted from local newspaper articles)

9 February 1970. *Richard Candee, architectural historian of Sturbridge Village, terms Laconia's mills "the best remaining examples of brick mortared mills in New England," and urges preservation.*

24 February 1970. *Laconia citizens give Save the Mills representatives solid support at City Council meeting.*

2 April 1970. *Save the Mill Society seeks $180,000 from Department of Housing and Urban Development to save mill buildings.*

1 May 1970. *City Council majority (Gove, Lakeman, Cellupica, Mayor Tabor) vote to build new City Hall building on Beacon Street property, instead of using Seeburg-Busiel Mill.*

5 May 1970. *Robert M. Vogel of Smithsonian Institution visits mills, strongly supports preservation of such important industrial buildings.*

8 May 1970. *City and Mayor served with petition from eleven pro-mill merchants requesting injunction preventing city from ever building a new City Hall building on Beacon Street property.*

10 May 1970. *Sunday tour of mills draws over one thousand people.*

13 May 1970. *Mayor quoted as favoring immediate demolition of mills — and is reminded by LHRA of City's obligation to rehabilitate mills "if feasible."*

15 May 1970. *City Solicitor Norberg denies merchants' petition of 8 May which requested injunction.*

25 May 1970. *Former State Senator James P. Rodgers presents petition to City Council and Mayor with 2,750 signatures asking that mills be saved.*

27 May 1970. *Mayor seeks to discredit petition, claims only one thousand signatures are valid.*

16 June 1970. *Anti-mill group (Laconia Citizens Committee) pops up, urges demolition, says no tax or public funds should be used on mills.*

29 June 1970. *Former Mayor Dyer presents minority report on mills, recommends renovation, points out that 1967 study for city determined that Busiel Mill "has every potential for being renovated into a fine City Hall."*

22 July 1970. *Local law firm announces interest in Busiel Mill as office building.*

18 August 1970. *Mayor Tabor pushes demolition forward by formally advising LHRA of City Council's decision of lack of feasibility to retain and restore mills for public use.*

18 August 1970. *Life magazine announces article featuring Laconia's mills will appear in September 4 issue; support for mill preservation increases immediately.*

12 September 1970. *Mayor Tabor changes stance on mills without apparent reason, drafts resolution urging preservation.*

29 September 1970. *City Councilmen Lakeman and Gove walk out of City Council meeting to forestall passage of Mayor's resolution; they want no discussion of saving mills, and say the will walk out of any Council meeting in which mill preservation is brought up.*

22 October 1970. *LHRA sets deadline for mill preservation. Director Lafond says unless firm plans and funds shown by June 1, 1971, mills will be razed.*

23 October 1970. *National Trust for Historic Preservation grants $500 for mill restoration — an honor previously only given to historic residences, such as those of Presidents.*

17 November 1970. *46 merchants file six point petition suggesting mills be razed, property be paved as parking lot.*

30 November 1970. *LHRA and City Planning Board move to okay new City Hall construction on mill site.*

22 December 1970. *Davis, Weeks, Karagianis seek injunction to restrain city from "partially or totally razing mills" on grounds that city is not giving required consideration to preservation and restoration.*

31 December 1970. *Court grants temporary injunction.*

1 January 1971. *Crowd of several hundred takes turns ringing in the New Year with Belknap Mill bell; Save the Mills Society announces plans to make bell-ringing an annual community event.*

9 January 1971. *LHRA takes sides on mill preservation issue, supports destruction of mills by filing a court motion that Karagianis-Davis-Weeks petition to delay action on mills be dismissed.*

14 January 1971 *was a turning point for the Save the Mills Society. The judge hearing the Karagianis-Weeks-Davis petition had sent the three parties concerned — the Save the Mills Society, the City Council, and the LHRA — into conference with instructions to work out a compromise.*

On 14 January this was done. The agreement stated that the Busiel Mill would be reserved for private development, and would be protected at least until 1 June 1971, while a developer was sought; and the Belknap Mill would be reserved for non-commercial development and would be protected at least until 1 September, while a developer was sought. The LHRA would have responsibility for judging which developers would be satisfactory.

The Save the Mills Society stopped worrying about the mills being torn down overnight, and turned their attention to fund-raising and development plans.

3 February 1971. *Mills become listed in National Register of Historic Landmarks.*

4 March 1971. *City Council gives contract to build new City Hall on Beacon Street property next to mills to local developers; need for parking for City Hall plus downtown businesses — because new City Hall will cover a parking area — encourages talk of demolishing mills.*

15 March 1971. *Department of the Interior gives $37,500 to save mills.*

20 March 1971. *Dinner-dance-rally held to raise money for restoration of mills — one of many social events which keep Save the Mills movement going strong.*

25 April 1971. *Save the Mills Society plans Senior Citizen Multi-purpose Center for Belknap Mill — would satisfy LHRA criterion that mill be used for non-commercial activity, would also generate income required for post-restoration maintenance.*

Mill is located adjacent to two housing complexes populated by senior citizens — senior citizen groups are excited by plan.

28 May 1971. *LHRA gives tentative approval to One Mill Plaza Realty Company (formed by local law firm of Nighswander, Lord, Martin, and Kill-Kelley) to buy Busiel Mill and restore into office buildings.*

5 August 1971. *Save the Mills Society officially begins major fund-raising drive.*

18 August 1971. *One Mill Plaza, Inc. purchases Busiel Mill.*

23 August 1971. *Belknap Mill hit by vandals — arson is attempted.*

26 August 1971. *Twenty merchants in letter to local paper oppose restoration of Belknap Mill — not enough parking.*

27 August 1971. *Small fund-raising party nets $325; interest in saving mill continues strong.*

1 September 1971. *Save the Mills Society submits plan for use of Belknap Mill as Senior Citizens Center.*

5 November 1971. *LHRA refuses to name Save the Mills Society as developers of Belknap Mill on grounds of insufficient funding available. Save the Mills Society has raised over $130,000, but this is short of the $165,000 necessary for primary phases of restoration. Save the Mills Society meets to decide what to do next, decides on all-out fund-raising effort.*

25 November 1971. *Belknap County Commission on Beautification disbands, leaves money to Save the Mills Society; fund-raising drive looks to be succeeding.*

14 January 1972. *Save the Mills Society announces they have raised $180,000 — $15,000 more than LHRA set as requirement — and await LHRA decision.*

29 February 1972. *Second arson attempt on Belknap Mill; Save the Mills Society outraged, urge immediate decision in favor of restoration.*

31 May 1972. *New LHRA Chairman Messer declines decision, leaves fate of mill up to City Council. Parking dispute still unresolved.*

22 September 1972. *New LHRA Director Albert LaBonte names Save the Mills Society as tentative developer of Belknap Mill — decision had been returned to LHRA. Determining factors are (1) new mayor and several new councilmen have been elected who are favorable toward mill redevelopment; (2) Save the Mills Society's re-use plan is popular, and Senior Citizens programs scheduled for the mill are already functioning; and (3) the Save the Mills Society has raised more money than it was asked to.*

25 October 1972. *Parking dispute is resolved — city will build a parking structure elsewhere.*

June 1973. As this book goes to the publisher, the future of the Belknap Mill is still uncertain.

The battle to save the mills inspired art and poetry on both sides of the issue. Councilman Harry Gove submitted the poem below to the Laconia **Evening Citizen** *after reading a similar offering on the opposite side.*

The Old Mill

I am the mill, alone and still
In Laconia town.
Broken and old, filled with cold
I hope to come down.

My windows leak, and winds shriek
through my empty halls.
My bell is still in belfry chill
no more the worker calls.

My rafters groan, cracked walls moan
with aged infirmities.
My beauty shorn, weary and worn
I live with my memories.

There was a time, when in my prime
that many came to me.
Within my walls, in dim lit stalls
they worked on endlessly.

My bell would ring, and daily bring
the workers to my tower.
Throughout the town, it was the sound
that told of my power.

In summer heat, and winter sleet
they trudged through my doors.
The long day thru, in twilight too
they toiled on my floors.

The young and strong, all came along
and gave to me their best.
Their youth I stole, then bent and old
I sent them to their rest.

Then came the day, for me to say
that now my task was ended.
My own youth spent, my timbers rent
no more could I be mended.

My work was done, the course run
I had a date to keep.
I did not cry, at my time to die
I sought the long long sleep.

Then man came by, and wondered why
I could not stand forever.
A building old, a monument bold
to his own selfish endeavor.

Now God must frown, as He looks down
on such futility.
For can't man see, that only He
can make immortality.

None can stay, it is god's way
for all of our race.
So let me go, you here below
to my appointed place.

Harry E. Gove

This is the story of three college students who applied what they learned in the classroom to a real-life situation — and helped a whole town rediscover its history. In 1967, the San Luis Obispo City Council made plans to widen the city block in front of the town's Spanish Mission. Ralph Taylor, Walt Conweil and Jack Reineck, architectural students at the California Polytechnic Institute, decided to actively oppose the street-widening, because they knew it would totally spoil the aesthetic value of the city's most beautiful and meaningful structure.

Here is Jack Reineck's account of the Mission Plaza Project:

"Erected in 1772, Mission San Luis Obispo de Tolosa was, in an earlier age, the cultural and geographic center of the town of San Luis Obispo. In the old days there was an Indian settlement, a creek and an adobe mill adjacent to the mission grounds. When the town began to thrive in the early part of this century, construction and commercial activity originated near the mission and spread in all directions. The Indians were driven away, the beautiful creek was systematically covered with streets and buildings and the mill was abandoned. The appearance of the automobile exaggerated the trend of the town to sprawl and lose its once-close relationship to the mission.

"By the 1960's the central business district was suffering from the battles of deteriorating vacant stores and modern outlying shopping centers. The mission attracted approximately forty thousand visitors annually, but few could be persuaded to remain in the city longer than the time required to reload the Instamatic.

"In 1966, the city of San Luis Obispo decided to spend $185,000 in order to widen an already discontinuous and unnecessary street which separated the mission from the only remaining exposed section of the tree-lined creek and the adjacent business district. Two other architectural students and I began to realize that the proposed street widening would defeat any future hope of making a pedestrian area near the mission and a focal point in San Luis Obispo. We hoped that the mission could be surrounded by landscaped walks and a plaza, exposed to the picturesque creek and stand in harmony with the characteristic brick rear facades of the town. In this way we planned to renew the town identity and help to bring life back into the central business district.

Wedding parties no longer descend the steps of the Mission San Luis Obispo Chapel into downtown traffic. Now they walk out across the new Plaza, and have a peaceful place to talk and enjoy the Central California sunshine.

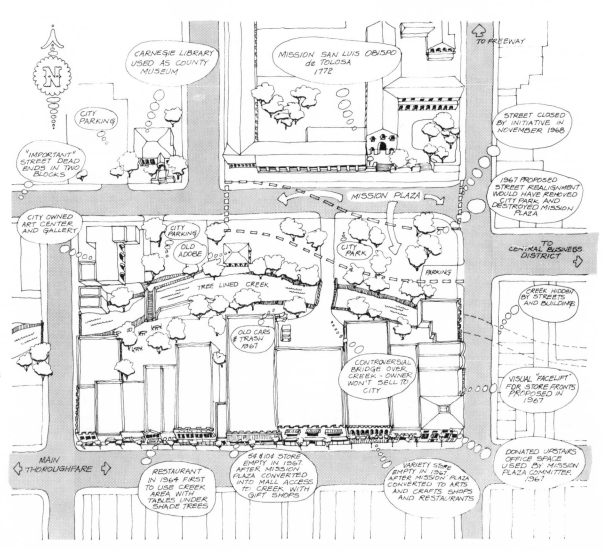

The top two pictures are Before and After, and show how Mission Plaza has done nothing but good for a formerly spiritless business district. **Just above:** *That street running diagonally to the right is gone forever, because townspeople made up their own minds instead of letting city officials do it for them.* **Below, far right:** *As soon as the referendum vote was announced, students brought planters out and erected a verdant barricade to signify the change.*

"In 1967, we applied for, and received, a planning grant from the America the Beautiful Fund in order to accomplish our goals. We were soon given the use of some vacant second floor office space in the area which was beginning to be known as 'Mission Plaza.' In the meantime, the City Engineer — against his will — prepared the construction drawings and requested bids for the proposed street widening and realignment.

"We soon discovered not only planning, but traffic and economic reasons to support our theory that the proposed realignment was an utter waste of city and state tax money.

"We naively approached the City Council with our findings and a plan for closing and landscaping the street facing the mission. Needless to say, the reaction of the City Council was violent, indeed. Not to be discouraged, we took our cause to the people and the newspaper. This tactic finally produced a great deal of publicity and support.

"In the following year citizens were aroused, petitions distributed and an initiative proposal placed on the November ballot to close the infamous street. The initiative passed in 1968; the mayor and two councilmen who were opposing 'Mission Plaza' were defeated in the same election."

Now, in 1972, the Mission Plaza Project has become a reality. The city closed the street, purchased the land adjacent to the mission and the creek, and built Mission Plaza. There are now pedestrian bridges, tree-lined paths and landscaped public areas which serve to relate the historic mission to its natural setting and to the surrounding town. It's a pretty nice 200th birthday present for both the Mission and San Luis Obispo.

d favors closing Monterey ncilmen remain unconvinced

STUDENT JACK REINECK OFFERS MISSION PLAN
Col. Frank Warden (seated right) isn't buying any.

The presentation that Jack Reineck (far right) and his fellow students made to the San Luis Obispo City Council convinced just about everybody who heard it or heard about it — except a few downtown property owners, a construction company, and their friends on the City Council. The students did a terrific job, but they probably wouldn't have succeeded without strong support from several businessmen and the **Telegram-Tribune** *newspaper.*

1784 ◉ 1785

New York City becomes temporary Capital — John Jay heads foreign affairs — Slavery abolished in New Hampshire, Connecticut, Rhode Island, New York — Empress of China opens Far East trade — US commerce recovers from British blockade — Basic Land Ordinance established township system — First state university (U. of Georgia) established — John Fitch begins steamboat experiments — Ben Franklin invents bifocals.

PARTIALLY COMPLETED MISSION PLAZA MODEL.
The public inspects it after last week's controversial City Council meeting.

Rochester, New York

Saving the Soul of Rochester (On Less Than Half a Shoestring)

It only takes one person to visualize a way to save a town's unique character, but the spirit must spread and gain support before any effort can succeed. In Rochester, New York, Douglas Fisher's energy was so contagious that now most of the people there support his project to preserve an unusual section of town called Canaltown, where the Erie Canal once intersected the Genesee River. Fisher's work shows that large and small towns have some things in common: an architectural heritage, special traditions and forces which were responsible for the town's existence, and most important, people who want to save what they've got.

Rochester is a big city. From its beginnings, its history and its looks have been influenced by the Genesee River and the Erie Canal, which flow through it. Canaltown is in the middle of the city and is one of its most distinctive neighborhoods. Brick buildings over a century old line the Genesee near where the Erie Canal crossed over the River contained in a concrete aqueduct, like an antiquated freeway overpass. The district had an unusual charm, and now the whole section will retain its distinguished air, from the old reddish stones of South Water Street to the buildings which line it — the Claude Bragdon Security Trust Building with its classical interior, the old Wilson Mill, and the 1891 Cook's Opera House. Douglas Fisher's plan includes the restoration and reactivation of the mill, the remodeling of the Trust Building into an Italian-Mediterranean restaurant, and the rescue of the Opera House. Downriver a ways, an 1822 Erie Canal warehouse will become a canal museum. Eventually a half-mile section of the original Erie Canal through town will be restored in its original bed, linking Canaltown with the museum. The restored section will function as a strip park, with rides available on canal boats pulled by mules.

Luckily, town politics moved in favor of the Canaltown project. Douglas Fisher says: "I talked to each of the City Councilmen, and John Paranello — who is now the vice-mayor — picked up on it. He was quite cooperative from the outset, while many others were still sitting on the fence. In mid-1971, a proposal to spend $150,000 to demolish the Trust Building suddenly came before the Council for a vote — that demolition certainly would have killed Canaltown — but Paranello stopped that from happening.

"The Canaltown plan didn't come into the press, though, until December of 1971. That was when we presented a complete plan to the Planning Commission — what would be done. They reacted favorably to it. Then the City Council passed a resolution endorsing the concept of Canaltown — in a unanimous vote. It was co-sponsored by the minority leader. I thought it was very important to have bi-partisan support on this. The council has since set policy prohibiting any actions inconsistent with Canaltown. Now they are re-writing the renewal plans for the area from demolition to preservation."

A key part of the plan for Canaltown is the restoration and reconstruction of the 1891 Cook's Opera House into a complex of four theaters. The main auditorium will retain the still-intact proscenium arch over the stage which gave it such fine acoustics. The South Avenue wing of the Opera House structure will be converted into two legitimate theaters for 400 people each, and one 400-seat cinema theater. An evening at the theater will be made even more enjoyable by the presence of half a dozen new restaurants, evening shopping and convenient access.

Projects like Canaltown are gaining momentum all over the country. Douglas Fisher is just one of the many citizens who know that a sense of identity springs from knowing where you came from. They know that it feels good to walk down the same streets your father or your grandfather did, especially if they look like they did then. Rochester's pride in its heritage is spreading to every citizen, and even newcomers can feel the security of that enthusiastic and solid movement.

To the right is Douglas A. Fisher standing on the top floor of one of Canaltown's loft buildings. He is 26 years old, and his background includes studies in history, linguistics, physics and mathematics. He started out with no experience in saving buildings, but his energy and determination have made him an expert. Reusing history creatively runs in his family — he is the son of J. Sheldon Fisher of Fishers, New York, who runs one of New York State's most interesting private museums.

Douglas Fisher describes his involvement with Rochester and Canaltown: "I discovered the Opera House and saw how the buildings fitted together when I was an undergraduate at the University of Rochester in 1965. It wasn't till I was doing graduate work down at Columbia and I just happened to see a Rochester newspaper which described plans to demolish the whole block that I thought seriously about doing anything.

"So I got on the telephone and called the urban renewal people here in Rochester, and found out more about it — at the time, I didn't know anything about urban renewal — I got in touch with Washington and got all the official handbooks, so I knew all the regulations — better, it turned out, than the people in Rochester.

"I spent all 1971 commuting back and forth between Columbia and Rochester — I was still doing graduate work — not only finding out about urban renewal, but enmeshing myself in the whole political structure, getting to know everybody on all levels that would have anything to do with the project. And I had to learn all about how real estate is financed and developed.

"Everybody I talked to for the first couple of months had reservations about whether the project was financially feasible, but they all said they liked it very much. They didn't know that people would support it, but personally they liked it. And I heard this so much that I got the feeling that, well, all these people who say they like it, that's enough of a market. I don't really need to know what they think other people think — if I know what they think themselves.

"Did I have trouble getting people to take me seriously because I didn't have experience? Because I'm young? I don't know. It really helps to know what you're talking about. I started out as a physics major, and a lot of that background is very helpful in the architectural and engineering aspects. For example, in dealing with a utility substation on the site — the utility company people were initially very much opposed to having anything happen here that would affect operations. But since I knew about electricity I was able to persuade them that I knew what I was talking about. They were saying that if they had to move someplace, that for a week the whole electrical system of the city of Rochester would be very much in jeopardy, because this was a very vital substation. But I knew how power networks are pooled, and they finally admitted that they did have nine substations around the city, and that if one went out, the others would take up the slack. So this kind of specialized knowledge which I have in relevant areas — I've been able to carry the day on that."

1786 ◉ 1787

Farmers up in arms: Shay's Rebellion over paper money — Import-export trade declines — First major strike: Philadelphia printers walk out — Depression sets in — Interstate commerce convention at Annapolis — New Jersey outlaws slavery — Model for first amendment: Virginia adopts religious freedom statute — Fitch's first steamboat plods Delaware River — First cotton mill opens in Beverly, Mass. — Northwest Ordinance establishes Ohio jurisdiction — First Federalist Paper stresses need for new government — Constitutional Convention opens in Philadelphia

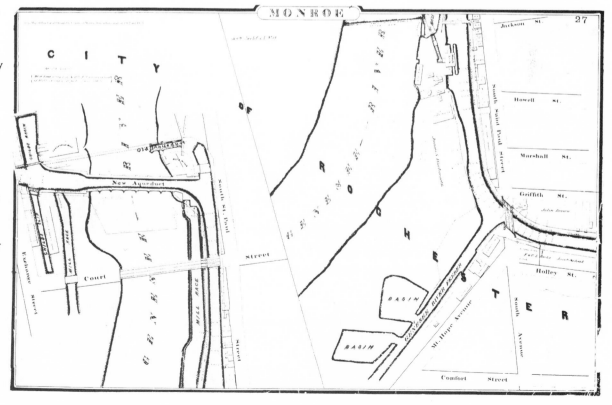

"For me, the Canaltown project is the most satisfying thing I could be doing. With Canaltown, I find that I can express a vast array of interests and I'm not confined. A lot of people deserve a lot of credit for Canaltown's success to this point, though. I could never have done it by myself. To date I've used forty-seven consultants on the project — only one received money for his work, and that was because we got a grant from the National Trust for Historic Preservation. The grant was for an architectural study of the restoration possibilities of the Opera House. My lawyer has run up over $10,000 in legal fees. He's agreed not to charge unless the project begins paying. He's having a ball with it. Really, this has all been done on, well, less than half a shoestring."

Fisher and friends inspect the original mill race. Water was diverted off from the Genesee River to run water wheels which supplied power for industry. After running through the mill race, the water returned to the river. The restoration planned for Rochester will save this curiosity. If the demolition plans had gone through, it would have been destroyed.

"The Canaltown project is really very important to Rochester. It's extraordinarily relevant to day-to-day life. It'll make all the difference in whether somebody would want to live in Rochester or elsewhere — because Canaltown is the soul of the urban center."

Tucson, Arizona
Who Cares About the Barrio?

Tucson, Arizona, began many years ago as a dusty Sonoran village. Now it's a cosmopolitan city with a population approaching 300,000. The small adobe village is still there, and is still populated by Mexican-Americans. But it is surrounded — and threatened — by modern Tucson.

It's called the Barrio, and it's poor and run-down. But to the people who live there, the old district is synonymous with their way of life. When a freeway project started that could have broken the Barrio into pieces, residents and ex-residents banded together and forced a change of plans. That's a neat trick when you have no money, no power, and a language problem, too.

The Battle for the Barrio isn't over yet. The freeway is just part of a struggle that will take years to resolve. But it has begun to teach a quiet minority that if they don't work together and learn how to fend for themselves, even their way of life can be taken away in the name of progress — a fact which is clearly evident in the episode which started the whole affair:

One day Mrs Miguel Rodriquez, a long-time resident of the Barrio, decided to make a trip to city hall because her tax bill hadn't come. She found her way to the tax assessor's office, and inquired why she hadn't received her bill. The man got down the book and thumbed through the pages until he came to her street. And then he looked at her, "There's nothing there." The assessor's office records did not show a residence at 361 S. Main. Mrs Rodriquez understands English better than she speaks it, but she was confused by this report and didn't know what to do. She assumed a misunderstanding, and went home to get a friend who could speak English better. On the second trip she was again confronted by the absence of records. By now Mrs Rodriquez knew she was not misunderstood by the official who was telling her all this. With the help of her translator she told the man she had lived at that address for fifty years and had paid her taxes each time they were due. Finally she and her friend were directed upstairs to the city planning office. The man in there had large maps. Surely the maps would show her house that had been there so long. The man got down his maps of her neighborhood, pointed to the area where her house was sup-

posed to be. The map showed that all the homes in that area had been sold or were condemned. Mrs Rodriquez told him that her house was very much there — neither sold nor condemned, and no one had offered her any money for it — and that she would not sell if they had. Before she left, Mrs Rodriquez was told not to pay her taxes. But she didn't want to do that. She told the man that she wanted to pay her taxes anyway, even if no records showed her house was there. For the next three months she put the money in a special place and waited for her tax bill to come. Finally it did, and it was then that the citizen whose house didn't exist paid her taxes. She found out that the same thing had happened to others. Evidently it is easier to begin condemnation proceedings if the city can prove non-payment of property taxes. Mrs Rodriquez' house lay in the path of a new freeway. And the freeway very likely would have been built with little opposition — though it certainly wouldn't have been welcomed by anyone — except that its path also fell on El Tiradito, just across the street from Mrs Rodriquez' house.

El Tiradito, the Wishing Shrine, is a 50 x 80

plot of ground. At the back of it is a shrine which seems much too small and insignificant to be the focal point of a major urban controversy. But El Tiradito is the symbolic center of the Mexican-American neighborhood; it has invested in it the spirit of life itself. During the second World War, Mexican-American soldiers from Tucson would write home asking their families to light a candle in front of El Tiradito for them. And in those years the earth was covered with small votive candles from the Wishing Shrine wall all the way to the street. The candles burned constantly, and the smell of burning wax drifted for blocks. At night the light could be seen from far away. The men who returned from the war knew that it was the spirit of El Tiradito that brought them back safely.

When a local Mexican-American group called Los Tucsoneses got wind of the freeway — and its proposed routing — they formed a committee to act as a pressure group. Purpose: save El Tiradito. The battle was on.

The story about Mrs Rodriquez' visit to city hall — plus reports of other questionable

Here you see Mr and Mrs Miguel Rodriquez in the house that the city said did not exist. The picture at the top of the page shows Harris Sobin, Mr R. S. Perez, Vicki Welch, Father Cantrell and Dr Arnulfo Trejo standing in front of El Tiradito.

tactics — made the Tucson papers. Residents of the Barrio quickly found they had sympathetic and vocal support from Mexican-Americans outside the Barrio, and from many Anglos as well.

A Legal Aid Society attorney announced that his group had accepted seven Barrio residents as clients. He stated that the matter could be taken to court and encouraged other Barrio residents to seek legal help.

On September 24, 1971, three days after the newspaper story, a small but noisy protest march was made from San Cosme Chapel to a State Highway Department Information Office near the Barrio. Three days after that, a petition containing 858 names protesting the planned freeway were presented to the City Council. On October 2, another petition was filed, this one with 1,000 signatures, including those of five state legislators and six members of Tucson's own City Planning Office.

The same day, the Arizona **Daily Star** carried an announcement that Harris Sobin and Robert Geibner, two Associate Professors of Architecture at the University of Arizona, were going to give a special course for about twenty fourth and fifth year students that would concentrate entirely on a survey of the Barrio: its history; buildings; its residents and their way of life. The professors believed the survey would document the great history and cultural wealth of the Barrio.

On October 5, the Tucson **Daily Citizen** reported that "The City Council, although willing to restudy aspects of the proposed Butterfield Parkway (as it was called), has voted along party lines to keep plans rolling unchanged while it takes its second look."

Suddenly, the Butterfield was a political issue — not terribly surprising in view of the uproar and the coming municipal elections. Incumbent Mayor Corbett was identified with the Butterfield route, even though his actions indicated he was not wholeheartedly in favor of bulldozing aside the Barrio and its residents. Opponent Murphy, who was Corbett's eventual successor, was loudly opposed to the Butterfield. Gradually, as the controversy grew, the principal figures in the defense of the Barrio began to emerge. It was a coalition, each part of which had its own reasons for wanting the Barrio saved.

Dr Arnulfo Trejo, a tall and reserved academician who began his life in the Barrio and is now a Professor of modern languages at the University of Arizona, was appointed by Los Tucsoneses to be Chairman of the Wishing Shrine Committee. His was the responsible and reasonable voice often heard as the official spokesman for the community. His co-workers, Mrs Annie Laos and Mrs Vicki Welch, both energetic and much more volatile than Trejo, had a way of reaching the viscera of Mexican-Americans and Anglos. The ladies seemed to be the principal organizers of the protest effort.

Father Cantrell, "working" Episcopal priest (and ex-city planner), made meeting space available in his church, but more importantly, gave both his experience and support as a respected community leader. A local attorney filed an action against the Arizona State Highway Commission which helped force re-study of the proposed route. Architecture professors Sobin and Geibner became more deeply involved. And there were many others.

One highlight of the campaign was an extraordinary appearance by a contingent of Mexican-Americans at a session of the State Legislature. Sixteen year old Ernesto Perez brought the legislators to their feet applauding after he made a plea for saving his neighborhood. Ernesto also started a newspaper, **La Voz del Barrio,** to keep citizens informed of developments affecting the Barrio.

Finally, on October 26, 1971, the City Council reversed its position and voted to ask the State Highway Department to refrain from proceeding with preparations for demolition while alternate routes were studied.

The Barrio was apparently saved from the freeway. But that struggle brought into focus some serious questions about the Barrio's future. The Barrio is a living, breathing unity of unique architecture, history, culture and life-style. Development of one element at the expense of another weakens the fabric of the neighborhood. But development of some sort is inevitable — since the Barrio is in the middle of a growing city — and necessary — because most of the people in the Barrio are poor. The question was left: What development? And by whom?

Kelly Rollings has one answer. Rollings is a successful Tucson automobile dealer. He is a student of the old adobe architecture of the Barrio, and knows as much as any Anglo of its history. He has been a supporter of its preservation for a long time. He also owns a big hunk of it. Mr Rollings' plan for the Barrio (now partially executed) is to restore the buildings to their original condition, adapting them for use as shops, restaurants and offices — beginning with the block he owns. His plan is a good one. It is being lovingly executed under Mr Rollings' personal direction. Mr Rollings will save the buildings — but not the Barrio.

Development like the Rollings effort is another kind of threat to the people of the Barrio. In a way, it is more ominous than the freeway, since it threatens to kill the heart of the neighborhood while restoring the body. Since by all objective standards careful restoration solves at once the physical and economic ailments of the district, it cannot be fought as though it were a freeway. The people know that. But they also know that the district is theirs, and that their way of life as a people depends on it.

Fortunately for everyone, Kelly Rollings evidently understands the need of the people to be there, and seems willing to try to help them. There appears to be emerging *in Tucson an unusual alliance* between Rollings the developer and the people of the Barrio through their Wishing Shrine Committee, which has remained intact as a kind of community development council. Compromises have been made on both sides. Rollings has spoken of helping to form a private, non-profit Mexican-American development corporation. There is talk of setting up craft guilds within the Barrio, to use native skills and knowledge to supply the weaving, tiles, furniture and decorations needed for restoration, putting unemployed Barrio residents to work. There is also talk of a school and a community center, and the promise that the entire Barrio district will become a historic district.

There seems to be a unity of purpose now. And there is hope. The poem on this page speaks of the hope of the people. It was written by Rene Gonzalez and appeared in the April 1972 issue of Ernesto Perez' paper, **La Voz del Barrio.**

Ernesto Perez and Mr R. S. Perez, his father, continue to work to increase community consciousness in the Barrio.

"el tiradito, pray for us"
"don't destroy our homes"
"where will we go?"
"help us build, don't destroy"
cried the people,
but the man did not hear

and the people were brown
and the people were black
and the people were white
the people were young
and the people were ancient
and the people were proud

and the man said,
"destroy the old and ugly"
"build the modern and beautiful"
but the man did not see,
the beautiful jardines, macetas, enredaderas
the beautiful: "que paso carnal?"
the beautiful: "prestama una taza de azucar?"
the beautiful shrine of faith
the man saw only a map
and the man had money
and the man hired machines
and the man started destroying
and the people had only togetherness
and the people won.

1788 ⊙ 1789

Constitution adopted — First 12 states join new union — Washington inaugurated first President — Congress holds first session in New York — Federal Judiciary Act established Supreme Court — First tariff passed — Bill of Rights drawn up — French Revolution begins — Mutiny on HMS Bounty — 200 Connecticut farmers form first temperance group — Christopher Colles publishes first US road maps — 800 French-Spanish style buildings lost in New Orleans fire — Thanksgiving becomes national holiday.

Annapolis, Maryland
The Twenty Years War

Annapolis, Maryland, is full of history — and its residents have had to fight for almost every inch of it. The people of Historic Annapolis made a decision to win *every* battle. They believe you can't indiscriminately drag ill-conceived modern structures into eighteenth century neighborhoods and come out with anything special. Since there is always somebody ready to put up something new — or change a neighborhood to suit their pocketbook — Historic Annapolis has been in and out of the papers, the courts, the legislature . . . ever since it was started, back in 1952.

The amazing thing about it is they keep winning. And when Historic Annapolis wins, almost everyone benefits. Here is the organization's own capsule account of the Twenty Years War.

"Do you remember when many people thought Annapolis an ugly, obsolete, outmoded town? Perhaps they had a reason — there was once a visible degradation of environmental values. Two large ugly buildings hid the water in Market Space; a forest of signs disfigured business districts; the fine architecture of historic structures was often obscured by tasteless additions.

"Businessmen and residents alike fled the old city. Only dreamers imagined a bright future for Annapolis. Now that goal is almost won. What was once a vision is now a happening.

"The Old Town is recognized as a unique place for pleasant living — a Registered Historic Landmark District. Views of sparkling waters have been regained. Historic buildings and sites, restored and protected by easements, are preserved as a part of America's architectural heritage. Suddenly, life in Annapolis has recovered a quality that heightens the sense of community and fosters a relationship to environment that is crucial to a well-ordered society."

The woman who has led Historic Annapolis to victory in campaign after campaign doesn't wear any medals. But Mrs Anne St Clair Wright is indeed a leader among leaders.

Indirectly, she has had a hand in the fate of every building in Annapolis by working to have Annapolis designated a National Historic Zone. As a result of her efforts, many buildings in the city have been saved and rejuvenated. She has found angels to underwrite many projects, and she has located sources of grant money. She has contributed to the economic resurgence of the Annapolis business district. She helped devise an unusual and very useful "Historic Easement" program — to insure protection of historic structures in future years. She has supervised countless community fund raising drives. And she fought the United States Navy — and won. When the Naval Academy sought to expand by knocking down three blocks of Annapolis residences, Mrs Wright did a study which showed twenty-four houses in the area to be of historical architectural merit. She went with this information to the House Armed Services Committee. The Navy was told by the Committee to expand within its boundaries. Pretty cheeky behavior for the daughter, wife and mother of Annapolis graduates.

Before enlisting in the service of Historic Annapolis, Inc., Mrs Wright was a professional artist — specializing in mural design and execution. Lately she has transferred her interest to garden design, and has done major work on the Paca Gardens restoration in Annapolis (as well as conjuring up $340,000 worth of support to make the project go). She worked with the archaeologists who unearthed what apparently is one of the earliest "Wilderness" Gardens known in the United States.

Mrs Wright doesn't have the time to devote to landscape gardening that she'd like to have. Besides her work for Historic Annapolis, she is associated with the Anne Arundel County Chapter of the Nature Conservancy, the Port of Annapolis Corporation, the Society for the Preservation of Maryland Antiquities, the Maryland Federation of the Arts, the Governor's Maryland Scenic Beauty Commission and the Annapolis Coordinating Committee on Beautification. Somehow she finds time in addition for five grandchildren.

Mrs Wright, you might say, is a Renaissance woman: author, designer, fund raiser par excellence, city planner, lobbyist, history scholar, public relations representative, horticulturist, lecturer and leader. Historic Annapolis would never have happened without her. Of course, if you asked her, she'd tell you that it was all those other people — the donors, the workers, the concerned citizens — who are responsible for the success of Historic Annapolis. And, of course, she'd be right in a way.

Mrs Wright is presently spearheading a drive to raise two million dollars for Historic Annapolis projects. So she's not exactly resting on her laurels!

The Market House at the head of the City Dock was granted a reprieve when widespread protests against its scheduled demolition reversed the decision of the City Council. It has been restored by the City and once again will become a vital social factor in downtown Annapolis.

The present 1858 building is the third market structure on this site. Three earlier buildings were on an adjacent site, nearer the foot of Main Street. The entire Market Space site was given to the Mayor and Aldermen of the City of Annapolis in 1784 for the express purpose of building and maintaining a City Market.

Though Historic Annapolis, Inc., is now a major force in determining the course of events in the city of Annapolis, though it is a highly professional group with its own research organization and fund raising apparatus, it started as a handful of amateurs and retains that somewhat inaccurate image of itself. The people who make up the group function as professionals, though they choose not to call themselves that. The important thing to remember is that they got that way by spending twenty years at it. Their professionalism wasn't hired from outside. It grew out of the experience of the Twenty Years War.

The battle goes on — in Annapolis as everywhere else. The end isn't in sight. But in Annapolis, with the passing of every year, people find out more about the history of their city, and become less willing to permit its random destruction in the name of progress, because there are people like Mrs Wright around who are willing to go on fighting without a thought of losing.

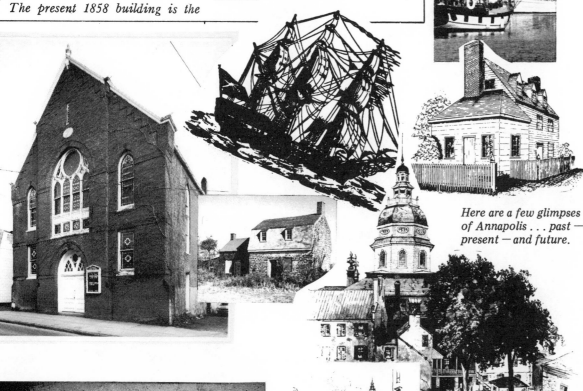

Here are a few glimpses of Annapolis . . . past — present — and future.

Annapolis, 1886

1790 ⊙ 1791

First US census: 3,929,214 people; 18 percent enslaved — Rhode Island, Vermont admitted to union — Philadelphia named Capital for decade — First patent, copyright laws passed — US Bank chartered — Samuel Slater introduces British methods to industrialize cotton mill — Anthracite coal found in Pennsylvania — Fitch tests new steamboat — Ben Franklin dies — Tom Paine publishes "The Rights of Man" — W.P. Sprague opens first carpet factory in Philadelphia.

Population Density 1790

Parents, pray with your children,
as well as for them. – Cotton Mather

I'LL SEE YOU THERE

*A teacher affects eternity; he can never tell
where his influence stops. (Henry Adams)*

✦ ✦ ✦
Alice
First and Last Wife of
Thos. Phillip
Talked To Death
By Friends
Epitaph in Pritchett Cemetery
near Boulder, Illinois

"Work while you work, Play while you play."
– McGuffey's Prim

Men need brotherhood and sympathy as much as they need the loaf.

The real end of the American year is not the thirty-first of December but the old festival of Labor Day. (Alistair Cooke)

Neighbors, you stand related unto one another; and you should be full of devices, that all the neighbors may have cause to be glad of your being in the neighborhood. (Cotton Mother)

A lit-tle girl and a lit-t'e lamb.

There is one thing the American people have got to learn, and that is to give scholars in school a half holiday when there is a circus in town. — George W. Peck, 1883

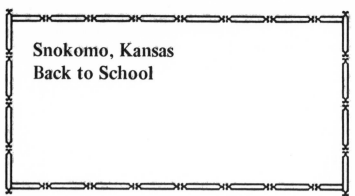

Snokomo, Kansas
Back to School

There's an old pot-bellied stove up in the Flint Hills of Kansas that's warming bodies once again, after standing cold more than thirty years. The Snokomo Silent Workers have restored their old schoolhouse.

Like other Americans of their generation, the Silent Workers remember when schools had inkwells, and blackboards were really black boards. They remember when the start of school was signalled by a clanging metal bell. They remember cloakrooms, double desks, pot-bellied stoves and the schoolteacher who cooked hot meals for her students. Like most of us, the Silent Workers have fond memories of the place where they spent so much time growing up.

Mrs Edna Rowe said, at the beginning of the project: "We all want to restore it for the sake of history. With today's schools, we're afraid our children will never know what an old one-room schoolhouse was like. They've taken the schoolhouse from old Chalk (a nearby district) and moved it to Knott's Berry Farm in California. We should care enough to preserve them here."

The Silent Workers did care. Except for the heaviest chores, like mending cracks in the stone walls (for which they had help from husbands), they've done all the work themselves. The interior needed complete refurbishing. Wainscoting had to be scraped and refinished, there was wallpaper to be hung, the whole place was repainted. This handful of Kansas ladies set to the work with the same kind of concern for the common good and determination that their ancestors exhibited when they set aside their plows to build the schoolhouse in the first place.

You're looking at five of the Snokomo Silent Workers, the Kansas ladies who restored their old schoolhouse with their bare hands (and some help from their husbands). The Snokomo Silent Workers is a venerable twelve-lady sewing circle that was founded forty-six years ago. (When pressed, present members admit there probably hasn't been a moment of silence since.) The founders never dreamed that their progeny would end up owning a hunk of Snokomo real estate.

The Silent Workers raised the money to pay their expenses by writing to everyone they could get an address for who attended the old Snokomo School. It worked. Enthusiastic responses and money came from all over the United States from people who shared the Silent Workers' memories of the old place. In addition to contributions, many offered valuable information, or schoolday relics. The Workers also made and sold wild berry jams and jellies, and handmade cloth goods, and staged rummage sales to help cover their costs.

Now the house functions as a gathering place and meeting room during the week and as a school museum (and a place to buy Silent Workers' jams and handiwork) on weekends. Best of all, this restoration has begun to kindle an interest in the history of the area among the young people who live around Snokomo. It turns out that the Workers did more than restore a childhood memory.

The Kansas farmers who, in 1883, built their people a schoolhouse (right), reported in their minutes that they were "ishued" insurance, and that they "highered" a teacher. Their spelling wasn't much, but, as the **Topeka State Journal** *put it, "their dreams ninety years ago reflect their knowledge of the needs of youth. They built a school."*

44

Decatur, Texas
Long Live Higher Education

It was like a death in the family when the administrators announced in 1965 that the Decatur Baptist College would be moved to Dallas. The College had been a visual and cultural focal point of Wise County since 1891. But the town of Decatur didn't waste much time mourning the loss. Mayor C. L. Gage promptly bought the empty Administration Building, and then gave it to the town. Rosalie Gregg, her husband Robert, and the rest of the Wise County Historical Society went to work in 1967 to make the castle-like structure back into the cultural center of Decatur.

Mr and Mrs G. C. Rann, both retired schoolteachers, have worked full time for three years — at no pay — reconstructing the Auditorium for use as a Community Theater. Though two more years of work remain, Decatur theater groups already use the Theater to present melodramas, musicales and other forms of entertainment popular during the early years of the College; it is also used for beauty pageants, homecomings and club meetings.

The auditorium is only part of the structure, and only part of the project. Fifteen other rooms will be put to use. The Historical Society so far has given the building a new roof, new windows, new lights, restrooms and either refinished or carpeted all the floors. Now one group is sorting out a multitude of donated tools and trinkets into exhibits for a town museum, and another is opening a gift shop featuring historic placemats, plaques, plates and craft items made by Wise County residents.

The College is gone, but another form of higher education is alive in Decatur. The renovated building will be an educational complex, teaching residents about their own past. Rosalie Gregg says, "We are finding some of our young people have no conception of how our pioneer people lived, and do not know the names of the tools with which they worked." With all the activity going on now, chances are they won't remain ignorant of their heritage for long.

The Ranns, who have spent three years making possible the opening of such a unique theater, received a standing ovation in appreciation of their efforts.

CLEO RANN SAYS HE HAS "Lost his farm, lost his garden and about lost his wife" over the remodeling job going on at the old college auditorium. Mr. and Mrs. Rann, both retired from school teaching, took on the project of bringing the auditorium back to a usable condition and it is taking most of their time . . . and there are thousands of hours to go . . . for two people. They would accept all the help they can get. The Musical Extravaganza will be held in the auditorium Friday night, though it is far from completed. (Messenger Photo)

Opening Plays To Full House

Friday night's opening of the Little Theater marked another milestone in the history of Wise County and made a dream come true for the theater's originators, Mr. and Mrs. G. C. Rann.

The premiere productions, "The Storm", a drama in one act, and "The Farmer's Daughter", a melodrama, were presented by local talent in the recently renovated auditorium of the Wise County Historical Society to a standing room-only audience. Surrounded by a Victorian decor, theater goers found all the elements of vaudeville and the thrill of love, suspense, and surprise in the 2 1/2-hour program.

Music Extravaganza
Volume II

ENTERTAINMENT FOR THE ENTIRE FAMILY
LOCAL TALENT — VOCALS — GROUPS — SOLOS
DUETS — GUITAR MUSIC — AND SPECIAL GUESTS

Saturday, Nov. 8 - 7:30 p.m.

Decatur Woman's Building - On Sheriff Posse Grounds

ADULTS $1.00   CHILDREN .50

SPONSORED BY

MR. AND MRS. CLEO RANN

On Behalf of Wise County Historical Society

H.N.S 1840

DIED

WILLIAM GRIFFIN SARGENT

Ap-ple.

Adze.

Arch.

The only reason the Albany Historical Society was formed was to save this tiny rural community's grand stone schoolhouse. Just a simple effort — maybe a month or two. But it didn't stop there. What started as an effort to preserve a remnant of early plains settler life, has grown like topsy into a twenty-five acre establishment for the preservation of the best parts of the history of rural Kansas . . . and it's all the work of community volunteers. Maybe saving old buildings is like eating peanuts. Once you start . . . .

Mrs May Wines, who taught in the school, is a charter member of the Albany Historical Society and the unofficial curator of the schoolhouse museum. She tells how she and her neighbors got into this:

"In Kansas, after a school has been closed for three years, the building is turned back to the County Superintendent, and it can be sold at auction — belongings and all. A number of schools have been lost that way. 1962 was the last term here — the schoolhouse served almost one hundred years — and when the three years were up, the people of the community didn't want their schoolhouse sold and used as a barn, or a stable, or torn down. The Superintendent said they would offer the building to the community as a museum — if we could form a historical society. We weren't sure what that meant, but we found out."

So they got their schoolhouse. It then seemed only proper that the people who took it on just because they cared about it would begin to think about using it as a place to keep other things they cared about. It wasn't long before

Twice 4 are 8.
Your bonnet is not straight.

A-corn.

attics around began producing the kind of stored treasure that is to be found in any community with a history — family relics, old tools, photographs, Civil War mementos, Bibles, bonnets, shawls, wedding dresses, school pictures, family folk art. It all went into the schoolhouse, and what wouldn't fit inside began to pile up in the yard outside: the old farm equipment, wagons, some railroad gear.

The neighbors who made a historical society in order to take care of their old schoolhouse now take care of a pioneer farm, complete with farmhouse and outbuildings, a nineteenth century railroad depot complete with repair shed and telegraph office, a fleet of ancient farm machines, trucks and antique cars and twenty-five acres, part of which is cultivated in order to have grain to thresh the old-fashioned way in the fall of each year. All of this is cared for by the members who enjoy putting aside their high-horsepower lifestyles for a few hours of fussing around each week with the things and ways of their settler forebears.

Why all this seemingly regressive behavior by serious and responsible people? Mostly it's fun. The people in Sabetha who come out to the old schoolhouse enjoy being together, and take a measure of pride in what they have accomplished together. There seems to be, in the doing, a certain bond that knits these plain plains people that almost anyone who has grown up in America senses is back there somewhere in his own past. May Wines puts it pretty well:

"People helped each other in those days. Families helped other families, and each child helped his own family. It was just part of life. Kids in those days had to milk cows, shock wheat, hoe, cut weeds. Everyone did something for everyone. People used to raise big kitchen gardens with watermelons, and pumpkins and all those things, and you helped harvest them. It was hard, but I wouldn't trade it for young folks' life nowadays. That's one reason I've been interested in keeping all this old history: these young folks don't realize that what their parents and grandparents and great-grandparents did together made this country what it is."

Classes aren't held in the old Albany Schoolhouse any more. But there is still a lot of learning going on just the same. And it isn't the kind that requires either a teacher, or a hickory stick.

This is the Albany Schoolhouse. The people in front stopped their work one Sunday to assemble for this picture. They are members of the Albany Historical Society, which, as you can see, is not a bunch of octogenarians. Like their ancestors who hacked the rock for the school by hand from nearby quarries, these people are building a community institution that works now, and they're doing it by hand. The Lincoln Zephyr is the pride of one of the members, and is kept on the premises, along with the farm and railroad equipment, below.

This is May Wines, the school teacher lady who presided over the old house back in 1922, and is now generally acknowledged as the group's historian, though all of them shun titles. She just does her thing, which happens to be to spread an interest in local history by making room for everyone to contribute something to the museum. The items on the opposite page are just a few of the treasures that fill the building's two floors.

1794 ◉ 1795

Whiskey Rebellion protests excise tax — Jay Treaty: seamen still unprotected against impressment — Ben Franklin's autobiography published — Philadelphia-Lancaster turnpike first macadam road in US — Yazoo Land frauds in Georgia — Naturalization Act restricts immigration: five-year residence and allegiance required — Prison reforms in Pennsylvania — Powder in men's hair goes out of style.

47

Carmichael, California
San Rafael, California

Relics in the Suburbs

Shopping centers, maybe, but not one-room schoolhouses. Suburban California is not a place where history is very visible. Even though settlement is not distant in time, it is light years from the nearest freeway. Somehow, in these two small communities, original schoolhouses have survived, along with the spirit to see them saved.

Carmichael, California

Even as late as 1920, some parts of the West were still a frontier. And here, as elsewhere, a decent education was high on the list of community priorities. Here is a first-hand account of the establishment of the Carmichael School, by the lady who was responsible.

THE EARLY HISTORY OF THE CARMICHAEL DISTRICT

My husband, Judge Clyde L. Warren, and I, were among the first settlers. I bought Tract 24, Carmichael No. 2, consisting of ten and two-fifths acres, without seeing it, through a friend, in 1914. We came west in 1915 to attend the Pacific-Panama Exposition in San Francisco. We met Mr. Dan Carmichael, who only recently had sub-divided the land, and my husband became so enthused over the idea of raising oranges, that he refused to go back to his prominent place in Wisconsin. We bought an improved ten-acre tract on Lincoln Avenue. My husband and older boys, remained here to see that the house was properly built, while I and my young daughters, returned to Wisconsin to break up our home and

come west to pioneer. We had such fine schools in Wisconsin, that it broke my heart to send my children to a one-room school in the San Juan District. I had five children and I was determined to do something about it.

I took my horse and buggy and covered the whole district, interesting the people in a PTA and a new school. I organized the PTA in 1916, and affiliated with the Third District. I had the school board as members, and the County Superintendent of Schools. We were determined to build a Carmichael Grammer School.

My Tract 24 was the show place of the Colony for years, having been carefully developed and under one man's special care. Mr. Carmichael used it for the sale of other property, so when I asked him for land for the school, he graciously donated ten acres on a high point of land. Mr. Carmichael was then the Mayor of Sacramento, so when the school was built, we had him and his wife, and all the Council members, out for a day's celebration. The Sacramento Boys' Band furnished the music, and Mayor and Mrs. Carmichael were presented with baskets of fruit and flowers by the children. It was a gala day with lots to eat and great rejoicing. Although we had kerocene lamps and stoves, we were happy at the great improvements in our circumstances. We gradually bought playground equipment, and planted fruit and nut trees to help pay expenses. The members of the PTA donated their services and labor in building the school, and in whatever work there was to be done. For all this, and for those who came later and followed through with so great a work, and so much accomplished, we are most grateful.

Mrs Mabel Carr Warren
First President of Carmichael
Grammar School PTA

In 1972, the school district decided the old schoolhouse had outlived its usefulness and that it should come down. It was then that Mrs Felicia Leis got the Carmichael P.T.A. to work at fixing up the old building. Mrs Leis says, "The people responsible for building this school took a lot of pride in building it for future generations and we have no right to tear it down." This argument against the divine right of expediency has not gone unheard in Carmichael. It looks as though the old schoolhouse won't be destroyed after all.

The Dixie people found a batch of old school records and a map showing the school's original surroundings drawn from memory by a man who shows in this old photo as the little boy on the far left.

San Rafael, California

The heart of Dixie isn't to be found only in the deep South. There's a little bit of it in a community near San Rafael. It takes the form of a tiny one-room schoolhouse, built in 1865 by James Miller, a rancher who gave the land and even hauled the redwood himself so that his children could get a decent schooling. The Dixie Schoolhouse is Marin County's only remaining mid-Victorian one-room school. It retains most of its original features. Thanks to a group of volunteers, it also retains a safe place in the world (in December, 1972, it was designated a historic site by the Department of the Interior), and a new chance to serve the people in the neighborhood. The same people who painstakingly restored it are finding it a good place for a range of community activities. And they do it with a kind of flair that has great appeal.

THE FAMED DIXIE SCHOOL MOVES AFTER 110 YEARS IN MARIN
Josephine Leary, who taught there 14 years, guides it to a new location.
—Examiner Photo

After 110 Years

Marinwood School Moved

The white paint is peeling, the whole building is perhaps a little wobbly, but after 110 years the Old Dixie School house still stands and friends of the school are determined that it will stand for a long time to come.

Today the school was moved about six city blocks from its century-old home just off Highway 101, near the Marinwood exit, to a site near Miller Creek school on Las Gallinas Avenue in Marinwood.

There the school will be restored and used as a museum and historical landmark — the school being one of the oldest one-room school houses in the state.

Heading the restoration drive is Mrs. Josephine Leary who spent 14 years teaching in the school until it was finally closed in 1954.

Mrs. Leary, who is retiring this year after 45 years of teaching, decided that the school had too important a place in history simply to be left as a maintenance office. So with the help of friends, parents and teachers she persauded the Dixie School Board to give the school the dignity of a permanent home.

If you read the handbill below, you'll see that the rededication ceremony of the relocated Dixie Schoolhouse was no mean affair. The determination of the people who saved this school is exceeded only by their imagination, and a canny sense of what the neighbors enjoy doing with their spare time.

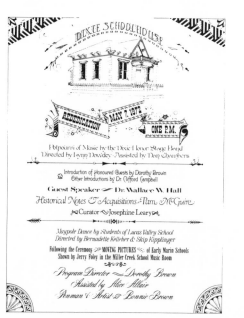

[Handbill:]
DIXIE SCHOOLHOUSE
REDEDICATION MAY 7, 1972 ONE P.M.
Potpourri of Music by the Dixie Honor Stage Band
Directed by Lynn Dowdey, Assisted by Don Chambers
Introduction of Honoured Guests by Dorothy Brown
Other Introductions by Dr. Clifford Campbell
Guest Speaker — Dr. Wallace W. Hall
Historical Notes & Acquisitions — Pam McGuire
Curator — Josephine Leary
Maypole Dance by Students of Lucas Valley School
Directed by Bernadette Kelleher & Skip Kipplinger
Following the Ceremony MOVING PICTURES of Early Marin Schools
Shown by Jerry Foley in the Miller Creek School Music Room
Program Director — Dorothy Brown
Assisted by Alice Allair
Penman & Artist — Bonnie Brown

Moon

Castle

Pidgeon

Joan

Thrush

Swan

Spinning wheel

Wind mill

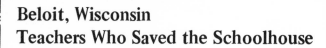

Beloit, Wisconsin
Teachers Who Saved the Schoolhouse

The schoolhouse in Beloit, Wisconsin, was built in 1850. It might still be a seed storage building on Ron Dougan's farm, but in 1970 a group of women in the Upsilon Chapter of Delta Kappa Gamma (a society of women educators) launched a four-year, $4,000 fund drive, and got the schoolhouse moved from the farm to the grounds of the Bartlett Museum. Now they are restoring it so that visitors will know what a pioneer schoolhouse was like. The building was renamed in honor of Daisy W. Chapin, a beloved Beloit educator and historian who is still active in community affairs.

Here is Daisy (with her successor, C. Ober and children of former students) having a fund drive in Cunningham amid st familiar surroundings. Daisy is now 83 yrs. old and in a Nursing Home, not able to get around.

Above, Daisy Chapin herself participates in fundraising for the school rebuilding. Mrs Evlyn Beck writes: "We also held an All Day Bell Ringing Drive in a shopping center. Every time someone came to our little booth with a donation, a genuine country school bell was rung." Evidently, the idea worked.

Below, one of the boys on the roof is Ron Dougan, whose memories of the old schoolhouse have helped restoration efforts. Some of his memories have also enriched the folklore that surrounds the old building: "At times the mothers would try to send things for a hot meal. One day there was a pot of soup heating on top of the stove, and it blew the cover off, putting soup all over the ceiling." Besides a soup-stained ceiling, the schoolhouse had a blackboard at one end, and a raised platform for the teacher's desk. There was no provision for lighting (when it got dark, school was over), and heat came from the wood-burning stove. "There was a ventilation pipe which went from the jacket of the stove through the outside wall. When someone had to stay out and there was to be some excitement inside the school, two children could get their heads down by the ventilation pipe and hear what was going on inside."

Wren

All schoolhouses have their traditional legends. In Boone County in Iowa, one of the more famous (and favorite) stories was retold at the dedication of the restored Hickory Grove School.

Mrs Edythe Mountainarry Tilley taught two stints at the school, first in the Depression years in the 1930's and then again from 1946 until the school was closed ten years later. Her memories could fill a book. She recalls that the first teachers taught despite freezing weather, that they did all their own janitorial work, and received monthly wages which would barely buy a week's groceries today. Asked about humorous or unusual things that happened during her teaching years at Hickory Grove she said:

"Probably the thing we laugh most about (though it wasn't funny then) is the booger man scare in the school. It began when we kept hearing sounds and we kept hearing someone talking or humming to himself. Then the children began missing food from their lunch pails. This was all very mysterious. We would look everywhere around the schoolhouse and in the coalhouse but couldn't find anything. This went on for several days. One day, I remember, I accused the older pupils in the back of the room of singing and humming, but they denied it. We kept hearing these sounds and I felt sure it was a prank. Then one Sunday, some neighbors heard the school bell ring. A nearby neighbor reported seeing a stranger walk from the schoolhouse across the school grounds. Well, by that time everyone, especially the younger children, were getting very nervous. Finally the sheriff was called in and some members of the board came and they searched everywhere, but could find nothing. They looked in the attic of the main part of the building, but no booger man. But after that we never heard or saw any signs of him. Then sometime later, someone had reason to go up on some boards that lay across the rafters in the cloak room addition and there they found evidence that someone had indeed lived in the schoolhouse for a while! He must have watched us search for him!"

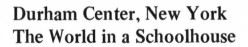

Durham Center, New York
The World in a Schoolhouse

Helen and Vernon Haskins are the gentle couple who preside over a little red schoolhouse which is the sort of place that people who save schoolhouses dream about. It all began when Haskins, as a boy, began collecting birds' nests and pioneer relics. Well, you know how it is with boys who collect things. One thing led to another, and before long Mr Haskins filled up his boyhood schoolhouse with collections which now jam two buildings. It's a kind of historical Fibber McGee's closet. A wonderful place.

That's how a lifelong hobby became a New York State Institution. Recently, the Haskins deeded their property to the New York State Board of Regents. It's hard to tell who should feel more honored. For Vernon and Helen, it's some reward for forty years of hard work with no pay. For the state, it's probably the only educational establishment of its kind.

Haskins writes: *"Ours is a humble little institution, but we are proud of our record of service. You will not find our story in the headlines of the great publications of the land, but we believe that you will find it instead in the hearts and minds of those who have visited our museum. . . . We measure our success not so much in attendance as in services rendered. And we are mighty proud of that record."*

Boone County, Iowa
The Girl Who Stopped A Train

Kate Shelley
July 6, 1881

"Hers is a deed bound for legend...."

Boone County, Iowa, has its share of heroes and legends. And there isn't any doubt that the County Historical Society there is making the most of what they have. First they successfully restored the Hickory Grove rural school as a museum. Now they want to pay tribute to a local heroine named Kate Shelley by putting up a replica of the Northwestern Railroad Depot where Kate served as Station Agent in the countryside near her home.

Boone County also hopes to make a park out of the Shelley homesite, near the proposed depot, and run excursion trains from Moingona to the Shelley home. Although Kate's dramatic story took place over fifty years ago, her memory is very much alive in Boone County today.

One of the few railroad legends we know of that involves the "gentle" sex, Kate Shelley's story (see news clip) is not only a saga worth reading, but has inspired townsfolk to ambitious restoration efforts.

Kate Shelley Anniversary Today

Boone News Republican, July 6, 1972

A Moingona girl risked her life on a stormy night 91 years ago to save the lives of two railroad men and hundreds of passengers on a midnight train to Des Moines.

It was the night of July 6, 1881 that the Shelley family sat huddled in their farmhouse between Honey Creek and the Chicago and Northwestern Railroad, about a half-a-mile from the Des Moines River.

They were waiting out an unusually heavy Iowa thunderstorm when they heard a train attempting to cross the Des Moines River bridge about 11 p.m.

The train was a single engine stationed at Mongona that served as a "pusher" that helped pull trains up steep grades on either side of the river.

The crew of four men had been ordered to Boone and back to Moingona in search of washouts along the track.

The year had been unusually wet, causing the river to stand at the high water mark for several days.

Many embankments had been undermined and the bridge pilings had weakened.

The Shelley family was aware of the danger because their father, who had died three years earlier, had been a section foreman for the railroad.

Soon they heard a horrible crash followed by the hissing of steam.

Kate Shelley looked at her mother. "Oh mother, they have all gone down," she said.

She later recalled, "It seemed as still as death; as silent as the grave," after the train crash.

The pusher had attempted to cross the bridge at Honey Creek but it had collapsed under the engine's weight into the torrential flood waters below the bridge.

Kate wasted no time. She knew that the midnight express was due in a few minutes to cross that collapsed bridge.

The entire Honey Creek valley was flooded when Kate left the house with her little miners lamp to help the men on the pusher and to save the lives of the hundreds of passengers on the late night train.

Because of the flood she could not go to the tracks and follow them to the station house. Instead she had to climb the steep bluff in back of the house and detour to the southwest until she found an old wagon trail that crossed the tracks.

Finding the tracks, she at once ran to the broken bridge.

There she found two men stranded in the tops of trees in the middle of the flood. The other two men were nowhere to be seen.

Not being able to help these men she turned and started toward Moingona, hoping to avert another disaster.

Between her and the village lay the awesome Des Moines River bridge. It was a high wooden trestle that stretched over the Des Moines River Valley for over a mile.

When she reached the bridge she was greeted by a muddy, raging river below that could at any minute rip apart the pilings.

The railroad had tried to discourage people from using the bridge to walk across by removing some of the planks. The ties were a good two feet apart and were studded with twisted rusty spikes.

To cross the bridge in pleasant weather was dangerous, but to do it in gale strong winds on rain slippery ties would test the courage of an army.

As Kate stepped on the structure she could feel the bridge sway in the wind. Immediately she dropped to her knees and began to crawl across the long trestle.

Many times on the long journey, guided only by the rails, she nearly lost her balance when her skirt became caught on the protruding spikes.

Finally she felt the ground of the west part of the valley under her.

Yet her ordeal was not finished. It was over a quarter of a mile to the station.

Knowing that it could only be a few minutes until the train arrived she got to her feet and ran the rest of the way to the station.

One can only imagine the scene at the station as the water soaked little girl appeared at the door screaming that the bridge was out on Honey Creek.

At first she was admonished for being a crazy little girl.

Then one of the men recognized her as the daughter of a former section foreman and realized that she must be telling the truth.

Her strength and courage still lasted as she guided a rescue party back across the bridge and to the bluffs above the washout where the two men clinging to the trees were

rescued.

It was three days later after the flood and the excitement had subsided that Kate

collapsed. She spent the next three months in bed recuperating from her courageous feat.

Kate Shelley

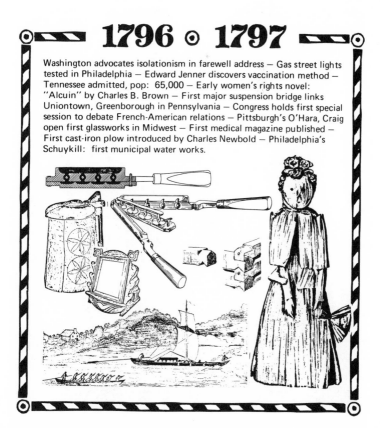

1796 ● 1797

Washington advocates isolationism in farewell address — Gas street lights tested in Philadelphia — Edward Jenner discovers vaccination method — Tennessee admitted, pop: 65,000 — Early women's rights novel: "Alcuin" by Charles B. Brown — First major suspension bridge links Uniontown, Greenborough in Pennsylvania — Congress holds first special session to debate French-American relations — Pittsburgh's O'Hara, Craig open first glassworks in Midwest — First medical magazine published — First cast-iron plow introduced by Charles Newbold — Philadelphia's Schuykill: first municipal water works.

The railroad station was the door to the future and the entrance to the outside world for small town America for over one hundred years. Trains brought news from New York, letters from Peoria, shoes from St. Louis. They took sons off to war, brought the folks to see the grandchildren, and carried the likes of Grover Cleveland on Presidential campaign tours. Almost everyone and everything new and strange came by train, and the first step in town was on the platform at the railroad station.

Now the news comes by satellite, and the shoes by interstate, along with all the visitors, so the little railroad stations in the land are mostly idle. Or they were. Like other public buildings that may appear to have outlived their functions, the old railroad station is being recycled into community life — refurbished, renovated and rewarding. Here's what you do with an old railroad station in these small towns.

Mound City, Illinois

In this small Illinois town, they're going to use an abandoned station as a library and history information center.

Mound City desperately needed a permanent home for its library. The area is economically depressed. Seventy-five per cent of the school-age children come from impoverished families. The library has a good collection of books for children, but no building. And they've spent so much time moving from one temporary location to another that no one even knows where the library is. The railroad depot is a perfect answer — after painting, re-wiring, some concrete work, insulation, roofing, plumbing and chimney repairs. Mayor Frederic Winkler says, "Everyone here is enthusiastic about the program."

But that isn't all. At the station, visitors will be able to learn about Mound City's very important role in the Civil War; they'll be headed toward the docks where the ironclads were prepared for battle, directed to the first United States Naval Hospital — in fact, the success of the railroad project will speed restoration of such landmarks as the Hospital and the Navy Yard. The old railroad depot looks like it will be a very important part of Mound City's future.

Kenwood, California

When N. W. Griswold founded the town of Kenwood in the Sonoma Valley wine country back in 1889, he demanded that the railroad build a depot which would match the elegant architecture of the rest of the town. Now, eighty years later, most of the rest of Griswold's town is gone, except for his station, and the people of Kenwood are using their picturesque depot for purposes as refined as Mr Griswold's taste — such as chamber music concerts and dramatic performances.

The Kenwood Improvement Club has owned the depot since 1940 (shortly after railroad service was discontinued). But it was only last year that Club members started to push to improve the aging station. Kenwood people are becoming "Depot Doers" as they contribute to the Building Fund or bring down a hammer and a broom and get to work. The stage has been enlarged, new paint brightens the meeting room, the huge fireplace is back in good repair and installations of such conveniences as modern electric circuitry and forced heating are finally in progress.

You can't even see where the railroad tracks used to run in Kenwood. But as the Kenwood Improvement Club says, "The Depot is still as much a part of the community as when trains were rolling through with passengers and goods bound for the San Francisco Bay Area."

Kenwood Railroad Station 1887

MERWINSVILLE

RESTORATION

It always did look more like a clubhouse than a railroad station. Now, the old depot at Kenwood is actually functioning as a gathering place for residents of the little wine country town.

Gaylordsville, Connecticut

The Merwinsville Hotel in Gaylordsville, Connecticut, is a three-story colonial-style structure built in 1843, and it may be the fanciest railroad depot ever built in America. It was an elegant luncheon stop for the mahogany-paneled excursion trains, with dining rooms, a wine cellar, a ballroom and twenty-one guest rooms. Gaylordsville citizens started three years ago to restore the glory of the station-hotel from its low point as a carpenter's warehouse. They jacked up the building, re-built part of the foundation, removed wheelbarrowsfull of decrepit plaster and began period redecoration. Money for materials was raised by selling $2 memberships in the project — as a token, each new member received an original freight bill from the elegant railroad days. When final trimmings set and dry, Gaylordsville will have one of the fanciest community centers in America, and probably the only one with a restored railroad ticket office right smack in the middle.

Cazenovia, New York

This newspaper photo shows where Cazenovia, New York, will be spending some of its spare time from now on. The old building was acquired by the Cazenovia Preservation Foundation, will be fixed up by young people who have volunteered their services, then used as a community center.

Community Center Opening Is Sunday

An open house for the public will be held at the Fairchild Kennard Community Center in the old railroad station on Williams St. Sunday, September 12.

Mayor Charles H. S. Pace will dedicate the center at 1:30 p.m. Ceremonies will include guest speakers, refreshments and entertainment.

The open house will give Cazenovians an opportunity to

hear plans for renovation of the building into a center serving young people and adults.

ACCORDING TO THE center's directors, the building will be a place for organizing and conducting recreational activities, an information center serving village and town, and a permanent meeting place for groups and organizations.

Young people have

volunteered to clean the building and grounds, and several service organizations have indicated support for the restoration of the building.

The building, once the Lehigh Valley Railroad station, is being acquired by the Cazenovia Preservation Foundation Inc. and will be leased by the Fairchild Kennard Community Center Inc.

Mt. Washington, New Hampshire

While the rest of us think about railroad stations, Mrs Ellen C. Teague is saving an entire railroad, just by keeping the engines stoked. For over one hundred years, the Mt. Washington Cog Railway has been climbing to the top of New England, carrying passengers. And for over forty of those one hundred years, it has been operated by members of the Teague family. When Arthur Teague died six years ago, the old railroad's future was thrown into doubt. He had placed principle above profit (no one gets rich running cog railroads any more) and had kept the Cog running with an absolute minimum of modernization. Who would be willing to take on such a nice but unprofitable antique? Mrs Teague herself, that's who. She took over, and in the act she preserved both a family tradition and one of the country's most interesting remnants of the days of steam locomotion.

Littleton, New Hampshire
Woodland, California

Saving the Opera House

Municipal egotism has been blamed for the destruction of many splendid old (but "old-fashioned") municipal buildings like this one. But the town fathers in Littleton must be credited with some straight thinking. They have chosen to keep their splendid Victorian Town Hall, and in the process have guaranteed a future for the town's old Opera House which happens to be in the same building.

In the days when entertainment came on the hoof rather than on the screen, the best towns had opera houses, and often they were in the town hall. Since there was no such thing as electronic amplification, the acoustics had to be good, and many of these old theaters are better than anything built since.

Once the decision was made to keep the town building, rather than try to build a new one, local people began a push to restore the old Opera House. Letters like the one from Evangeline Machlin of Boston University (right) helped. Mrs Machlin and her husband now live near Littleton and are volunteers on the restoration project.

One of the events people remember best is the appearance of Tom Thumb and his wife at the Opera House around the turn of the century. They were billed as Count and Countess Magri.

Dear Editor:

Although I think the whole Town Building is unique and historically valuable, my particular interest is in the beautiful "Opera House" or theatre auditorium that occupies one end. It needs much renovation, but as a theatre person I was astonished at its potential. Rarely does a town possess such a fine and historically valuable auditorium.

According to the history, it seated 750 when built; but it is so compact and so functionally designed that I would guess when the seats are replaced, each one would command a good view of the stage. The auditorium is handsome also; the graceful windows and fine curving lines of the balcony with the handwrought frieze decorations on the plaster, are examples of the artistic details that can hardly be reproduced today at any price.

The stage is large and open, as a good stage should be, and its acoustics are excellent; being a teacher of speech for the stage, I tried them myself, and was impressed. It would be easy to produce all kinds of shows here, musical comedies, modern plays, Shakespeare, ballet, opera — the possibilities are unlimited.

Recently I heard Elliot Norton, the well-known TV personality and drama critic of the Boston Globe, *lecture on the value of old theatres, and their irreplaceability. He said that it is a tragedy that so many have been pulled down to make room for other structures, because citizens do not understand their value. He said they are often not only historically significant, but also that functionally, in design and proportion, they are far superior to many of the modern, sterile theatres replacing them. He said communities should make every effort to preserve them, and I hope that our community will make such an effort.*

Yours sincerely,

Evangeline Machlin
Professor of Theatre Arts

Boston University

Woodland, California

The prosperous farming community of Woodland let its brick Opera House stand vacant "collecting dust and the wine-bottles and epithets of illegal entrants" for sixty years — until the Yolo County Historical Society bought it in 1971, with the idea of giving the town a center of culture once again.

Sixty years is a long time. The exterior of the structure (built in the days when great buildings were built to stand forever) needed only a vigorous bath, but just figuring out what carpentry was called for inside to make the structure usable and safe for crowds, took months. And fund-raising to carry out sixty years' worth of repairs doesn't just mean a few dollars for brushes and paint.

A general building clean-up (enough so citizens can get far enough inside to see what they've been missing) has been accomplished, and the re-painting of the original Opera House exterior lettering shows passers-by that something is finally happening. The vacant lot next door has also been purchased (from the city of Woodland, at a conveniently low price) and is becoming a mini-park with an outdoor stage for sunny-day events.

The community was welcomed back into the Opera House in May of 1972 to see — appropriately enough — the original "Phantom of the Opera" film. Soon afterwards, Old Timer's Day took place — and more than 130 people over the age of seventy showed up! A quartet — the youngest member was seventy-eight — entertained, and one of the singers told the crowd that he had sung in the Opera House once before — in 1912. The Historical Society took advantage of the gathering to tape record reminiscences, and these tapes will be the start of a collection of oral history and lore related to the Opera House.

An innovative way of celebrating the return of culture while raising some bucks is the giving of parlor concerts of light classical music, several of which have been hosted by the President of the Historical Society, Dr Cleve Baker, and his wife, in their home. Another type of music will also be heard — loud and clear — as a part of the Opera House restoration activities: the Plaza is scheduled for rock and roll street dances. Someday, rock concerts will happen inside the Opera House, too, as will classical music events. But the entertainment that the Historical Society is really looking forward to is the turn-of-the-century stage shows for which Woodland originally built its Opera House.

The Phantom Welcomed Them Back

GRANT — Dr. Cleve Baker, president of the Yolo County Historical society, receives a check from Mrs. Alice Medrich of the Rediscover America program. Looking on from left are Roger Landucci, Mayor Harold A. Roberts and Keith Long.

1800 ⦿ 1801

Washington DC becomes capital of US — Thomas Jefferson elected President — Naval war with France ends — Spain cedes Louisiana Territory to France — Library of Congress established — John Marshall appointed Chief Justice of Supreme Court — War with Tripoli — Virginia assembly proposes African resettlement of slaves — Sailors strike and riot in NY — Ben Waterhouse performs first cowpox vaccination — Johnny Appleseed begins his mission — First crackers baked in Josiah Bent's Dutch oven — Total US pop. 5,308,483.

The Woodland Opera House restoration will take years of work — not easy for modern people "conditioned to expect instant results like instant coffee" (in the words of Dr Baker) — but the Opera House itself has been patient for sixty years. And it looks now like the final results may be worth waiting for — and working for.

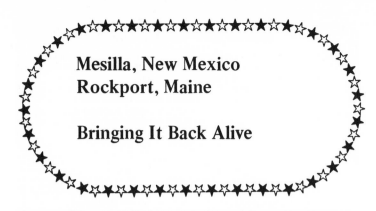

Mesilla, New Mexico
Rockport, Maine

Bringing It Back Alive

These two towns couldn't be farther apart in lots of ways, but they have at least one thing in common — townspeople in both places have decided to revive old palaces of community entertainment, built back in the days when if you didn't have your own, you went without. And in a funny way, it's still true. Ask the people in Mesilla or Rockport.

Mesilla, New Mexico

A seventy-four-year old adobe theater in Mesilla, New Mexico, has been renovated by Max Freudenthal, Mary Lou Leger, Luis Estrada and several other members in the Las Cruces Community Theater Group. The theater is called "The Fountain of Pleasure," and there are, besides the name, several unusual things about the "Fountain": (1) it operated as a playhouse for thirty years without charging admission; (2) it had its own editorial policy when it presented films; and (3) it is haunted.

The name of the theater is a play on the name of founder Albert Fountain. Fountain was an uncommonly devout man who believed that the talents of his family — all of whom were performers — were divine gifts, and that to reap profit from such gifts would be sinful. His moral stance showed itself later when films supplanted live theater. Mr Fountain personally accompanied each showing in his theater with a narration laced with moral interpretation. Moviegoers were taught Christian principles as Fountain "explained" the actions of the silent movie greats.

The Las Cruces group is not as morality-minded as old Albert Fountain, but they don't make a profit either. And they did save the soul of the theater from its limbo as a chili pepper warehouse.

The ghost? Her name is Maria. She is seen now and again standing in the ticket booth at the first light of morning. And sometimes she plays with the theater's stage lights. Once an actor, angry at her antics, swore oaths to drive her away. It worked for a while. But now she's back. And everyone is glad.

Little by little, as there is any extra money, the Las Cruces Community Theater people patch up the old adobe building, adding "new" used seats here, something else there. Albert Fountain might not approve of all of the plays, but he couldn't deny that the "Fountain" is again bringing pleasure to Mesilla.

Rockport, Maine

Rockport, Maine, has just converted its Opera House into an Opera House. Actually, the building served its middle years as Rockport's Town Hall. A new Town Hall structure then made the old building obsolete, and for a time it stood at a crossroads between re-use and destruction. Then along came the Rockport Garden Club. They launched a campaign to "Save and Use the Rockport Town Hall" — as an opera house — and high-quality music is the result.

The first performance, presented in September of 1971 by opera impressario Boris Guldovsky, was "The Telephone" by former Rockport summer resident Gian-Carlo Menotti. At that time, Guldovsky decreed that the Hall had unparalleled acoustics, was a "gem" of a theater, and certainly should be saved.

Musical offerings are usually accompanied by considerable community involvement; for instance, the ladies of the Megunticook Grange preparing a whole "downeast" supper for the busload of hungry symphonists on arrival from Bangor before the December 9, 1972, performance of works by Wagner, Handel and Rimsky-Korsakoff — which may explain why the musicians performed so well that evening.

And besides providing the community with a music hall, the ladies of the Rockport Garden Club have resolved the building's long-time identity crisis. During all its years as a Town Hall, the lovely old red glass transom above the entrance insisted that the building was an "Opera House." Its insistence seems to have paid off.

Little Falls, New York

Is This Urban Removal Project Necessary? or,
The Bank Stands Alone

In Little Falls, a Greek Revival bank that was built of hand-hewn stone in 1833 now stands alone at the corner of Ann and Albany Streets, at the end of a row of rubble. The Little Falls Urban Renewal people hope to level it as soon as possible — even though it's structurally sound, architecturally valuable, and historically a key part of the community.

The 115 members of the Little Falls Historical Society have been fighting for four years for the Herkimer County Bank's life, against some remarkably stubborn opposition. Urban renewal is, of course, not primarily responsible for saving historic structures. But the U.S. Department of Housing and Urban Development does have funds available to restore buildings listed in the National Register of Historic Places which stand in urban renewal project areas.

The Herkimer Valley Bank is now on the National Register, but the local Urban Renewal director, at the time of this writing, has not asked for the money. He points out that the building was not on the Register when the Little Falls redevelopment scheme was approved (which is true), and concludes that he doesn't have any responsibility to ask for funds for restoration (which is what everyone is upset about). He says it will be harder to interest a commercial developer in a block that isn't completely cleared (which may or may not be true). And he isn't certain that local people will have money to maintain the Bank if HUD does agree to provide a majority of restoration funds. There you have it.

Despite bureaucratic shuffling, the Historical Society has solicited contributions, held garage sales, bake sales, crafts shows, hobby shows and two "Taster's Luncheons." They have raised over $6,000 in an area which has the highest unemployment in New York State — and proven

The Herkimer County Bank was built when Little Falls was blossoming into a commercial center at the point where Western New York's farmlands met the newly-important river traffic. But elegantly-clad gentlemen such as those above probably haven't been near the building in many years now. The Little Falls Historical Society is fighting mightily to help the building shed the ignominy shown in the lower right photograph.

CENTENNIAL REVIEW

LITTLE FALLS N.Y.
1811 – 1911

at least that some people care very much about the old Bank and are willing to work hard to keep it from the rock pile.

The Historical Society has been polite, energetic and sincere in trying to convince the Urban Renewal people to save the Bank. They haven't failed, but they haven't succeeded, either. It looks like the Society is going to have to do something big — something that will rally the whole town into active and vocal support.

It is ironic that a renewal project designed to revitalize Little Falls should disregard the town's first important commercial structure. The Herkimer County Bank epitomizes the pride of a farm settlement that built itself into a trade center. What does the planners' map suggest that the Bank lot be used for? A forty car parking lot.

Warrensburg, Missouri
The Living Legend of Old Drum

Every town should have at least one great old building to show off to visitors, and there certainly ought to be at least one amazing story that goes along with it. Warrensburg, Missouri, has got 'em. The energetic members of the Johnson County Historic Society (with much help from local college students) are 80% finished with the restoration of the Johnson County Court House — a Georgian-style building of brick with walnut and oak. The story that goes with it is about a faithful hunting dog named Old Drum, and a trial that took place back in 1870.

Old Drum, the favorite hound of one Charles Burden, was shot by a neighbor, Leonidas Hornsby, who had sworn to kill the first dog that came onto his property because he had lost a number of sheep. Though Hornsby had hunted with Drum, and acknowledged him to be one of the best hunting dogs he had ever seen, he insisted on carrying out his threat when he found Old Drum prowling in his yard. Burden sued Hornsby for damages, and — with each man determined to win his case — the argument went all the way to the Missouri Supreme Court. It was in Warrensburg's Court House that the case was decided in favor of Burden and Old Drum (Hornsby had to pay $50 in damages) — mostly because of a stirring eulogy to the hound delivered by Senator George Graham Vest. He appealed to the hearts of dog lovers everywhere when he said, "The one absolutely unselfish friend that a man can have in this selfish world, the one that never deserts him, the one that never proves ungrateful or treacherous, is his dog." The drama of that trial was re-enacted during the "Old Drum Centennial" that Warrensburg celebrated in 1970.

Besides hearing about Old Drum, Court House visitors can browse public history exhibits showing Johnson County's role in the Civil War, or visit a little Country Store run by the Historical Society. When restoration is finished,

public events will enliven the Court House too. If you visit friends in Warrensburg, don't be surprised if they waste no time in showing you the Court House, and filling you in on the story of a certain legendary hound.

1802 ◎ 1803

Military academy opens at West Point — Library of Congress issues first catalog — First sheet copper produced in Boston — Louisiana territory purchased; US area doubles — Marbury vs. Madison: Supreme Court establishes judicial review — Ohio admitted, pop. 46,000 — Fulton tests steamboat unsuccessfully in France — First tax-supported library opens in Salisbury, Conn. — Ezekiel Case begins glove manufacturing in Gloversville, NY.

New Orleans, Louisiana
No Money for the Mint

New Orleans is one of only seven American cities to have a United States Mint operate within its bounds. From 1838 until 1909 the dies stamped the letter O on millions of silver and gold coins. Since the 1909 closing, people have been dreaming up uses for the stately grey money factory, but all that's happened during the past sixty-five years is decay . . . almost.

Jack Cosner is a young architect with red hair and a strong desire to keep old buildings alive. Cosner, who lives in a restored Vieux Carre mansion, decided in 1970 to try to put a little life in the Mint. What he did was give a group of fourteen eager Tulane architecture students the chance to do a full-blown study on restoration and re-use. The students drew up not one but six excellent plans — including features such as a museum of jazz, art exhibition areas, concert halls, shops, restaurants, children's play areas, even living quarters for an artist-in-residence program. But although the students' work was a hit on the front pages, it was a miss in the financial section: no money for restoration of the Mint anywhere. So the interior walls crumble and the Mint approaches oblivion, in spite of the young planners' spirited effort.

To look at it, you would never know that the serene white church in the middle of this classically quaint little New England town was once the symbol of a community controversy that raged for over a hundred and fifty years (a social phenomenon that, in itself, may be possible only in New England). Somehow, the old church survived it all, and, restored as a community center, could be what it takes to knit the town back together.

"At the turn of the century, Francestown was the religiously benighted possessor of two doctrinally distinct churches, the two congregations acting toward each other, individually and collectively, in as unchristian a way as is to be expected of Christians, but also with a personal spitefulness which cleaved the town into two intolerant factions which would have nothing to do with each other. Any organization which sought to bridge the gap — even if it only involved school children — would inevitably keel into this joyless rift between the two faiths," writes Dr John Schott in his book *Frances' Town*.

Finally, financial pressure forced a series of attempts at religious unity, and the Old Meeting Hall, after agreements and disagreements, mergers and schisms, finally became the central hall for The Federated Church of Francestown. Unfortunately, even economic necessity could not mend the rift, and the building eventually became the property of the Unitarians.

Despite (or perhaps because of) all the tempest and fury, a community-wide effort was mounted to save the building when, in 1972, it was discovered that parts of it were in danger of falling down. Although technically it still belongs to the Unitarians, it is maintained by the community and is now used for many non-religious community events, including occasional performances by the highly-regarded orchestra of the local Monadnock Music group, and is still very much in the center of community attention.

How has the Old Meeting Hall become such a symbol for this unusual little community? The answer is not simple, but it centers around three points. Dr Schott comments:

Francestown, New Hampshire
Sunday Go To Meeting

"One reason for the importance of the Meeting Hall is simply the fact that the building is so especially handsome from an architectural standpoint that it is hard to imagine any community not taking civic pride in its presence. Also, it is the first thing one sees upon entering the village, and probably the last thing a visitor forgets after leaving.

"Rather ironically, the Meeting House has undoubtedly become a symbol by having been for so long a center of town controversy. There are still a few in town who'll say, 'the church can collapse into its cellar hole before I'll contribute a penny to support those damned Unitarians.' But the righteous indignation this prompts among non-church goers, preservationists, the religiously devout, old-timers and new-comers alike, as well as the small children of the town, far offsets the irrational antagonisms engendered by family hostilities going back several generations.

"Lastly, and at the risk of sounding maudlin, anyone who has lived in a New England village knows the sense of serenity and peace one can feel on a crisp winter's night upon hearing the church bell steadily tolling the hours, a sound heard miles around. For those who have grown up to that sound, as well as to those escapees from suburbia, it epitomizes in some special undefinable way what New England is all about. Had not the present preservation effort been successful, that bell tower would have either collapsed within a year or two, or would have had to be torn down as a hazard owing to rotted timbers."

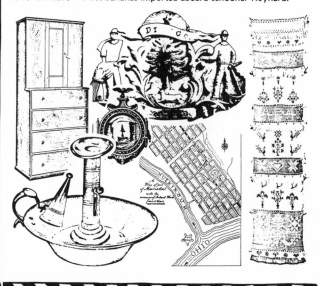

1804 ⊙ 1805

Lewis and Clark set out from St. Louis — Hamilton dies in duel with Burr — Middlesex Canal opens — Andrew Jackson completes "The Hermitage" in Tennessee woods — Coonskin Library opens in Marietta, Ohio — Tripoli War ends; treaty grants US Navy freedom in Mediterranean — Zebulon Pike begins search for Mississippi River source — In vogue: French Directoire furniture — First bananas imported aboard schooner Reynard.

Buckfield, Maine
Pultneyville, New York
Buena Vista, Colorado

The Old Church on the Hill

From all approaches a Beacon seen
Piercing the blue above the green
O'er looking the scene, a befitting
    crown
of the landscape fair and the beautiful
    town.
The pride of our fathers, tall and still,
the old white chapel that stands on
    the hill.

"The Old Church on the Hill in Buckfield, Maine, is being renovated. A group of civic minded citizens have formed a steering committee consisting of Chairman Roger Kimball, Vice-Chairman Virgil Tilton, Secretary Mary Harris, Treasurer Elizabeth Tucker, Publicity and Historian Chairman Georgia Prescott Robertson, Grounds Chairman Sandra Perkins, Artifacts Co-chairmen Alice Parks and Virginia Smith. Myra Irish is an honorary member and advisor; Ruth Scott has volunteered to handle Art Work.

"This well-preserved old building belongs to the people of Buckfield, having been purchased in 1895 for the sum of $75.00. It is hoped that, as soon as this year's planned portion of the work is finished, it will be used by the people of Buckfield. As the building was once used as a gathering place for town meetings and other activities, as well as having been used as a chapel and church, possibilities for its use include meetings of senior citizens, youth groups, local organizations, weddings, annual church services and many others.

"Beautifully white from a fresh coat of paint on the outside, it is a maintenance project voted for and accomplished by the townspeople. If you would like to see one of the remaining old churches with its unique spire still intact, come to Buckfield and see our part of the past that we are working to keep for the future: The Old Church on the Hill."

If building the school came first, building the church came next, and in some early settlements, the order was reversed. Like schools, churches were a gathering place for simple folk without any of the present day distractions from work — and devout though they were, the builders of early churches needed the socializing that church provided as much as they needed divine providence. Like the old one-room schoolhouses, the white spires of little wooden churches still dot the landscape, many of them abandoned for some more modern, or more grand, house of worship.

Here are the stories of three quite different churches, and the efforts that are being made to restore them once again to a place in the center of community life.

See you in church:
Buckfielders of all ages — from the high school musicians to eighty-six year old Church Board Member Myra Irish — are finding the church a friendly place for community activities.

Buckfield, Maine

The following account appeared in the Norway, Maine, Advertiser-Democrat. The accompanying photographs are evidence that the hopeful tone of the writer was justified. The Buckfield Church is once again the scene of social gatherings, and like restored churches in other towns, is providing the community with a certain something that was missing for a long time.

Pultneyville, New York

John Westerburg calls himself "The Yankee Peddler," and earns his living selling books. He and some of his neighbors are using an old church as a place to rediscover Pultneyville's empyreal religious history.

"We are the Burnt Over Society — we formed in October of 1971. The main subject matter of the Burnt Over Society's work will be a dramatic review of each of the spiritual and religious groups in this area. For this, we are restoring Pultneyville's old Union Church building, which is called Gates Hall.

"In the early 1800's, there were hundreds and hundreds of itinerant preachers, circuit riders, maneuvering through this area, competing with each other. Religion became fierce because each wanted to outdo the other. They'd have five-day meetings where four or five preachers would get together and really put on a show, almost a dramatic show. People cried. A man would stand out in the street because he didn't want to go into the church and all the women would sit down in a circle around him and pray that he'd enter the church. Women wouldn't make love to their husbands unless they agreed to be converted. This developed into a revival tradition and overflowed into new sects and religions: Mormonism, Millerites, Never-Sweats — a sect of Quakers — and many spiritualist groups. They all started in this area. From 1800 to 1850 was the period of the "burnt-over district" — everyone got burned over from fire and brimstone. Our area is still called the Burnt Over District. We're researching the social history of our county before 1850, and the Burnt Over Society's dramatic effort is going to be based on that.

"Our Society is giving the maximum effort toward restoring the Hall, but there are others in the community involved, too. We want to put gas lights back in, and red seats and red curtains. It's being continually used for one thing or another while we clean it up. The people in Pultneyville own the building, anybody that lives here has a share, and we hope they all make use of it.

"Our intention at this point is the first time we give a performance not to charge anything for tickets but to move around the entire community and say: 'Here are two tickets to the first effort of the Burnt Over Society. We are remodeling Gates Hall. Please give what you want to.' We think they'll like the way we're giving the building this kind of attention, and also bringing the Burnt Over District's religious history back to life."

Buena Vista, Colorado

This account of the near-death of "the prettiest little antique in the West" is one of the best such sagas we've run across. So we reprint it here.

CAN

YOU

GIVE

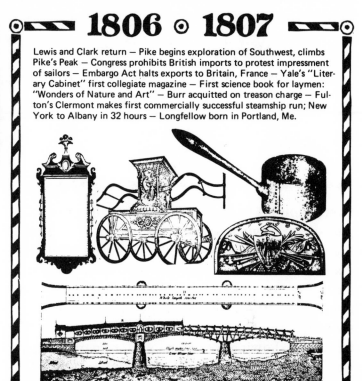

1806 ⊙ 1807

Lewis and Clark return — Pike begins exploration of Southwest, climbs Pike's Peak — Congress prohibits British imports to protest impressment of sailors — Embargo Act halts exports to Britain, France — Yale's "Literary Cabinet" first collegiate magazine — First science book for laymen: "Wonders of Nature and Art" — Burr acquitted on treason charge — Fulton's Clermont makes first commercially successful steamship run; New York to Albany in 32 hours — Longfellow born in Portland, Me.

When the high little mountain town of Buena Vista, Colorado, was a brawling, burgeoning, dusty mining center with freightwagons pouring through en route to the silver boom town of Leadville and the fabulous gold fields of St. Elmo, and a heavy traffic of creaking wagons brought rich ores to the local smelters; when the town consisted mostly of hastily constructed tents and shanties and there were 68 places where a man could get a drink; it was then that a group of folks put their resources together to build Buena Vista's first little church building. That was 1879---a very early date for the gentler cultural things to be happening in these parts!

Nearly 90 years later, after continuous use, the little frame church-house was abandoned in favor of a move to a new, starkly modern assembly hall. The little church-house was condemned to demolition. As nobody wanted the job for its salvage value, and several tentative efforts by aesthetically and historically minded individuals to have the little church-house moved had trailed into nothingness, the fire department volunteered to use it for practice and burn it neatly to the ground.

Although cries of dismay and dazed disbelief went up from many quarters, especially from oldsters whose childhood memories centered around the little church, nobody came up with money or an effective plan.

Then, practically on the day of the proposed cremation, a woman of some means and lots of determination came flying down the street waving a restraining order, figuratively speaking; and within a few weeks the little structure was sitting on a new foundation in a grove of old cottonwood trees beside the highway, in a city park.

For three years it sat there, praying for a future, fallen plaster littering its hardwood floor, its quaint pine pews all in disarray, ancient white paint flaking off with every breeze. The disgruntled firemen made threatening noises from time to time and the Town Council spread its collective hands helplessly whenever the subject came up. None of the old established clubs wanted to touch it with a ten foot pole. The Park Department even permitted the cutting of park trees in front of it to open up the view of a new gas station sign a block away!

Then, last August, a small committee got itself together with determination to restore the "Little Chapel in the Park" to usefulness as a community center for art and history, club meetings and perhaps weddings---simply because it was THERE. (The only "community house" in town had been destroyed during highway construction.)

With publication of this aim, support has gradually rallied. With donations of cash, labor and good discounts on building materials, an aura of hope now surrounds the project. Installation of water heating, electricity, the painting and repair of walls, etcetera, are being achieved.

Bethel, Missouri
The Gospel of Hard Work and Sharing

Every building in Bethel, Missouri, is, in a sense, part of the original community church — because the community was founded as a religious colony dedicated to God, sharing and hard work. Present day residents — almost all of whom are descended from colonists — now are saving the buildings that their grandparents and great-grandparents built, and showing the same extraordinary cooperation that was characteristic of Bethel colonists.

The Christian commune of Bethel prospered as a frontier manufacturing and trade center from 1844 to 1879. Even after the dissolution of the commune, the town continued to grow. As the years went by, though, trade activity moved away from Bethel. One by one, the small factories ceased operation. Homes were vacated. In 1970, Bethel's population had dropped to 150, and community activity was at an all-time low.

The inevitable conversations about the town's predicament compared to its lively past caused a meeting to be called — of all people interested in the original Bethel Colony. Sixty people showed up (and how many towns could get forty per cent of their population to a meeting about *anything*?). The interest was there: my father did this, I want to fix up that, I haven't seen you in ages, I know just the person, and so on.

The energy behind the Bethel Colony Foundation comes from three ladies, each of whom is a member of either the original Bower family, the original Bauer family, or both: Mrs Marion Gonnerman; Mrs Lucille Bower; and the postmistress of Bethel, Mrs Nedra Garrison. The ladies, their husbands, or their friends or relatives have bought — individually or collectively — several of the sturdy colony

buildings. They have begun restoration, and hope to encourage similar efforts for all the remaining colony buildings.

More important, they appear to have revived the fine Bethel traditions of hard work and sharing. Their efforts have restored the faith of the people of this small community in their past, and in their village's future. And who could ask for anything more?

To the left are the three ladies from Bethel who started out bravely enough, but weren't sure they could do it. One year and several successes later, they know better. Bethel hasn't seen such a future since old Dr Keil was in charge.

1808 ◉ 1809

Congress halts slave importation — First Bible society formed in Philadelphia — "Worthless" anthracite coal burned for first time to heat homes — John Stevens' "Phoenix" first US oceangoing steamboat — Commercially unpopular Embargo Act repealed — Jefferson retires to Monticello — Boston Crown Co. makes first window glass — Washington Irving's "History of New York" first American literature to impress Europe.

Dr. William Keil and "Elim"

Pictured above is Dr. William Keil, founder of the Bethel Colony and his Bethel home known as "Elim". As can be seen, the brick house included 3 complete stories. One of the floors was used as a community room. Social functions and community entertainment were held on this floor. A debate has arisen in recent years as to the occupancy of "Elim". According to some Bethel historians and records, Dr. Keil never lived in "Elim" but preferred to take residence in another house directly in the colony.

Russell Springs, Kansas
Summing Up

Here are parts of a letter from Michael Baughn of Russell Springs, Kansas, who writes about a local project, but speaks for people with similar feelings all over the country:

It is my sincere belief that our organization, chartered in 1964, has grown so rapidly and become so widely recognized as a concern on the move simply because it is a "labor of love" to us. We want to preserve the old Courthouse and adjoining buildings for generations of Americans, yet unborn, to enjoy. It will serve as a repository for antiques, diaries, manuscripts, paleontological displays and American Indian displays as long as we can afford to keep it open. We are not out for the almighty buck that some organizations are; we simply want to show people our past, of which we are rightly proud.

It has required a lot of time, talent and money from our local people to keep our projects going, but we enjoy our "hobby." We are all amateurs and don't want to accept any money with "strings attached." Our museum is the focal point of community life, along with the Church and the grade school. We respect our history and traditions and will do all we can to see them preserved.

One mile east of Bethel is a three story house, Elim, built around 1848 by the Colony Craftsmen for their leader Dr. Keil. Made of Colony bricks, 36 x 60 feet in size this house has a full basement and wine cellar of hand hewn limestone rocks. On the main floor four large rooms open from a wide hall. Double doors of paneled walnut open to the outside at each end of the hall. Fireplaces in each room provided the heat. The entire second floor was used for a ball room. Here the Colonist celebrated holidays with music and dancing.

Lend a hand to one another in the daily toil of life.

And thus we came both weary and welcome, home; and delivered in our corn into the store to be kept for seed.

My only suit to all men is, that, whether they live here or there, they would learn to use this world as if they used it not.

Every farm should own a good farmer.

THE QUIET FIELDS OF MY FATHERS

Miller owns this field, Locke that, and Manning the woodland beyond. But none of them owns the landscape. (Emerson)

Santa Susana, California
Saving Them Thar Hills

"In an eighty square mile area where so many different periods of history are still evident — it would be an injustice to our descendents not to save this living history for them, too. When all the Indians, Mexicans, Spaniards and pioneers used it without spoiling it, why should *we* be the ones to allow its destruction?"

Jan Hinkston said that. Who is Jan Hinkston? She's a Los Angeles housewife who's trying to save those eighty square miles of wild canyon country from residential development. She originated the idea, and now the Santa Susana Mountain Park Association, the Chatsworth Beautiful organization, the Simi Valley Beautiful group, several Boy Scout troups, many local business firms, a Congressman and various unaffiliated residents are united behind her.

Jan and her friends see great historic and environmental value in preserving what some people would call a wasteland:

"The unspoiled Santa Susana Mountains rise above the heavily-populated San Fernando Valley and the rapidly growing Simi Valley. These mountains are rich in oak-filled canyons; high, but accessible peaks bathed in sun even when the valley below disappears beneath a sickly yellow blanket of smog.

"In these mountains can be seen clues to each age of our history since the time of the dinosaurs — when the towering mountains were uplifted from the floor of the sea; through the age of the ancient Indian tribes who dwelled throughout the Santa Susanas as evidenced by archaeologists' findings; to the time of the Mexican and Spanish settlements and large ranchos; on down to when the pioneers made the long, hard migration west, and stage coach trails (such as the section of trail the Santa Susana Mountain Park Association is seeking to purchase) were the freeways of that day."

The all-star cast of the SSMPA hams it up on the Iverson Movie Ranch acreage, where all those Hollywood "oaters" were filmed. (It's part of the proposed park.) Leading lady Jan Hinkston is third from left.

It's not easy to say "no" to land developers — especially in Los Angeles, where the developers and land speculators have usually had their way. But the people of Chatsworth, Santa Susana, Newhall, Simi Valley, Valencia and Saugus are saying "no," because they almost unanimously prefer a natural park to another vast housing development (for which much of the area is zoned). If the mountains are developed, people already living in the area have a lot to lose, and very little (if anything) to gain.

They are saying "no" by publicizing park plans . . . by organizing merchant support . . . by leading hikes through the mountains . . . by holding junior bicycle rallies . . . by sending speakers to PTA's, to civic organizations, and to youth groups . . . by raising money to buy land options . . . by writing local, state and national park and recreation departments . . . and by raising more and more money, because any landholder who has a half-million invested is not likely to give it away, no matter how public-spirited he is. The Santa Susana campaign has such a high activity level that they fill a two-page newsletter every month (edited by Doris Murphy) with news like this about the project:

1810 ○ 1811

Madison annexes West Florida — Boston Philharmonic Society forms first regular orchestra — First theater in West opens in Lexington, Ky. — John Jacob Astor organizes Pacific Fur Co. — Cape Disappointment, Wash. becomes first Pacific NW colony — Earthquake shakes Ohio-Mississippi valleys — First steamboat navigates Mississippi — Charles Deslandes leads Louisiana slave revolt — Harrison defeats prophet Tippecanoe; Indians flee to Canada — Total US pop. 7,239,881.

"Thoreau said: 'Each town should have a park, or rather a primitive forest, where a stick should never be cut . . . a common possession forever for instruction and recreation.' Thoreau didn't say it was easy to accomplish this — but, working together, we hope to be able to leave Los Angeles a better place, with a regional park people can be proud of."

"SSMPA IS PLANNING another two-day Hike-In on the Stage Coach Trail. The tremendous success of the January Hike-In and numerous requests from individuals and organizations who missed the first ones led to this decision. Once again volunteers are needed to serve as guides, speakers, parking attendants, group organizers and publicity assistants. We'll need volunteers to man food, information and other booths, and special guides to conduct slower tours for those who because of age or physical handicaps cannot keep pace with a faster moving group. If you or anyone you know can donate oranges or home-baked food ... or wish to donate the wholesale cost of soda and other commercially produced food to sell, let us know as soon as possible."

The Santa Susana Mountain Park Association is fighting against tremendous odds, because they are arguing that dollar profit should take second place to cultural worth in the determination of the Mountain area's fate. If they win the argument, if they permanently save more than a token area of their mountains, Jan Hinkston and her co-workers will have proved to several million other Los Angeles people that you don't *have* to say "yes" to the bulldozer.

"COLLEGE STUDENTS are being scheduled to lead younger people on various types of hikes and we need even more to help guide and inform these young groups. IF YOU ARE A TEACHER with knowledge of nature or geology, you are also urgently needed to lead hikes on weekends so we can keep our hiking program operating successfully.

"IT'S BEEN A GOOD month (February, 1972). We are happy to report that only $250.00 more in donations will enable us to obtain the option on the upper forty-two acres of the Stage Coach Trail. $250 is a lot of money, but not when we stop and realize that we have already raised the balance of the $5,300. Especially significant is the fact that $4,000 of it came from many small donations, none over $60 from any one individual.

"THE PUBLIC is no longer asked what it wants, nor is it often given a choice. Instead it has been led to believe 'the professionals' must determine its needs and what is best. More often than not, we find that when a question of profit is involved, the welfare of the community takes a back seat."

Sun Valley, California
Saving the Natives

There are some people in Southern California who are saving a special kind of history, natural history. It's a real "grass roots" project. They are running a nursery where anyone can purchase native California plants and seeds, and learn about their growing habits. Some of them are extinct in the wild, and their delicate nature has made them unpopular with commercial nurseries. It all began with a horticulturist named Theodore Payne who devoted his life to saving the plants of his state.

In 1903 Mr Payne started a nursery in downtown Los Angeles. When he retired at ninety, the Theodore Payne Foundation was formed to carry on his forty years of cultivation and preservation of 430 species of native plants.

The fledgling Foundation had some problems. In 1961, a new site for the nursery had to be found. Five years of uncertainty followed before a solution presented itself: Edwin Merrill, owner of a native plant nursery north of Los Angeles, offered to donate his nursery and lands to the Foundation. The Foundation and its "vanishing natives" had found a home, and they have been there ever since. Merrill lives there, volunteers run it, and people come from all over to get acquainted with California's "living history." If you're interested, contact the Theodore Payne Nursery, 10459 Tuxford Street, Sun Valley, CA 91352.

Tannehill, Alabama
The People's State Park

When the state of Alabama designated sixty-six acres surrounding the old Tannehill blast furnaces as a State Park in 1970, they made it known that there was no money available for improvements. So sixteen local residents who thought the Park was a good idea — the Tannehill Furnace and Foundry Commission — agreed to somehow provide what the state of Alabama couldn't.

This unusual do-it-yourself approach is working. One reason is that the Commission hired Ed Nelson, who understood immediately *what* the Commission was trying to do, and wasn't put off by the impossible-sounding task of *how* to do it. Nelson took the job of Superintendent — which means everything from long-range planning to emptying garbage cans — at a salary determined by what the Commission could afford. And, as if that weren't enough, he agreed to provide his own place to live. Ed Nelson could have found a job that pays a whole lot more money — but he says he couldn't have found a better job anywhere.

What is Tannehill Park now? If you are used to the asphalt-and-landlord-green style of most institutional parks, you'll notice something right away: this is a welcoming place. No you-are-being-watched signs on arrival. You might be met by a flock of noisy white geese who waddle furiously to greet anyone who has food (otherwise, they're not interested). There is Roupe's Creek for swimming, simple campsites, trails to hike, a concession stand that sells Confederate flags and orange drink, and about half a mile down a green and shady path stand the silent ruins of Moses Stroup's twin furnaces (see box). It's a nice place for people.

Here's Ed Nelson inside the furnace.

Tannehill Park also has something special for children: the private zoo of Mr and Mrs Stamps. The Stamps' menagerie is a double row of pens and cages containing animal visitors — most of whom are kept only a little while, and then released. The Stamps love their animals and the children. The children love the animals and the Stamps. The animals don't seem to mind the arrangement. The zoo is a popular attraction.

The future? The Commission has big plans — they hope to expand the size of the Park (the dream is one thousand acres). They plan to rebuild and reactivate one of Stroup's two furnaces; to establish a one-of-a-kind museum on the history of the iron industry; and to re-establish the old charcoal pits. And it may all happen — because people who come to see Tannehill sense that special feeling about the place, and want to stay — or help. Nelson has had help moving and rebuilding a number of old log cabins and other antique structures, which are now in use as park buildings. (If you ever visit Tannehill, better bring your work clothes.)

Mrs Stamps makes crafts pieces (such as this bottle filled with natural colored sands) for sale — and the proceeds go back into the Park's general fund.

Tannehill is already an impressive example of what people can do without much money. It's probably the way parks used to be made in America — before everyone learned how to let the government do it. Maybe it's time to revive the tradition. A few more parks wouldn't hurt us any, and the price is right. Ed Nelson will tell you that it's one "hell of a lot of work," and you'd better not plan on any other hobbies while you're at it. But when your friends ask what it is you're doing in the woods every weekend, you can tell them you're making a State Park, and we're willing to bet you won't find anyone who can top that.

Mr and Mrs Stamps were actually the first official visitors to Tannehill State Park — and they liked it so much that they've never left. The zoo and the crafts store above are the results of their decision.

VISIT HISTORIC TANNEHILL IRON FURNACES

The iron works started small in 1831, with a single forge built by Daniel Hillman. The property changed hands several times, finally coming under the control of legendary Southern ironmaster Moses Stroup. Stroup saw the value of the site's proximity to iron ore deposits, sandstone cliffs (for construction material), water power, wood (for plank structures and charcoal), and solid stone (for constructing the furnaces and stacks), and he created and brought into production the first of the great stacks in 1859. But the Tannehill Works' days of glory were to be few: seven years later, Captain James A. Sutherland and his three companies of the 8th Iowa put the torch to the cast houses, tramways, trestles and settlement houses. The stacks were soon hidden by the thick, sleepy forest, and remained so until the Tannehill Furnace and Foundry Commission created Tannehill State Park with the furnace ruins as the centerpiece.

"Its ruins still stand in silent watch at the base of a lonely cliff, above Roupes Creek, that slender dark-flowing tributary of Shades Creek. Two massive stacks of solid masonry builded as the Romans builded twenty centuries ago, great stone on stone — vine-veiled these forty years — are all that is left today of Moses Stroup's handiwork. Solemnly the old furnace speaks of the heavy ways of toil, long since dead, that our fathers had before us." — Ethel Armes in *The Story of Iron and Coal in Alabama* (written c. 1905).

1812 ◉ 1813

War with British and frontier Indians (War of 1812) — First war bonds authorized — First foreign aid: $50,000 quake relief to Venezuela — Louisiana admitted, pop. 78,000 — Philadelphia Academy of Natural Sciences founded — Jethro Wood patents iron plow — William Monroe of Concord, Mass. makes first lead pencils — Troy, NY meatpacker Sam Wilson becomes the original "Uncle Sam."

Carroll County, Ohio
Hammering and Threshing and
Hand-Sowing and
Square Dancing and Quilting

Living on the land: not "suffering," not "enduring," not "getting by," but *living*. Tilling the soil, building shelters, raising livestock; working with two hands or with tools, alone or with neighbors; growing, harvesting, preparing, storing food — the farm has been home for millions of Americans, and farming has been, in general, a good life. The people in Carroll County, Ohio, think so, and they don't want any part of it forgotten. They want to remember farming as a way of life — not an industry — the way it was before weather satellites, crop subsidies and frozen beans in butter sauce.

How do you save a way of life? Certainly not by running farms as if William McKinley were still President. (You'd have a hard time selling that to people who have to work hard to make ends meet using the best of modern techniques.) People in Carroll County are saving their past simply by devoting some of their spare time to the rediscovery of things that gave their grandparents sustenance and joy. And it's working. How are they doing it?

The difference between any potentially good restoration project and a really successful one is at least partly a matter of organization. Carroll County's secret is a retired school principal named James Steer: he's an organizer with an appreciation for traditions. He's been all over the world but always comes back to Carroll County. Steer is president of the Carroll County Historical Society, which is a collection of people who care about their past and enjoy doing something about it. Take the Algonquin Mill, for example. Somebody noticed an old grain mill building that was left to fall apart, and they asked for some help. At one of the Society's regular meetings, Ellis Wiley stood up and right out of the blue asked if people would like to see the mill actually running again. Just because he likes steam engines, he spent a year

tinkering with an old engine in his shop at home, and restored it to like-new condition.

Then there is Wendell Oberlin who volunteered to raise a few acres of oats last year in the old-fashioned way, so there could be an authentic threshing demonstration at the Annual Festival. The Mill wasn't ready to grind by Festival time, but Paul Ross had a 1916 Case thresher he wanted people to see running, and Charles Harrison had just the sort of Russell Steam Engine that was perfect to drive it. And that's how it went. By now, the Algonquin Mill is back in business, and it's the pride of Carroll County.

Festival? Well, Carroll County people enjoy getting everybody together once a year to share in old-time activities like making apple butter in witches' brew size pots. It's held at the Mill, so it also gives them a chance to show off what they've done with that "old pile of boards." Of course, it takes about four months of preparation. There are all sorts of special projects to be done — preserving, whittling, fanciwork, and, later on, the baking. *"The Festival is the event, and it's a grand time, but the getting ready is more than half of it!"* The Festival also raises money and always manages to bring a few more people into the Historical Society as enthusiastic workers. Finally, listening to the Black Mountain Rag played at the Festival's Old-Time Fiddle Contest with a cup of freshly-pressed cider in hand or seeing a nine year old smile with her first taste of homemade butter makes an old-time fair pretty well worth the trouble.

He won't come right out and say it, but James Steer, Historical Society President, must feel a special kind of pride every time he turns the key to open the old mill. Ellis Wiley, pictured below, is the man who's changing the mill from a silent relic into a hum-dinger.

SUGAR PUMPKIN

Carroll County's Finest: *Late afternoons in summertime, you hear the hum of power saws as these men take a few extra hours to do "just a little bit more" on the County's Algonquin Mill. James Steer is second from right.*

And if the Festival isn't enough, people in the Carroll County Historical Society never have to look very far to find more to do. They saved the first church built in their area. (It had never been remodeled, and looks just like 1850.) And they built a park and a historic monument on a plot of land which was occupied by the New Hagerstown Academy, a nineteenth century institution known nationally for its high standards. Nobody ever forgets that these are *community* projects either — not when one family comes and plants flowers in the park "because it needed some" . . . and a brick barbecue appears because somebody "thought it might be a good idea."

All of this hammering and threshing and hand-sowing and square dancing and quilting and so forth keeps Carroll County people in touch with local history, with the land and with each other. Funny how doing things the hard way can sometimes make life a whole lot nicer.

1814 ☉ 1815

Ghent Treaty ends war with British — Battle of New Orleans fought after treaty — Francis Scott Key writes National Anthem — Hartford Convention: secret sessions held for states rights — Lewis & Clark journals published — War with Algiers over ship incidents — "North American Review" founded in Boston — Whaling industry thrives: oil and tallow light homes — Cost of college: $300 for one year at Harvard.

Grains have been staple crops in America since the first settlers tilled the fields. And the grinding of grains for flour and meal is one of our oldest industries. Old grain mills which served communities one, even two or three hundred years ago are being restored by concerned Americans (many of them quite young) — not as museum pieces but as the food production machinery they really are.

Millford, Virginia

The Clark County Historical Association is restoring the old Burwell-Morgan Mill. Richard Plater supervises the operation, and his young nephew Will Robinson shows visitors around during the summer. Fifteen year old Will tells them how millstones were fabricated in the eighteenth century — from thin stones, iron bands and a mortar made of creeksand, lime and horsehairs; he describes the grinding machinery that changes corn kernels to corn meal; and he tells this yarn about a former Millford mill supervisor L. H. Mongrol: *"His nickname was 'Sledgehammer,' and he got it because once when he was down in Louisiana he was challenged by a very short Creole man to a duel. He didn't want to fight, so when the little Creole gave him the choice of weapons, he picked sledgehammers — in six feet of water. The smaller man couldn't stand up, and had to forfeit the duel."*

The Clark County Historical Association is bringing back some of the color of their forefathers' lives . . . and also happens to be helping the town of Millford live up to its name once again.

Wye Mills, Maryland

The old mill was built 292 years ago and ground grain that nourished General Washington's men during the Valley Forge winter. Young people re-opened the mill and saved it from being just a decaying curiosity. Richard McComas, one of the millers, tells how:

"It really started with Mr John Bronson. He's the head librarian over at Chesapeake College and he passes the mill every day on his way to work. One day he brought up an idea — to the Phi Kappa campus service organization — of coming to Wye Mills and cleaning up the old mill. He talked it over with college officials and whatnot, and pretty soon everyone was convinced that the mill should not just be cleaned — it should be re-opened. The Phi Kappas came out here and cleaned up the grounds, and provided people to work here and the college put them on work study. But now that it's going, it's not limited to Phi Kappa members any more. Anyone can apply for work here during the summer."

1816 ◉ 1817

Virginia Dynasty continues: Monroe elected President — Second US Bank chartered — Indiana, Mississippi admitted; Alabama territory formed — American Colonization Society forms, aims to transport free blacks to Africa — "Year of no summer": New England gets 10 inches of snow on June 6, 1816 — Rush-Bagot treaty limits naval arms on Great Lakes — First Seminole Indian war — First gas company forms in Baltimore — Erie Canal construction begins — George Clymer builds first hand-powered printing press in US.

The old mill produces white flour, whole wheat flour, buckwheat flour, rye flour and corn meal . . . and offers young people in the area a chance to learn history first-hand. And John Bronson deserves congratulations for bringing new life to a worthy remnant of colonial America.

Busti, New York

In Busti, New York, the kids succeeded where the adults had failed. Three young girls couldn't bear to see Busti's last link with its bucolic beginnings — a weatherbeaten grain mill — become firewood and memories while the community elders shrugged their shoulders. So they announced that *they* would save the mill — and then, to the astonishment of most of the town — they *did* save the mill, and have parlayed that project into a growing rural home-life revival.

Actually, it could have started with a duck pond, a water tower or an ice house instead of a mill. To sixteen year old Mary Sienkiewicz and her friends, the mill was important because it was all that was left: *"In 1965, there was an attempt by the Town Board of Busti to form a committee to restore the mill. But nobody seemed to want to take charge of the project, because there would obviously be a lot of work involved. After waiting six years for someone to step forward, the Town Board gave up and was about to have the mill demolished. So Louise Carlson, Diane Pangborn and I decided to do something about it, because if we didn't, our last link with the past and its people would be gone."*

PIONEER FESTIVAL

Benefit for
BUSTI MILL RESTORATION

SAT. and SUN.
September 16 and 17
BUSTI FIREMEN'S GROUNDS

Saturday — 12 to 8 pm   Sunday — 1 to 5 pm

- CHICKEN BARBECUE
- FISH DINNER
- 4-H FAIR
- SQUARE DANCE (Sat., 8:30 p.m.)
- PONY PULL (Sun., 1:00 p.m.)
- PIONEER CRAFTS
- COMMUNITY CHURCH
- OLD FASHIONED CHILDREN'S GAMES

Adults $1.00
Children FREE with an adult

Front of Busti mill — the porch roof has been re-designed and rebuilt. The porch floor and stairs are in the process of being rebuilt.

This photograph shows the side of the mill and the need for new clapboards.

New beams to replace structural beams in the mill, that we have just received.

Bottom of photograph shows the isolation necessary to drain the water from the bottom of the mill.

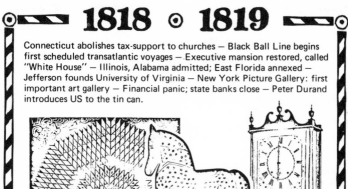

1818 ◉ 1819

Connecticut abolishes tax-support to churches — Black Ball Line begins first scheduled transatlantic voyages — Executive mansion restored, called "White House" — Illinois, Alabama admitted; East Florida annexed — Jefferson founds University of Virginia — New York Picture Gallery: first important art gallery — Financial panic; state banks close — Peter Durand introduces US to the tin can.

Mary's snapshots speak eloquently of the great effort she and her friends have put forth to give the community back its mill. The fund-raising process has been true to the historical spirit of the mill restoration, re-introducing the townsfolk to long-forgotten skills such as log-hewing, quilting, bread making, horseshoeing, weaving, butter making, spinning, and the making and playing of an instrument long heard in American hill country, the dulcimer.

The spirit of Busti's agricultural past is alive today — even though time has changed its economic identity to "suburb" — because Mary, Louise and Diane saw a special meaning in an unwanted mill.

73

Shakopee, Minnesota
Making It Big in Minnesota

Margaret MacFarlane never dreamed it would be like this. Some time ago, she had a recurring daydream about saving some of the history and landscape around her part of the country (the forest valley along the Minnesota River not far from Minneapolis). Fifty months, one hundred acres and a half a million dollars later, Mrs MacFarlane is directing one of the biggest history projects in the country, and it's no longer a daydream. It's a full time job.

Little by little, she and others are assembling along the Minnesota River a gigantic slice through the nineteenth century, represented by the buildings, artifacts and crafts from the earliest settlements on. They are constructing out of scattered relics an environment of history. The idea is not anything new. There are already a lot of historic reconstructions, villages, that employ the "living museum" notion. But generally these tend to be institutions, excluding people except as an audience. Things may be different in this instance.

The Minnesota Valley Restoration Project, which is its official title, though it started as a gleam in Mrs MacFarlane's eye, has outgrown its humble origin. Even in its early stages, project workers thought big. They decided to obtain professional assistance in planning and in other matters in which they felt weak. The infusion of large amounts of money have also taken the project out of the "backyard" category. This kind of success as often as not brings with it the attendant evils of large scale administration, record-keeping and public relations that work at cross purposes with the whole notion of preserving traditions.

What is important about the Minnesota project is not its size, but that, despite its ambitious scale and big government money, it remains very much a people project. The work is still done mainly by volunteers. They may think big, but they know how to act small . . . and accomplish much.

Here is a catalogue of what they've done so far.

1844 Fur Trading Post. *Moved in, restored to 1844 appearance. The first house built for white occupancy in Scott County.*

1850 German Immigrant Farm. *Moved in, restored to 1854 condition. Six timber buildings originally located along the Minnesota River in Sibley County.*

1885 Train Depot. *Moved in, part of the 1880 village. Being restored as nineteenth century depot. Plans include adding a track and tourist train of the period.*

1867 Bloomington Ferry Church. *Moved in by barge over the river, being restored to portray typical Protestant church of the period. Part of 1880 village.*

Civil War-era Atwater House. *Moved in, being restored.*

1860 Realander House. *Moved in, being restored to original log cabin frame construction.*

Dakota Indian Village. *Bark huts, skin tipis being constructed by Dakota Indians from reservations of Prairie Island and Shakopee, Minnesota.*

Murphy Inn and Ferry Crossing. *Being reconstructed (original building burned in 1960's). Will be constructed on the original site using original stone. Plans include the restoration of a working stage coach and stables, a tavern, and a period room for meetings and special events.*

Pond Grist Mill. *On original site, being restored to 1875 condition. Pond was the first Protestant missionary in Minnesota.*

In the Planning Stage: *shops, homes, industries for the 1880's village, including a Catholic church and 1880 farm; an Interpretive Center which will serve to integrate the whole Project.*

Minnesota Valley Restoration Project

We Need You

Stroudsburg, Pennsylvania
The Farm With the Open Gate

There's a farm in Stroudsburg, Pennsylvania, where anyone is welcome, and where you can step back into pre-Civil War days. You can go out to feed the sheep, help with shearing or carding or spinning. You can even begin to learn to weave. You might help bake bread, or hoe and weed the garden. You could do all these things because Mr and Mrs William Wicks had the vision in 1948 to buy Quiet Valley Farm just in order to keep it like it was.

The woman they bought it from must have been in a hurry to get away because she left everything there — "the stew on the stove and the dog on the porch" — and the Wicks just picked up where she left off. They're still at it. They have succeeded in preserving a unique tradition of two hundred years of German farming life, and visitors can make themselves a part of the farm — if they want to.

Ten years ago, the Wicks-Oiler family (three generations of them) opened the Farm to schoolchildren, and conducted informal tours. Some of these grew into all-day projects in which the children could help the family with actual farm work. Now, thousands of children visit the farm each year, and teachers make reservations well in advance.

Each summer, there are tours for the public: some people just visit the farm and watch. But others come to stay — for a few days or a few weeks — and really work. Many visitors get hooked by the farm crafts that are daily chores, like broom-making or butchering or candle making, and want to come back and do it themselves. What the Wicks want is a chance for everyone to get a good hold on a part of their past that they may never have experienced.

All the buildings are for real; the farm is stocked with animals; the garden is planted. The Wicks live there. They need and appreciate the help of volunteers from the community, from the visiting schoolkids and from the people who come to stay for a while, because making a farm go is very hard work. Sometimes there are special projects — seasonal activities which are a part of farm life — like ice harvesting from the pond in January, apple butter making and canning in the fall, and regular clean-up days.

A growing number of local people and returning visitors have been concerned about the future of what has become an authentic, unique and delightful museum. In August of 1970, they formed an association to help support and assure the continued existence of Quiet Valley Farm. In December of 1970, they were incorporated as the "Historical Farm Association," complete with a board of directors and by-laws. They signed a lease with option to purchase the farm itself. It looks like the Wicks' dream is becoming a reality, and a lot of people are going back in time with them to the days of do-it-yourself living.

GOLDEN CUSTARD SUMMER SQUASH.

Goat

1820 ☉ 1821

Missouri Compromise postpones slavery-statehood showdown — New York, New Hampshire open first state-supported libraries — First Hitchcock chairs manufactured in Connecticut — Maine, Missouri admitted — Treaty exiles Seminoles to Everglades — Stephen Long's Platte River Plain expedition uncovers unknown life forms — William Becknell blazes Santa Fe Trail — First natural gas offered for sale in Fredonia, N.Y. — First US high school: Boston's May English Classical School — Total US pop. 9,638,453.

The hill country of Texas is criss-crossed with little lanes they call farm-to-market roads. Back in the days when horsepower meant how many were hitched to your wagon, there used to be towns — little three-store clusters — at most crossroads... stores where merchandise was exchanged for produce, and long discussions about crop prices and impending rain were held. You can still find one of these towns if you drive out into the country from Fredericksburg. The crossroads is called Luckenbach, and it consists of three abandoned buildings and one shingled beer-parlor-and-general-store. Two long-time patrons recently bought the whole shebang, partly so they could continue to share a cold **Pearl Beer** now and then with friends.

This is what Guiche Kooch has to say about how and why he and Hondo Crouch came to buy a whole town: "My family came to Texas with an early German migration. They settled around here in the 1840's. We had been coming up here for family re-unions forever. Then, about five years ago Beno Engel, whose family settled this place in 1849, decided he wanted to retire. So he put this little town up for sale, and advertised in the classi-fied section of the Fredericksburg paper. The ad read: Town For Sale (and the egg route would pay for it, it said).

Household Measures

120 drops water=1 teaspoon
60 drops thick fluid=1 teaspoon
2 teaspoons=1 dessertspoon
3 teaspoons=1 tablespoon
16 tablespoons=1 cup
1 cup=½ pt.
1 cup water=½ lb.
3 tablespoons flour=1 oz.
2 tablespoons butter=1 oz.
3 teaspoons soda=½ oz.
4 teaspoons baking powder=
  ½ oz.
2 cups granulated sugar=1 lb.
3¾ cups confectioners' sugar=
  1 lb.
2½ cups wheat flour=1 lb.
3½ cups whole wheat flour=
  1 lb.
2¼ cups buckwheat flour=1 lb.
5⅓ cups coffee=1 lb.
6½ cups tea=1 lb.
2 cups lard=1 lb.
2 cups butter=1 lb.
2 cups corn meal=1 lb.
2 cups powdered sugar=1 lb.

Don't these pictures make you relaxed just looking at them? That's Guiche in the middle, and his wife Trish is next to him. Hondo Crouch (right) proves that even smiles are bigger in Texas.

"I came up to talk to him about it, and he said no one had shown much interest. I talked to Hondo Crouch who ranches up here about going in with me because I didn't have much capital to put into it. So we bought it just to save it. I really wanted Dal-las, . . . I thought it would be nice to own Dallas, but we settled on Lucken-bach. So we came down and got the town — the Blacksmith Shop, Dance Hall, Syrup Shed — and the saloon-and-general-store. The saloon was the original building. It first opened as an Indian Trading Post in 1849, and it's been in operation ever since. Still about a third of our business is barter. People bring their eggs on Monday and Tuesday and we take them to San Antonio and exchange them for groceries and feed."

Guiche Kooch doesn't really depend on the egg route to support his family — he's a television personal-ity down in Houston, and minding the Luckenbach store is a spare-time project for him and his wife Trish. Hondo has his ranch, of course, and their new partner Cathy Morgan also does it for a side line. But the fact that these gracious people make their living elsewhere than Luckenbach doesn't make the store one bit less historic — or any less of a success story. Luckenbach is being talked about all the way to San Antonio as the place to spend a Saturday after-noon (maybe because it takes people back to a Texas that's a little easier-going, a little more neighborly).

Mrs Esther Babcock won first prize — a $50 savings bond — for her essay about "Meachland," a farm which has been in her husband Eugene's family for 140 years. Mrs Babcock's essay included the exciting story of how four wealthy bachelor brothers — George, Lorin, John and Jarvis Meach — thwarted a band of armed robbers who invaded Meachland in 1902. Hers was but one of many excellent entries.

Americans move quite often these days — it's said that one family in five moves in any given year. But in some parts of the country there are families who have lived on the same land, in the same homes, for over one hundred years. Long-time newspaperman Ernst Henes realized one day that he knew quite a few families near his town of Wellington, Ohio, who had been settled on the same ground for several generations. He made a decision that such an unusual achievement deserved public recognition, and he took it upon himself (and the Southern Lorain County Historical Society, of which he is President) to issue gold-seal award certificates. But do you think a man who's been in the newspaper business for forty years would just collect registration forms and issue certificates without bothering to find out what went on with each family during those hundred-odd years? Not likely. Not Ernie Henes anyway. He sponsored at the same time a Centennial Homes, Farms and Churches essay contest. People who lived on hundred-year family farms were invited to put their historic legacy down in prose, and congregation members of churches which had one hundred year buildings were asked to write up their church's history.

Ernie Henes continues to hear favorable comments from hundreds of people who have rediscovered their own family's past as a result of the Centennial recognition program. It looks like the energy he put into the program may have primed the pump in Wellington: such other community history projects as the Spirit of '76 Museum are really moving. The ingenious Ernie Henes approach to history has helped Wellington folk to take a good look at themselves and their heritage — and they're liking what they see.

W. HERRICK-AV-ANY SATURDAY

1822 ⊙ 1823

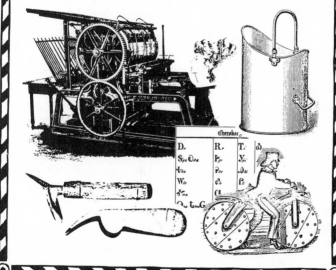

Mexico breaks with Spain, forms republic — Monroe urges recognition of Latin American republics — Yale prohibits student football — 37 executed in Vesey Slave Plot — Cumberland Road toll charge authorized — Coffee comes into general use — Monroe Doctrine tells Europe "hands off" Western hemisphere — C.M. Graham patents false teeth — Home remedy for asthma: ½ oz. senna, ½ oz. flour of sulphur, 2 drams ginger, ½ dram pounded saffron, mix in 4 oz. honey. Drink fast.

Fremont, California
Just What the Doctor Ordered

It's no accident that Dr Robert Fisher has his medical office in Fremont, California, just a hundred yards down the road from the 1797 Mission San Jose de Guadalupe. The Mission is the historic soul of Fremont, and Dr Fisher has been in the middle of Fremont's very successful heritage preservation movement ever since — well, ever since he started it.

Dr Fisher was on the local recreation commission back before Fremont existed (Fremont was born in 1958 as a legal union of five hamlets) — and he kept noticing that every time a verdant area was mentioned as a potential park, it just happened to be one of the great estates surviving from the pioneer agricultural days. The sagging Victorian buildings and rusting machinery sitting on each estate struck Dr Fisher as worthy of attention: they were the area's last links with pre-Gold Rush settlement days. (It was rich soil, not easy gold, that made California grow.)

Dr Fisher started talking (this is still early 1958) about municipal acquisition of whole estates — grounds, buildings, old tractors, whatever — as recreational areas. He talked fast — because endless waves of suburban development were already spilling onto Fremont's pastures of plenty from the general directions of Oakland on one side and San Jose on the other. Local residents listened, probably because they liked the quaint and rustic atmosphere which instant suburbia would wipe out — and what Dr Fisher said made sense in terms of preserving it.

Among the people who agreed were Fremont's first city administrators. They gave Dr Fisher the green light for the preliminary stages of his vision: Dr Fisher and several

The Best Idea of the Year

When the developers came to Fremont, they were asked please not to destroy any of the properties listed on the Historical Resources Commission survey. Of course, they balked — on the grounds that leaving old buildings on property they bought cost them money without giving any return. Fortunately, one developer made a suggestion that sounded good: the city of Fremont should give density credits (a right to build more units on a plot of land than would normally be allowed) to any developer who agreed to deed the historic sites on his land to the city of Fremont. What a bonanza! Overnight, developers who had been cursing preservation efforts were suddenly falling over each other to keep Fremont's heritage alive.

IN THE EARLY DAYS of Washington Township, long before Fremont was incorporated, the Peralta Boulevard estate of James Shinn and his wife, Lucy Ellen Clark Shinn, was one of the township's outstanding show-places. This old photograph from the files of the Mission Peak Heritage Foundation shows Lucy Shinn, in lace cap, seated beneath the magnificent canopy of LeMarque roses which once graced the whole side of the house where Lucy lived until her death in 1916. The other woman has not as yet been identified.

others were named to a Historical Resources Commission, and from 1960 through 1965 the Commission discovered and documented more than 350 sites and structures from Indian burial mounds to relics from the late nineteenth century which still stood within the City Limits.

Then they put the community to work. Fremont's first Historic Park is the Shinn Estate. Three and a half acres of apricot orchard, a large Victorian ranch house built in 1876, a barn and a Shiplap cottage of 1852 are becoming living examples of an early California farm. But that's only the real estate.

The Shinn project puts into practice two of Dr Fisher's theories about historic preservation. He thinks that groups should work on what interests them, and he also thinks young people should be involved in rebuilding their community's past. So, the exotic specimen gardens planted by James Shinn in the 1850's and 1860's that still surround the house are tended by local garden club members. The antique society is organizing furniture for the house, and, just a few weeks before this was written, an interior decorator called Dr Fisher up and offered to hang antique wallpaper.

Dr Robert Fisher (third from left) gives America the Beautiful Fund Executive Director Bruce Dowling (left) a Thanksgiving Day tour of the Shinn Gardens.

Above: *Just like bucket brigades of old, Fremont junior high schoolers "pass it on" in order to clear the debris from years of neglect.* Upper right: *It's always more fun to work on somebody else's house.* Snapshots: *(left) The Sim Cottage, built in 1852. (center, right) Wooden wheels will roll again over the fertile fields of Fremont.*

1824 ⊙ 1825

Jedediah Smith discovers gateway through Rockies — Erie Canal opens, coastal and frontier commerce linked — First iron steamboat built in US — First women on strike: weavers in Pawtucket, R.I. — 600 Boston carpenters strike for 10-hour day — Gibbons vs. Ogden establishes federal control of interstate commerce — Library of Congress fire destroys irreplaceable documents — First secular utopian society forms at New Harmony, Ind.

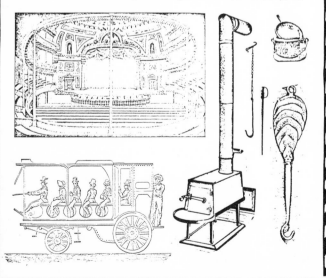

4-H'ers and Future Farmers are at work painting and re-designing the barn, and they also prune and harvest the trees. Junior high schoolers have done Herculean clean-up jobs. And high school students (chosen because they were considered to be potential drop-outs) have repaired the farm machinery and done much of the heavy carpentry — they've shown real enthusiasm for learning construction and machinery skills while contributing to a real-life project. School officials are enthusiastic, and hope to expand the program as more restoration projects begin.

Several similar projects are in the works — and, what with 300-plus projects waiting for attention — there's no end in sight. And though the fields of wild grass between Dr Fisher's office and the Mission will undoubtedly soon fill with new apartments, the people of Fremont will have their minds — and their hands — on the agricultural past of their community for generations to come, thanks to the foresight and ingenuity of Dr Robert Fisher.

Hayward, California
From Seeds of Sorrow

William Meek left his home in Keokuk, Iowa, in 1847 at the age of thirty after the tragic deaths of his young wife and two sons; he headed west to the unknown lands driving a wagon filled with seeds and grafted fruit trees. From these seeds of sorrow grew a new life for Meek — and a new enterprise for Northern California. Success in the nursery business enabled Meek in 1869 to move his new family into a palatial Victorian mansion amidst three thousand acres of flower and vegetable gardens, pasture land, grain fields and perhaps 30,000 white and pink blossomed trees bearing almonds, cherries and plums.

William Meek's acreage now sprouts new crops of three bedroom homes every year, and only a few natives remember the halcyon days. But the peace and tranquility of that genteel life have not vanished — the Meek Mansion still stands, surrounded by ten acres of yesterday. The Hayward Park and Recreation District showed wisdom akin to that of its neighbor Fremont when it purchased the Meek estate in 1964. Visitors who walk through house and garden today gain a touch of San Francisco Bay Area history that's much easier to see than to describe.

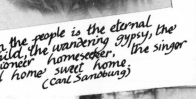

In the people is the eternal child, the wandering gypsy, the pioneer homeseeker, the singer of home sweet home.
(Carl Sandburg)

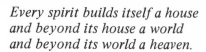

Every spirit builds itself a house and beyond its house a world and beyond its world a heaven.

A man must have aunts and cousins, buy carrots and turnips, must have barn and woodshed, must go to market and to the blacksmith's shop, must saunter and sleep and be inferior and silly. *(R. W. Emerson)*

In those days the typical American family of modest means was held together by the fireplace or the huge coal stove in the living room. — Lloyd C. Douglas

All the philosophy in our house is not in the study; a good deal is in the kitchen, where a fine old lady thinks high thoughts and does kind deeds while she cooks and scrubs. *(Louisa May Alcott)*

THE HOME FIRES BURNING

GOD BLES OUR HOME

Every log in my house is as straight as a pine can grow.

Families are the nurseries of all societies.
Cotton Mather – A Family Well Ordered

Bible – belonged to C.H. Isely. Published – The American Bible Society in 1859.

The great treasures of a dwelling are, the child's cradle, the grandmother's chair, the hearth and old fashioned fireplace, the table, and the window.
– Henry Ward Beecher

Spencer, Indiana
Making A Place for the Past

Any house that's held the baby-crying, birthday-partying, banquet-feasting, affection-showering, grief-sharing and grandchild-spoiling of several generations of one family's life shouldn't have to face an old age empty of people. Spencer, Indiana, is one of several American towns to discover the gratification which comes from bringing life into a family home again.

The Robinson House is not a home any more — it's a Civic Center. And it's a real monument to the generosity and public spirit of the people in one small Indiana town.

Back a few years when the Owen County State Bank needed space for expansion, they purchased the quarter-block on which Judge Robinson's house is situated. They didn't need the building, so instead of knocking it down, they said they'd give it to the city. A Civic League was formed, and people like Wade Allbritten, Mr and Mrs Perry Wesley of the Chamber of Commerce, and craftswomen Ruth McCarty and Irene Brock formulated an idea for a kind of Civic Center inside the building — an art gallery, a crafts showcase, an Owen County Museum, a general meeting room, a place for Chamber of Commerce materials . . .

Most of what's going on in the Civic Center (besides the hammering) is historical in nature. Crafts classes teach pioneer leatherwork; the museum holds objects of the Hoosier past (including a collection from Laymon's World's Products Company — H. B. Laymon once had the largest carded merchandise firm in the world, located in Spencer — Laymon's aspirins, Twenty Grand razor blades, and a lot else); and a good portion of art (both on display and in creation) deals with images and memories from Spencer's early years — like Dick Viquesney's bronzes and Lorraine Money's landscapes.

Spencer Jaycees Tom Paris, left, Jerry Ruble, center and Glenn Savage, are pictured above as they worked to place a new ceiling in an upstairs room at the local Civic Center in the old Robinson house on Montgomery Street here this past week-end. The Jaycees have taken on the job of refurbishing the room which will later be used as an Owen County museum.

"The Spirit of the American Doughboy" symbolized to many Americans the courage and fortitude our soldiers showed in World War II. Dick Viquesney of Spencer designed this statue; the new Owen County Museum — located in the Spencer Civic Center — will house a large collection of Viquesney bronzes, including one of the original edition of the "Doughboy."

Shown here, left to right, at Monday night's leathercrafts class session are Mr. and Mrs. James Brock, Gosport route; Marjorie Whitaker, and standing at right, Mrs. Pauline Mercer. Nine members are enrolled so far in the newly-formed crafts class, the first of what is expected to be a number of classes in various crafts which will hold meetings in the civic center. Present Monday night for the first class also was Mrs. Wade Allbritten.
Mr. Allbritten, President of the Spencer-Owen Civic League, said indications are that several additional crafts classes will be formed in the near future.

Spencer people have always had especially strong feelings for each other and for the old days. They've been keeping up a town "Hall of Fame," which records the exploits of Spencer people both in the town and elsewhere — such as the career of "Babe" Pierce, the first talking-picture Tarzan, a native of Spencer.

The people of Spencer showed their gratitude to the bank by making dreams into achievements. The roof was repaired; the front porch painted; sixteen broken windows replaced; rain gutters replaced; cracked chimneys made safe; wooden shutters carefully restored — not to mention the interior work. A hundred volunteers have donated time, skill and muscle. Every material needed has been purchased from local stores — at a discount. A recent progress report mentioned thirty-nine separate projects done by individuals or organizations to improve the old house.

Spencer is not a large or a wealthy community, but you'd never know it to see the Civic Center. Besides the outstanding revitalization of the Robinson House, the town has recently built a new high school and two elementary schools. What's the secret? Isobel Goldberg says, "The people in Spencer are warm-hearted and care about each other." That's powerful medicine anywhere.

Cucamonga, California

The Kids Do It Again, or,
Out of the Mouths of Bulldozers

The John Rains house is the second-oldest fired brick house in California. It stands outside the community of Cucamonga on a secluded hill, surrounded by a new chain-link fence and a century-old curse. Vandals, bulldozers, souvenir hunters, mobile home park and land developers, reluctant councilmen and the passage of time almost toppled the 112 year old "Casa de Rancho Cucamonga" — before a junior high school class finally convinced townspeople to put away their usual apathy long enough to save their primary link with settlement days.

When Mrs Ralph Strane and her history students took a field trip up to the Rains house one day in 1970, they couldn't believe their eyes. A bulldozer was at work on the side of the house. Already there was an eleven foot hole in the wall. Mrs Strane — furious and frantic — told the workmen they were making a terrible mistake. The workmen said no, the owner had hired them to push over the old building. Mrs Strane ran to call the owner — and her students decided to sit down in front of the bulldozer. After what was described as "an intense conversation," the owner agreed to give people in the community a chance to save the house.

It was a full year after the kids' last-ditch stand for history that a handful of people (Esther Block, Dr Jerry Smith of the San Bernadino County Museum, Jill Ritchie, Jimmie Stevens and Mrs Strane and Company) was able to mobilize an interested but phlegmatic community. Smith had said in the beginning, "Just about every citizen in Cucamonga is going to have to get behind the effort to save the historic Rains mansion to make it effective."

It turned out that he was right. Twice the city council voted to buy the house and then backed down, pleading "lack of community interest." It took $8,000 worth of contributions, hundreds of vocal locals and another en masse appearance of Cucamonga Junior High kids to get the council to keep their word.

Mobile homes still figure in the future of Rancho de Cucamonga. A family lives in one parked next to the Rains house. They and the fence (bought with proceeds from a traditional Mexican dinner done by the Junior Women's Club) are protecting the structure from more vandalism. The house is being restored by volunteers to a near-original configuration. Eventually, it will return to the world as a period-furnished early California residence. When it does, junior high school kids who trudge up the hill to see their last little piece of early Californiana won't have to stand in the way of a bulldozer to complete their history lesson.

The Rains House is no longer at the mercy of vandals. Mr and Mrs Gale Reeves now live on the property with their daughter and two German shepherds.

1826 ◉ 1827

Steam locomotive successfully tested — Smith completes first overland expedition to California — Harvard offers first college P.E. course — Josiah Holbrook launches Lyceum movement — Bestseller: James Fenimore Cooper's "Last of the Mohicans" — New York abolishes slavery — Martin vs. Mott: President has authority to call out militia — Massachusetts first state to require high school attendance — Ballet introduced in US — Creek Indian lands in Georgia taken — First swimming lessons offered in Boston.

Anyone who likes to poke around flea markets for bargains has technicolor fantasies of someday finding a forgotten cache of treasures to be had cheap. Well, friends and neighbors, this is the story of Buretta and Herbert Redhead, who found the biggest bargain of them all on the banks of the Des Moines River. And their lives haven't been the same since.

The Mason House, a twenty-one room inn built in 1846, was advertised for sale. Mrs Redhead came down from Des Moines to have a look. She thought there might be a few old things she could pick up. There were. A whole building full. From the basement to the attic the place was packed. Not junk. Real stuff. . . . clothing, bedding, furniture, kitchen equipment, paintings, the works. Chests of old toys, quilts, coverlets and doilies. A lifetime of antiques in one place. Everything was for sale in a lump. And it was a bargain. Mrs Redhead returned to Des Moines in a state of shock and told her husband. At that point, Herbert didn't share his wife's passion, but he knew a good thing when he saw it. They bought it, lock, stock and barrell.

First they bought. They then faced the question of what to do with it. They decided to restore it as a museum. That was seventeen years ago; their two daughters were children. If the first part of this story is fairy tale, the rest is soap opera, as Herbert and Buretta struggled against the elements, the neighbors and common sense to keep their treasure intact and their family fed.

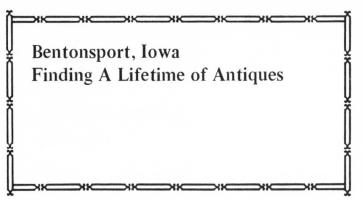

Upstairs, one of the bedrooms is furnished with all the things Todd, who is Redhead's grandson, likes best. Though called a museum, the old inn feels more like a home. The Redheads live in an apartment downstairs.

Herbert Redhead: *"When I first came down here, I couldn't borrow a dime on anything. I tried to do the restoration on weekends at first, and I'd drive back and forth from Des Moines. I could see I wasn't going to get it done that way, so I sold my home and quit my job and brought my family down here. I really got to work on the darn thing. I'd start at eight in the morning and work until midnight, seven days a week. When I finally got the door open, I was down to 110 pounds. I bet I didn't take in $50 that first year. I went back to Des Moines and found another job. I'd bring my wife and daughters down here in the summer and let them stay and try and catch the people that passed through town and I'd drive back and forth every weekend. I did that for about three years until finally I had to get back to work on it full time again. So I quit my job again and went back to work on it and my wife took a job. Finally, I got everybody paid off and I don't owe a damn soul, so . . ."*

FILLINGS
Gold and Silver

Redhead's daughter, Sally Ross: *"When we first moved down here to live we used the wood stove for heat. We got up one morning and it was 35 below zero outside. My sister and I had one hot water bottle so we'd take turns every other night with the hot water bottle and that way we didn't fight over it. The other got a peanut butter jar full of hot water. One morning we got up and the peanut butter jar had leaked and it was frozen along the edge of the bed. That's how cold it was. They didn't have electricity here until 1951. When it came in, the old lady who lived here put in two light fixtures. When we first came down here, the old crank phone was still here. Our ring was three longs, and there were about nine families on our line.*

"I didn't appreciate any of this when I was young. I had to take people through that museum. I hated it! How would you like to be stuck in a museum every day? I started taking tours through when I was eleven years old. My mother used to dress us up in those unbearably hot costumes and put us up there in the summer time.

"... it's beautiful down here. In the winter the river freezes over and we skated and went sledding in the hills. I don't think I'd want to live anywhere else."

"One thing we found is that people who collect buy up the stuff and pack it away, so other people don't get to see it. So we want to keep ours where people can see it and learn something about it." – *Sally Redhead Ross*

Redhead not only didn't know much about antiques or history when he started, he knew nothing about plumbing, electricity or restoration either. Faced with a community of indifferent, sometimes hostile, neighbors, no heat, running water and almost no money, Redhead and his family have invested seventeen years of their lives in an old building and a ghost town that no one would give a second thought to. Thanks to the Redheads, not only the Mason House, but the town of Bentonsport itself has a new lease on life, and Herbert Redhead says without a trace of bitterness:

"Those hard years were real living. I wouldn't trade them for anything."

Buretta Redhead was off on an errand when this was taken. That's Sally Ross, the Redheads' daughter, grandson Todd, and Herbert. Thanks to the Redheads, the town of Bentonsport has been placed on the National Register of Historic Places.

1828 ⊙ 1829

Democratic Party forms; extension of Jeffersonian "Republicans" — Andrew Jackson elected; "spoils system," "Kitchen Cabinet" follow — First factory workers' strike at Paterson, N.J. textile plant — Noah Webster publishes "American Dictionary of English Language" — American Peace Society established — Cincinnati race riot; 1,000 blacks flee for Canada — Samuel F. B. Morse founds National Academy of Design — Mexico refuses US offer to purchase Texas — Delaware & Chesapeake canal opens — First "luxury" hotel: Boston's Tremont with 170 rooms, 8 water closets.

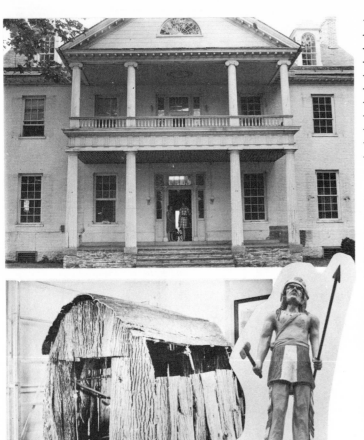

There it was — Rose Hill Manor, the old Governor's mansion, saved by a transfusion of half a million dollars of state, federal and county money — standing elegant, idle and empty — a white elephant — a dirty word in Frederick County.

Until Birch Hotz, Pat Sanner and Ann Lebherz decided that if nobody was going to do anything with the great house, they would. Their dream was a children's museum which would teach local history by exhibit and demonstration. They broached the plan to the County Commissioners and to the School Board. The answers were favorable, but confirmed the trio's suspicions: nobody was about to put another penny into the elephant.

It took the Rose Hill mob less than a year to change night to day. The museum opened at Christmas time, 1972, and in the first three months more than 1,500 children (plus hundreds of tourists) took the guided tour. The re-opening of Rose Hill also made meeting space available for community organizations — and it's already so popular that it's booked well in advance. All this at an additional cost of practically nothing — because volunteer help has been flooding in since life returned to the mansion.

The tour goes 'round from an Indian hogan to a painting of Barbara Fritchie's house to an open hearth bread baking demonstration to a quilt on which every visitor takes a stitch to a live horse to a hundred other pieces of early Frederick history. But nowhere is there a white elephant to be seen.

And special credit should be given to the kids of Frederick. Not only is Rose Hill a history house for kids to visit, but the youngest generation has also taken the initiative: they've done the lion's share of collecting and creating the exhibits.

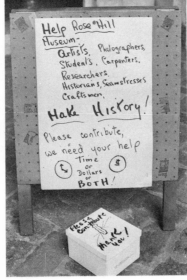

1830 ⊙ 1831

Indian Removal Act: thousands die on "Trail of Tears" — First wagon train heads for Rockies — B & O becomes first passenger railroad — Joseph Smith organizes Mormon Church — Webster-Hayne debate states rights — Robert L. Stevens invents T-rail for train travel — Horse outruns locomotive "Tom Thumb" in 9-mile race — W.L. Garrison published first "Liberator" — Nat Turner insurrection: 55 whites, 120 blacks die in Virginia — McCormick invents mechanical reaper — No lame feat. Philadelphia's Joshua Newsam walks 1,000 miles in 18 days — Total US pop. 12,866,020.

Canandaigua, New York

A Vintage Preservation Story: Saving the Homestead

Gideon Granger, a land speculator by trade, showed real acumen in 1812 when he selected acreage in what is now the center of Canandaigua upon which to build a mansion for his family. He picked level, well-drained land, accessible from several directions, amenable to shade trees. . . . Strangely enough, his choice of property was so good that it almost caused the destruction of the mansion 124 years later. If it were not for some fancy public relations footwork by a small group of local residents on behalf of the house, Granger's legacy would be long gone by now.

It happened back in 1945 that the Canandaigua Board of Education was looking for land for a new elementary school. Their eye came to rest on twelve acres right in the middle of town — level land, well-drained, with shade trees, accessible from several directions — and it just happened that the Homestead was then being vacated by an organization which had maintained a home for retired Congregational ministers. Not only was the Granger site ideal and idle — it was cheap. The will of Miss Antoinette Granger, last family member to live in the house, had specified a limited use for the land ("public, educational, religious or charitable"), and set the price at $20,000. The decision was as good as made.

Enter the Granger Homestead Society — a hastily-formed alliance of local people who wouldn't believe that Canandaigua had to cannibalize itself just to build a school. They raised money by public subscription to prove that Canandaiguans wanted the Homestead intact as living history for future generations. Sold! (And saved.)

The Homestead Society didn't deprive Canandaigua of an elementary school (they built it somewhere else). What they did do was restore and furnish the Granger Homestead, and then open it — giving the small community a gracious meeting place for social events. As the Society's booklet proudly proclaims, *"the old house gains warmth and charm from daily living."*

The Society is busier than ever now — twenty-eight years later — working on the various collections which have been gathered in and around the mansion. But they don't have to spend much time promoting the Homestead as an important part of Canandaigua — because the Granger Homestead and the people of the town have, during those twenty-eight years, gotten to be the best of friends.

Delaware County, Pennsylvania

America's Number One Nonstop Family Reunion

The Caleb Pusey House is probably the only colonial building in America ever saved by family subscription. The little stone house which dates back to 1683 is the earliest English-style and English-built house — unmodernized and intact — still standing in Pennsylvania. It is the only remaining house positively known to have been frequented by William Penn. And until restoration began in 1961, it was probably one of the most neglected buildings in Pennsylvania as well.

When the Friends of the Caleb Pusey House formed, a tarpaulin covered much of the structure, hiding a badly-burned roof. Whatever was capable of decay had decayed. Estimates ran about $70,000 for restoration. Despite all this, things looked promising, because the Delaware Historical Society owned nine acres adjacent to the Pusey House, and the word went out that the Pusey House would be the focal point for a historic park to be known as Landingford Plantation. Many of those who responded were Quakers who sensed the importance of this simple building. And then there were Caleb's relatives. . . .

The Pusey House Restoration Project has started what may be the most far-reaching and productive family reunion America has ever seen. Artist Maxfield Parrish and former Harvard University President Nathan Pusey are two of perhaps one hundred family members who have pitched in — not just in the house preservation, but also in helping to develop Landingford Plantation.

By the end of 1970, Landingford Plantation had several houses, a mill, gardens, a barn (which was restored by local Amish), a schoolhouse, beautiful antique furniture — some on loan from museums — and a huge collection of artifacts dug by an archaeologist and his volunteer helpers on the site. But 1971 turned everything upside down. First, the Pusey House was burglarized on the night of March 22, and many irreplaceable seventeenth and

eighteenth century household items vanished. Then, on September 15, the Chester Creek overflowed and flooded the property — the Pusey House was filled with mud up to the chandeliers.

Local people, Quakers, and Pusey descendents still work to regain their 1970 plateau. Almost every building was damaged; much furniture was lost; archaeological items were washed away; the gardens (except for some proud sunflowers) were destroyed. But the drive to revive Pennsylvania's beginnings is going stronger than ever (in response to the adversity), and the Friends of the Caleb Pusey House say they will be ready for the arrival of America's Bicentennial Celebration when it comes.

Woodcut of House, Sherman Day's Book, 1843

CALEB PUSEY HOUSE

Beaver County, Pennsylvania
A House Divided

Here you see the Beaver County Spring House before it was reduced to a pile of rocks. Hopefully, it will rise again. The Spring House stood at the bottom of that Pennsylvania hill for 120 years — protecting drinking water for local homesteads — before strip mining operators came through in 1970 to scrape the land bare. The Little Beaver Historical Society pleaded with the mining company to spare the house, but the most the strippers would do was dismantle it and pile the hand-cut stones in an empty field. Historical Society members marked each stone for position and stored the Spring House woodwork in their museum's new basement (dug by seventh and eighth graders for the purpose). The Spring House is still a house divided, because despite a variety show, historical bus tours and several annual dinners, there is not yet enough cash in the Society's coffers to finance reconstruction.

Burlington, New Jersey
The Gingerbread House

Henry Bisbee and his wife have a pre-Revolutionary bungalow on their property in Burlington, New Jersey, that they call the Gingerbread House. This little building, unlike Hansel and Gretel's discovery, is not edible. But there is a good story that explains the odd moniker:

"An eighteen year old lad by the name of Benjamin Franklin walked all the way down river from Perth Amboy to Burlington. On his arrival, a kindly lady on Pearl Street gave him some gingerbread and invited him to spend the night; Ben accepted. But he went exploring Burlington's river docks, and came upon a bateau with a number of people preparing to travel to Philadelphia. He rushed back to the gingerbread lady's house, grabbed his bag, and went on to Philadelphia — and to his many contributions to America and mankind."

Henry Bisbee is a man after Franklin's own heart: optometrist, historian, radio station owner, one-man town history booster, author and entrepreneur. He is definitely not a man to let a historic legend go begging. He and his wife oversee a Colonial Street Fair every year, modeled after those held around 1685 (which is when the cottage was built). Jugglers, puppeteers, costumed noblewomen and colonial lords mix with crowds of ordinary folk as they wander through a flea market (which makes money for the Colonial Burlington Society) and tour several historic homes which are opened for the occasion. The Bisbees themselves keep busy bringing that Gingerbread Legend alive by selling homemade gingerbread out of the little cottage to passersby. Which is a nice way to remind people of that day when Ben Franklin decided not to spend the night in Burlington.

Molalla, Oregon

Saving the Home At the End of the Trail

A good number of the wagons heading West in the 1850's and 60's weren't bound for the gold country. They were aimed Northwest by their owners, toward the fabled farmlands of the Oregon country. The people who now live in one of the settlements at the end of the Oregon trail still think a lot of those first pioneers. Here is the story of how they are saving two pioneer houses, as furnished by Thomas Lancaster, corresponding secretary of the Molalla Area Historical Society.

Molalla Area Historical Society

Molalla, Oregon 97038

"Way out here, in Molalla, Oregon, a group of energetic people are busy preserving two houses, which were a part of the early history of the area. One is called the Dibble House. Built in 1856-59, of hand-planed boards, it is one of the ten oldest buildings still standing in the state of Oregon.

"The response of the community was almost unbelievable last year. In fact, helping the Historical Society buy the Dibble House served to unite the community as it never was before. This year, when a call came for a new ambulance for the town, they swung right into action again, in the same manner, to start raising the necessary funds. So we can say that besides restoring the old historic Dibble House, we helped renew the old-time friendly 'all together now' spirit, toward our community needs."

"We have lately been hard at work raising funds to move the Von der Ahe House twelve miles and relocate it here. Since January of this year we have had seven different shows, two of which lasted three days; a Bake Sale in two markets; an Auction, which included a children's auction and such unusual things as a dinner for four at the home of the Mayor and his wife, an hour's service with a limosine and chauffeur in uniform, a week of 'house sitting' for vacationing homeowners, and a hat from a former First Lady of Oregon.

"Our group, the Molalla Area Historical Society, has only been organized for two and a half years, but we have over two hundred members. Last year we managed to get almost every organization in the area, including the Chamber of Commerce, to help raise the money--$7,000--to purchase the Dibble House.

"Why go out to raise money so quickly, you may ask. The answer is--the preservation of these houses was a 'somebody ought to' for so many years, that by the time the right people came together and said, 'Let's do it,' it was already almost (but not quite) too late.

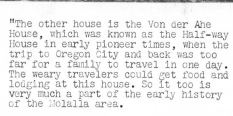

"The other house is the Von der Ahe House, which was known as the Half-way House in early pioneer times, when the trip to Oregon City and back was too far for a family to travel in one day. The weary travelers could get food and lodging at this house. So it too is very much a part of the early history of the Molalla area.

1832 ⊙ 1833

Force Act signed; Navy-Army authorized to collect tariffs — South Carolina Nullification Ordinance voids Force Act — Massachusetts becomes last state to separate church and state — Black Hawk War: Sac and Fox Indians pushed across Mississippi River — Thousands die in first Asiatic cholera epidemic — John Deere produces first steel plow — First street car in world: New York-Harlem line — President Jackson vetoes Bank of US charter renewal — Mass media beginnings: New York Sun becomes first penny paper — American Anti-slavery Society forms in Philadelphia.

Roland, Virginia

Saving the House
on the Mountain

"I believe that the Bull Run Mountains are among the most beautiful, natural, scenic areas in the state of Virginia. They have always been a population barrier, stemming from the Civil War. This area should continue to be preserved as a green strip around Washington, D. C., with the Bull Run Mountains as a barrier. The question that should be brought before the public is: *how* should these mountains be preserved?"

So saying, Mrs Alice Mills — President of the Chichester du Pont Foundation — gave one thousand acres of Virginia field, forest and mountain (and the question unanswered) to the Natural Area Council. The land, which includes a beautiful pre-Civil War manor house, was given with the requirement that the area be used for preservation and act as a focus for further protection of the historic Bull Run Mountains.

The America the Beautiful Fund, a branch of the Natural Area Council, accepted the challenge of carrying out Mrs Mills' wishes — which meant, among other things, generating enough revenue to maintain the property. And that's never as easy as it might sound.

The grounds are accessible to the public. Day use is encouraged; overnight use is restricted to special groups, by

reservation. The house — known as Roland Center — functions as a rustic conference center and retreat.

The proper use of the mansion has turned out to be a crucial part of the preservation effort — though it is just a speck on the thousand acres. The revenue it generates helps keep the open land from economic pressure. Roland Center also aids the preservation/conservation movement by providing a place for small groups of concerned people to gather.

At present, 3,000 of the Bull Run Mountains' approximately 20,000 acres can be counted as saved. The message that "no one should sit by while rich green rolling hills, criss-crossed with white picket fences and dotted with whitewashed cupolas become criss-crossed by nightmare patchworks of traffic-lighted, neon-lighted super-speed highways" will hopefully inspire others who care about America's natural beauty to follow the Roland model — or devise their own self-supported, people-oriented wilderness preservation program.

"Last winter the state deemed the mountain a 'Critical Environmental Area' worthy of preservation. More than 1,000 plant species have been identified and 45 species of mammals from the Bull Run Mountains. Rare plants such as the walking fern, slender ground cedar, meadow rue and pale cordyalis are found here."

1834 ☉ 1835

Whig Party forms to oppose "King Andrew" Jackson — Texas declares independence from Mexico, organizes Rangers — De Toqueville publishes "Democracy in America" — Department of Indian Affairs established — Seminoles ordered to evacuate Florida; fight to resist — Pro-slavery riots in New York, Philadelphia — Morse tests first telegraph — William S. Otis invents steam shovel — Thomas Davenport builds first electric motor — Tomatoes enter the American diet — Oberlin first college to accept blacks — Liberty Bell cracks.

THE FIRST TRAIN OVER THE PENNSYLVANIA RAILROAD IN 1835

I spun and wove this cloth at Adeline's, enough for me a dress and you a shirt, which I made. It is for the wedding, else to be buried in. *(Pauline Gorley, 1860)*

One of our most regular wanderings is the annual reunion, and they will come a long way for it. They stream into town by car, on foot, by interurban railroad, some bringing chocolate cakes, some ice cream, some sandwiches, some potato salad or punch. *(Wallace Stegner)*

Grandma's Quilt

With gentle and loving
*   fingers*
She caressed the well-
*   worn fold,*
'Round each piece a
*   mem'ry lingers*
Like a sweet story
*   often told.*

(Silvia Pierce)

It is dearness only that gives everything its value.

He put up a little shop, not far from the house, where he mended broken farm tools and various household tackle. *(Lloyd C. Douglas)*

Work which grows beautiful under ones own hands is truly a pleasure.

HANDS TO WORK

H.N.S
1840

Thus out of small beginnings greater things have been produced by his hand that made all things of nothing. *(William Bradford)*

Fredericksburgers know how to put together an old-fashioned picnic. On this hot summer day, everyone sat down under the pecan trees to sample a special feast of traditional favorites. Mrs Fritz Stieler (Aunt Lily) brought chicken and dumplings and fresh country butter; Mrs Rodolph Smith (Roberta) brought barbecued lamb and an artichoke plate; Mrs Caspar Real (Cynthia) brought a macaroni salad with artichokes and tomatoes, and Rose wine; Mrs Werner Keidel, Jr. (Mickey) brought a cucumber salad with cream, hot German potato salad and homemade pickles; Miss Margaret Keidel brought gefuellter kohl (stuffed cabbage) and a German chocolate marble Bundt cake (which was actually made by Mrs Stanley Wisseman); Mrs J. Hardin Perry (Nooky) brought barbecued sausage, sauerkraut salad, pickled peaches and rosetten (cookies); Mrs George Hill (Gloria) brought corn salad with nopalitos (cactus); Mrs Ruth Nettle brought rahm kuchen to finish everything up.

They were farmers, back in 1846. Families lived on large farms out in the hills and came into town on weekends to buy supplies and have fun. They built "Sunday houses" to stay in — usually wood, sometimes stone, with one room up and one down, often with outside stairs to the second floor. (Rumor has it that these were for father, who would get drunk on Saturday night and use the special entrance so as not to disturb the family.) Now, people in San Antonio, seventy miles away, are restoring the "Sunday houses" so they can retreat from the city on weekends!

Fredericksburg, Texas
Eating Your Way Through History

It's not unusual that America was called "the melting pot" when you look at the incredible variety of foods to be found in kitchens around the country. That pot contains not only foods but also traditions from every culture that has come to North America. Eating habits have all kinds of effects — from the transition of a whole nomadic hunting tribe to a settled agrarian community, to farming as a way to earn a living, to making a hobby of organic gardening, right down to the child at the dinner table refusing to eat his spinach. No one can ignore food, its production, availability or variety, and most people enjoy cooking and eating. What they eat often depends on where and how they were raised. Fredericksburg, Texas, was settled primarily by German immigrants. They brought their eating habits with them, and their descendants who live in this charming hill country town still carry on the traditions.

Mrs Henke's Recipe for Pfirsich Rahm Kuchen (Peach Cream Cake)

Cream together 1/2 cup butter, or substitute, and 1/3 cup sugar. Add 1 beaten egg; 2-1/2 cups flour; 1 tsp. salt; 1/2 tsp. soda; 2 tsp. baking powder and 3/4 cup buttermilk to make a biscuit-like dough. (When using sweet milk, omit soda and add 3-1/2 tsp. baking powder.) Roll on well-floured board to 1/2 inch thickness, and line large, shallow, greased pan with this crust. Almost fill with sliced peaches. Make a paste of 1 beaten egg yolk, 1-1/2 cups sugar, 2 tablespoons flour and 1-1/4 cups thick cream. Fold in beaten egg white and pour over peaches. Sprinkle with a mixture of sugar and cinnamon. Bake at 325 to 350 degrees F. for 15 or 20 minutes. Let cool until set before serving.

If you like the sound of this one, you probably ought to read the book it came from. Here's how to get your copy: Send $4.50 to Fredericksburg PTA Cookbook, Fredericksburg, Texas 78624.

Sausage Maker: Rodolph Smith

Rodolph Smith is one of the town's experts in the traditional skill of sausage-making. He learned it from his father-in-law, and uses the same equipment. He also smokes his sausage and other meat over a low fire of Spanish oak. He explains how he makes his specialties: "We have our own hogs. We use extra milk and scraps to feed them. From the pork loins we make Bratwurst sausage. We kill our first hogs about November, after the deer hunting season. The venison mixed with pork makes a good dry sausage or German smoked sausage, which you can eat raw.

Bratwurst

5 pounds pork loin, ground
5 eggs, beaten with 1 cup heavy cream
1 nutmeg, freshly ground
1 set of calf brains, ground

This sausage must be eaten fresh or frozen. To cook, sear casing ends to close and saute for about 25 minutes, turning once. Must be cooked gently.

Venison Sausage

(Mrs Henke's recipe from the Fredericksburg Cookbook)

To every 20 pounds of meat, 2/3 venison and 1/3 pork, add 1 cup (8 oz.) butcher salt, 1/3 cup coarse ground black pepper and 2 tsp. saltpeter. Mix salt, pepper and saltpeter together, sprinkle over meat, grind and stuff in casings. This sausage should be smoked for 2 or 3 days. May be frozen fresh or dried.

Meat proportion may also be 1/2 venison and 1/2 pork. For real dry sausage, use pure venison. Beef can be substituted for venison.

Rockland County, New York
A Mouthful of Antiques

Rockland County started its colonial crafts program in the summer of 1972 with a six week class called "Early American Cookery and Herb Gardens." Katrene Johnson taught the class all about colonial traditions with the hope that each student would leave the class able to cook a complete colonial meal and plant a small herb garden. She started by outlining the history of the period and the cooking equipment used, went on to actual cooking — Main Dishes, Breads, Desserts and Beverages — and finished up with a discussion of herbs and their uses. The class visited two formal herb gardens, and learned how the taste of traditional foods can be duplicated with modern ingredients. People who were experts in the cuisine of other countries learned how the tastes of food everywhere are distinguished by special seasonings.

The cookery class was a popular course, and introduced people to the Rockland County early American crafts program which offers a variety of classes, including spinning, weaving, natural dyeing, candle making and pewter work.

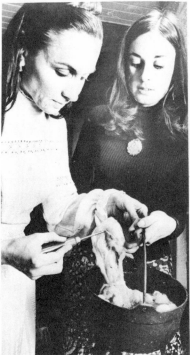

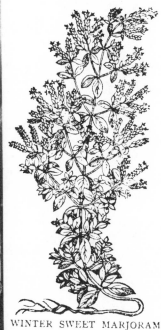

WINTER SWEET MARJORAM

A Main Dish Meal: Plimouth Succotash

This dish is traditionally served on Forefathers Day (December 21), the anniversary of the landing of the Pilgrims at Plymouth. It was first celebrated in 1769 when the Old Colony Club met together and dined "in commemoration of their worthy ancestors in this place." Plimouth Succotash was at that early date considered an "antique" dish, and it was said that during the winter the Pilgrims would freeze large portions of it with a string through it to carry with them on long trips. When meal time came, the traveler would chop off a chunk of succotash, place it in a pot over his fire, and soon have a good hot meal on his cold journey. This recipe comes from "The Plimouth Colony Cookbook," published by the Plymouth Antiquarian Society.

1 qt. dry pea beans
6 lbs. corned beef*
5 lbs. fowl
5 qts. hulled corn
1 medium turnip
5 medium potatoes*

Soak beans in water to cover overnight. Then cook and mash (makes thickening). Boil beef and fowl until tender. Save liquid. Cut up turnips and potatoes. Cook in the liquid. Cut up the beef and fowl into 1½" cubes. Combine all ingredients and let cook one hour. Stir frequently to prevent sticking. Let cool, always uncovered. Stir occasionally to keep from souring. Reheat and serve.

*Katrene says: "I doubt that these two ingredients were part of the original dish. Cows were not introduced until 1624, and then were valued for milk. They were slaughtered only when they no longer produced well. Therefore, there was no constant supply of beef in the New England colonies at the time of the first settlements. Most likely the meat used was pork or wild game. Also, potatoes were not introduced to New England until 1719; therefore, they should be omitted too if the dish is to be 100% authentic."

Alamo under siege — Narcissa Whitman & Eliza Spalding first women to cross North America — Michigan, Arkansas admitted — Emerson publishes "Nature," transcendentalist manifesto — First Dickens reaches US: "The Pickwick Papers" — First McGuffey readers published — Financial panic; 618 banks fail — Connecticut passes first incorporation laws in US — Supreme Court membership increases from 7 to 9 — In vogue: the English mustache — New York City pop. 300,000.

Shakopee, Minnesota
Minnesota Valley River Project

What started as a simple fund raising activity — publishing cookbooks in the basement of Margaret MacFarlane's home — soon became a growing concern in its own right, preserving the traditional recipes of the area. Proceeds from the sale of the books go toward activities at the MVRP.

Homesteader's Cookbook. *A collection of nineteenth century recipes, all adaptable to modern kitchens, lavishly sprinkled with humor and history. $3.50, postpaid.*

Caprine Cookery, How to Use Goat Products. *The only cookbook in the U.S. with complete instructions on how to cook with dairy goat products, including sections on Keeping, Choosing and Housing goats. $1.75, postpaid.*

Indian Foods. *A history of the foods used by Minnesota Plains Indians, including several recipes for authentic Dakota Indian breads. $0.35, postpaid.*

1850 Colorbook. *The story of pioneer life in the Minnesota River Valley during the homestead period for your child to color. $0.40, postpaid.*

All books can be ordered from Ginger Timmons, Minnesota Valley Restoration Project, 768 S. Jefferson, Shakopee, Minnesota 55379.

High Falls, New York
Soup's On!

Not only is the DePuy Canal House a four-star restaurant, but the Novis' concern for the environment and care for small graces spill out its doors and seem to be infecting the community all around. And it all happens with a simplicity and matter-of-factness that is the style of young people who live what they believe.

Sharing food has bridged a lot of gaps in American history — you can't really eat comfortably with someone until you're on speaking terms. Hence the good feeling about going out to a restaurant with friends, and the pleasure of a good meal together. In High Falls, New York, a young man named John Novi, with the help of his wife Rosa Lou, has created a restaurant which places personal comfort above all else, and in the process serves food which has rated a *New York Times* **four-star award. And it all started with John's interest in old buildings and history.**

The restaurant is called the DePuy Canal Tavern, after the man who built it in 1797, Simon DePuy, and because it originally sat alongside the Delaware and Hudson Canal. John bought it in 1964, and opened it as a restaurant in 1969 after a considerable amount of restoration. The story of how he managed to get the house probably starts with his own interest — "I can't pass an old building without finding out something about it" — and it's a real success story:

"I had worked in town for five years. My parents ran a bakery; that's where I learned most of what I know about cooking. I used to pass this building on my way to the post office, and one morning I thought of restoring it. I didn't have a dime at the time. But a businessman in town lent me some money, and, more important, gave me advice. I ended up buying the building for $4,500 (the original asking price was $12,000), and the lot across the street which contained an artesian well for $100. Everything just seemed to happen at the right time.

"I didn't open right away because I knew I wasn't ready. So I did some traveling through Europe, and I was lucky there too, since most of the time Americans can't get jobs there. I got apprenticed in Italy to some of the finest restaurateurs in the country. So I kept learning all around Europe, and when I came back, we cleaned and rebuilt and restored, and finally we opened the Tavern.

Right: John Novi's drawing for the DePuy House Christmas card.

High Falls is a town that enjoys parties. John and Rosa Lou gave tax parties every year until the restaurant opened, but there were a lot of other parties too. *"We had people, from sixty to ninety here at a time, all ages and all social classes. It was really amazing."* There were cleaning and building parties where people helped with the heavy work of rebuilding the Tavern — *"The people who helped are still complaining about their backs every time they come in!"* — and now that the restaurant is open there are Sunday brunches, Historical Society events and regular celebrations like the Log Party in October. Rosa Lou explains: *"The Log Party celebrates the official lighting of the fireplaces. Everyone is invited, and everyone brings a log. There's a prize for the most original. The first year, someone took the first prize with the back part of his bed! Then all the lights are turned out, and John flambes his special log cake which is baked in the shape of three logs with whipped cream all over it, and then the logs are lit."*

"I ended up borrowing about fifteen thousand dollars, even though when I started I only had one stove and one oven and a sink and a sideboard where you dried off the dishes which cost me $15 — galvanized — and the stove cost $35, and I put the whole kitchen together on $500, including the refrigerator. All the other money went into the physical reconstruction of the building — the floors, the ceiling, the windows, the fireplaces, everything. And we still don't have it finished to our satisfaction.

"I don't think of this as a business. I think of it as my house. The guests are guests in our home. I originally opened with the thought that if it didn't go over well as a restaurant, that I would still be able to get another job and keep it as a home. But it went over really well, so it just stayed the same." After the famous four-star rating, the only thing that changed was the size of the crowd. Says Rosa Lou: "We didn't really know how many people we could accommodate. We'd never had capacity crowds, and we started accepting more than our capacity. People would have a nine o'clock reservation and we'd seat them at eleven thirty." John adds: "That was still when I had one stove and one oven and one sink. Everything had to be done by hand. The way things got cooked half the time was I'd sit and pray! It took a good three months after the review to get organized, and then we weren't even really organized."

But by 1972, everything was under control — and a dinner at the Canal Tavern is a delight in every way.

An unusually quiet moment in the DePuy House kitchen. Normally, there are at least three to six people in and out of the kitchen constantly and how they manage to keep their balance and tempers and still get dinner on the table is one of the marvels of the place. Here, non-stop John cooks dinner for friends on his one night off, while Rosa Lou (left) entertains in one of the dining rooms.

This is an original Novi recipe which is an autumn favorite.

Cream of Almond and Chestnut Soup

3/4 cup almonds
1 qt. well-seasoned chicken stock
1-3/4 cups dried chestnuts, boiled until soft
1 cup cream

Combine above ingredients and cook for 20 minutes. Put mixture into blender and combine well. Pour into top of double boiler, allow to simmer 1 hour before serving. Just before serving, add 1 cup of hot heavy cream. Garnish with almond flavored egg white mounds as follows:

Beat two egg whites until stiff. Add a pinch of salt and 1/2 tsp. almond extract; mix well. Spoon into pastry gun, squeeze small rosettes onto a buttered baking sheet. Place rosettes under a hot broiler until lightly browned. Spoon one rosette on top of each serving of soup.

First transatlantic steamship service begins — Congress declares railroads legal mail carriers; demise of stagecoach — Van Buren claims neutrality in Canadian revolt — Troops evict Cherokees from Georgia — Amistad Incident: slaves revolt on ship; freed in US — Charles Goodyear makes first vulcanized rubber — Morse brings daguerreotype process to US — First manila paper made — Iowa territory formed — Liberty Party: first anti-slavery party forms in Warsaw, NY.

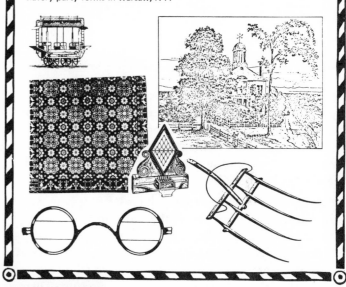

John Novi says he just sort of "fell into" the D & H Canal Historical Society because of his interest in history and old buildings, but he has done some careful planning since. The Society publishes a newsletter, and the whole town is involved in some pretty intriguing events: a Float-In down the river; the Canalaree held by the Boy Scouts (they camp along the canal and clean up the banks to earn badges); the Beard Contest; parades and talent shows; kite fly-ins; and the Canal Walk, which ends up at the Tavern with a prize for the person who walked the farthest to get there. The prize? A bottle of canal water!

The Tavern and the town of High Falls and John and Rosa Lou Novi are all a part of the same exceptional spirit. "It's a good thing to know that you are involved in something that is supporting people," says John, and it's not only the restaurant that is supporting people (the waiters and their families financially; the guests physically!), but also the energy and creative use of town history that is supporting the whole community. John has remarked that things usually get done in one of two ways: either an individual is so dedicated that he can pull along a whole group with his enthusiasm, or an entire community gets turned on to something and keeps energy high. High Falls seems to have a combination of both of those elements, and everyone is pretty happy with the results.

Warren, Illinois
The Cheese Man

A lot of the preparation of food isn't done by Americans any more; it's done by machines. In Warren, Illinois, John Bussman is preserving the traditional art of cheesemaking which was once the dominant industry in his part of the country. The result of his work? A two hundred pound wheel of Swiss cheese!

These pictures show the wagon which Mr Bussman made to take to various fairs around the state, and the making of the cheese — from start to finish. It starts with milk; that thickens (coagulates). Then it is stirred and the curd is cut up. Cheesecloth is slid under the curd (the "dip cloth"); this is pulled up and the whey drains out. Then the remaining product, the cheese-to-be, is placed in a round hoop which makes one round of Swiss. After the wheel is made, it takes another six to eight weeks of curing to get the eye formation (holes) in it.

John Bussman is one of the last remaining cheese-making experts, but he is trying to spread the technique to as many people as he can with his cheese wagon, "Die Alte Kaserei."

TYING THE ENDS AFTER SLIDING THE CHEESECLOTH UNDER THE CURD.

PULLING UP THE CURD AND DRAINING OUT THE WHEY.

PLACING THE CHEESE IN A ROUND HOOP WHICH MAKES ONE 200LB. WHEEL OF SWISS.

It all began when I was asked to contribute something of historical value to the county fair in honor of the Sesquicentennial for the town of Warren, Illinois. Then I realized for the first time that I had lived in an era already fading into the past, an era which helped mold our country. Can you imagine 368 cheese factories in one county (Green County, Wisconsin)? The cheesemakers were mostly Swiss immigrants, and brought with them their traditional pride in hard work, their wine making and their entertaining hospitality with mountain yodeling, polkas and festivities, including Swiss wrestling and the annual Cheesemakers Ball. Any two or three miles in any direction there was a cheese factory, necessary since milk was taken to the factory by horse-drawn rigs with thirty and forty gallon milk cans (240-320 pounds) twice a day. These factories were set up on a cooperative basis by a group of neighboring farmers.

I gathered all the old time equipment I could find that had been used by my father and other cheesemakers of the early nineteenth century, and made a Swiss wheel of cheese weighing two hundred pounds at the Sesquicentennial Fair in 1968, as they did a century ago. Since the fair, we have taken "Die Alte Kaserei" (The Old Cheese Factory) and made cheese at the Green County Cheese Days, held bi-annually at Monroe, Wisconsin, a Swiss settlement known as the Swiss Cheese Capital of the World.

The reward has been the look of awe in the faces of the youth, and the tales of yesteryear told by the old timers. It is to my father that I have dedicated "Die Alte Kaserei," as a way of life that will never be equalled or be again, as the advancement of technology has produced large concerns eliminating the small factories and the togetherness they had which was necessary years ago.

Letter from John Bussman

1840 ◉ 1841

Wilkes expedition discovers Antarctica — First wagon train arrives in California — Demise of the canals: first passengers ride Erie Railroad — Harvard observatory finished — John W. Draper takes first moon photo — 10-hour day established for federal employees — Congress passes Uniform Bankruptcy System — Horace Greeley founds New York Tribune — Slaves capture Creole ship, gain asylum in Nassau — New to the language: "OK" after Old Kinderhook, Van Buren's birthplace — Total US pop. 17,069,453.

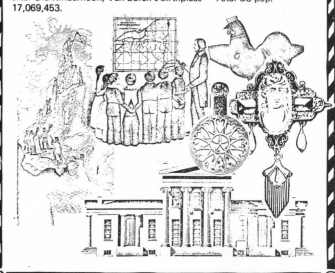

Fishers, New York

Saving, Among Other Things, Dr Came's Fabulous Electric Show

Scientific work hasn't always been carried on inside stainless steel laboratories by teams of white-coated technicians. A hundred years ago, the American man of science was usually a loner who doubled as his own traveling salesman. Geniuses in the Franklin/Edison mold were in the minority; but many wandering wizards did construct amazing devices. (If you were going to earn a living at science, you had to astound and bewilder your potential customers.) That era of science-and-showmanship is gone from just about everywhere except Fishers, New York. That's where J. Sheldon Fisher presents now and again the Fabulous Electric Show of Dr Charles Came.

Dr Came was a traveling scientist, medical doctor and cabinet maker who circulated through western New York during the 1830's and '40's. Fisher discovered an attic full of Dr Came's equipment in nearby Pittsford, and, instead of sealing it behind glass or selling it piece by piece to private collectors, he keeps the Came collection all set up in his Valentown "museum," ready for action.

"Those coils down there next to the medicines — aren't they beautiful? They're really unusual-looking and very decorative. What they did was change direct current from wet-cell batteries to alternating current. You hold the electrodes in your hand for treatment. Good for arthritis and rheumatism. If you're coming down with a sore throat, you hold the electrodes up to your throat.

"We also have this static generator and electric stool. Good for all-over treatment. The patient stands on the stool and is filled with electricity. Now if you want a milder treatment, stand next to the stool and hold your arms out over it. You'll be getting what Dr Came called an electric bath.

"And this lightning jar of Dr Came's will hold up to 100,000 volts. It will operate other things besides people, like chimes. The leather pad here has quicksilver, tin grains and bacon fat. This rubs against the glass jar and will generate static electricity. It goes on into the jar here and stores it up until you use it."

J. Sheldon Fisher has spent over thirty years of his life collecting, restoring, gathering, researching and teaching... keeping blacksmith operations, Indian burial mounds, Mormon landmarks, farmers' cottages and Dr Came's Fabulous Electric Show intact, vital and visible. Just think what an amazing world this would be if all museum curators had Sheldon Fisher's energy, his willingness to share, and, especially, his love of putting the past to work again.

His Valentown Museum, near Rochester, New York, is located in the world's first covered mall shopping center (but that's another story) and is one of the most unusual private museums to be found anywhere. What makes it that way, of course, is J. Sheldon Fisher himself, who knows how to make the past come alive and has, as well, a gift for sharing.

SCIENTIFIC EXHIBITION!

THE LIGHTNING MAN IS COMING!

With His Philosophical And Amusing

Entertainment

J. SHELDON FISHER

OF FISHERS WILL RE-PRESENT THE FAMOUS 1840 LECTURE WITH ORIGINAL LANTERN SLIDES AND DEMONSTRATE THE USE OF THE CENTURY OLD SCIENTIFIC INSTRUMENTS OF

DR. C. CAME

The celebrated Etherial Physician and Professor in Natural Philosophy, formerly of Pittsford, whose surprising experiments and Scientific Illustrations and astonishing cures have excited the wonder of thousands of spectators and have given him universal applause wherever they have been witnessed. This show will be repeated at

Rochester Museum of Arts and Sciences at 657 East Ave.

Under the Auspices of the Rochester Antiquarian League

on February 3, 1948 at 8 P. M.

ELECTRO-MAGNETISM AND ASTRONOMY

ELECTRO-MAGNETIC TELEGRAPHS!

Electro-Magnetic Engine,	The Charging Magnet
Illustrating the principle of applying Lightning for propelling machinery.	will be exhibited and ladies' scissors and gentlemen's knives will be magnetized free of expense.

ELECTRO-BIOLOGY

La Grange, California
The Last of the Gold Diggers

The little foothill town of La Grange was born in the early 1850's, when, it was said, bare hands could often scoop gold nuggets from California's gold fields. The easy gold went fast, though, and miners had to devise increasingly elaborate processes to force the countryside to yield up its treasures. The last mining device used near La Grange was a dinosaur of a dredging machine which dug thousands of yards of soil and rock from the landscape — eating twenty-four hours a day, biting seventy-five feet into the earth, digesting its meal in a hopper the size of a freight car, and dumping its waste ("tailings") as strings of fifty foot rockpiles — until it shut down in 1949. Thorne Gray, a young newspaper reporter, has had his mind on saving this last and most awesome piece of the Gold Rush for seven years now, and he's gotten an entire county interested in creating a Gold Dredge Museum.

Here is Thorne's story about how he fell in love with the monster:

"Rattlesnakes were more on my mind than gold digging machinery that September day in 1966 when I first visited the giant Tuolumne gold dredge at La Grange. Like so much of the Southern Mines country of California's Mother Lode, heaps of rocks, haphazard ditches, humps and swales left by the Forty-Niners made an ideal habitat for the big, dangerous snakes. I was watching my step.

"I was there to write about rocks — piles and piles of them in scalloped layers extending for miles along the Tuolumne River bottomlands. They were the by-product of gold dredging, as ugly as any mess I had seen in California. In the twenty years since dredging had ended here, scarcely a blade of grass had taken hold among the cobbles. The Tuolumne dredge was the only survivor in the San Joaquin Valley of the great machines which had dug to bedrock for gold after panning, and later hydraulicing, no longer would pay. Escorting me to tell me its story were Everett Brescia of La Grange, and Stanislaus County's remarkable self-made historian, I. N. 'Jack' Brotherton, president of the Stanislaus County Historical Society. My photographer-companion, Al Golub, was seeing the dredge for the first time, too.

"The machine loomed over us, mammoth, imposing, an incredible extension of the pick and shovel. It was four stories high. The idle bucket ladder reached toward the bank of the small pond in which the dredge rested, as if to make just one more 'step ahead' for a

"Then will come the restoration. The old dredge camp, which the County Board of Supervisors voted to add to the park property, is decaying fast. Its charming buildings are structurally sound, but they have suffered from vandalism and neglect. They will need renovation. The dredge must be redecked for visitors. Volunteers will have to do much of the work."

This picture of Thorne Gray, Al Golub and Dick Belt was snapped right after an overflow crowd filled the La Grange Odd Fellows' Hall to see a film presentation about the great dredge.

meal of gold. The stacker, a conveyor belt which had spilled the ugly tailings, reached precariously from the stern. The long gangplank was askew.

"Brotherton, an engineer by profession, was justifiably dubious about preserving this hulk of rusting steel, or even making the wooden deck safe for the public to stand on. Actually restoring the machine would be something else, he said, something gosh-awful expensive which the Historical Society could not dream of undertaking.

"In spite of Jack's hesitance, he had given me the ammunition I needed for a story or two. After all, journalists always have access to dreams without regard to cost, and so I dreamed in print about a dredge museum. For years, my gold dredge museum was a newsroom joke. The big machine became known as Thorne's dredge. No one took the museum idea very seriously, least of all the man who actually owned the dredge. He was I. L. Brooks, a San Francisco stockbroker who had bought the machine speculatively in 1961. The dredge had been considered so useless it had been dropped from the tax rolls for several years.

"When I reached Brooks on the telephone and asked him how much the dredge would cost for a museum, he was gruff. His price was $100,000, he said, entirely dashing my hopes. I quoted him in the paper, and to my surprise (and his), the assessor sent him a property valuation at his figure and the county sent him a bill for back taxes based on that amount. Heart failure killed Mr Brooks shortly after, though whether caused by getting his tax bill I will never know. His estate sold the dredge for $16,000, and the assessed valuation was reduced accordingly. The new owner, Dale Soulé of Susanville, has been trying to sell the dredge ever since, still asking $100,000 or more, but it clearly is a derelict.

"Then preparations were made for a new dam near La Grange. Its builders, the Modesto and Turlock Irrigation Districts and the city of San Francisco, bought large amounts of land in and around La Grange where the dredge tailings, and a clay deposit for the dam core, were located. I thought they might have purchased the dredge, but no one was sure just what had fallen into public hands, and everyone was too busy to find out. I figured the dredge idea was dead.

"I was wrong. California has a crazy historical society known as E. Clampus Vitus, a fun-loving group which delights in focusing attention on historic objects, and sometimes adorns them with brass plaques. In 1970, Richard Belt, a Modesto printer, became Grand Noble Humbug of the Estanislao Chapter, and Belt remembered the old dredge. He persuaded the conservation-minded Guy F. Atkinson Company, which was building the dam, to cut a rough road to the dredge, and sent out one of his elaborate printed invitations. History did not dare record all that went on at the Clampers meeting at the old dredge (it never does), but the derelict machine was back in the news.

"My interest in the dredge revived, stimulated by Dick and also because I had an idea some of the Don Pedro project landholdings at La Grange could be converted into a county park. A search of the assessor's records showed the dam partners owned a lot of river

frontage near La Grange, and some buildings in town. I thought they could be persuaded to give the property to the county. I spoke to County Supervisor Joash Paul of Turlock and he launched an effort to obtain the land through the Board of Supervisors.

"The dam partners made it clear there would be no gift of land, but they agreed to sell it for its appraised value. Since most of the property was in the floodplain, the price was not high and now more than three hundred acres of La Grange property, including the plot beneath the gold dredge and some of the oldest buildings in the county, are being purchased for $77,000, probably as good a deal for a park as anyone ever found.

"Then some good news arrived. In 1968 the county had submitted a list of historic places and buildings for inclusion in the National Register of Historic Places. At first no one had remembered the dredge, but Park Director Paul Morrisson skeptically agreed to include it at my insistence. Incredibly, we learned later that the dredge was the only county item to make the register.

"Much remains to be done. The dredge still is privately owned and deteriorating daily. We are searching old deeds and records for liens upon the machine which might be foreclosed. Maybe it can be leased from the owner, or purchased over a number of years. Certainly we must soon launch a major fund raising drive in the community.

"Is it worth it? Certainly. The La Grange Historic Park is a reality. And it's touching the hearts and the lives of just about everyone here in a very good way."

La Grange is one of many rollicking mining settlements connected by California State Route 49. By the time the giant dredge in question was put into operation, however, mining had settled down to a somewhat more staid occupation than is suggested by early town photos.

Thorne Gray is writing a book about the history of Stanislaus County, *Quest for Deep Gold: The Story of La Grange*. It costs $2.25 (postpaid) and can be ordered from Southern Mines Press, 410 Fleetwood Drive, Modesto, California 95350.

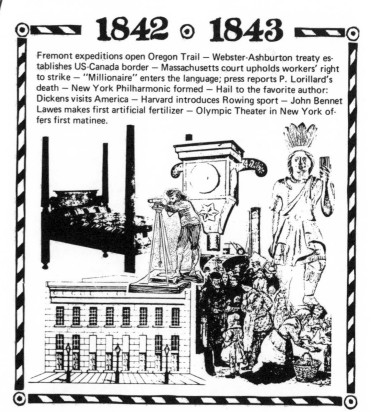

1842 ⊙ 1843

Fremont expeditions open Oregon Trail — Webster-Ashburton treaty establishes US-Canada border — Massachusetts court upholds workers' right to strike — "Millionaire" enters the language; press reports P. Lorillard's death — New York Philharmonic formed — Hail to the favorite author: Dickens visits America — Harvard introduces Rowing sport — John Bennet Lawes makes first artificial fertilizer — Olympic Theater in New York offers first matinee.

Rhinebeck, New York
Just Plane Folks

Almost the entire first generation of American flying machines has left our skies forever — most gone to junk piles, a few trapped inside museums. But thanks to a few wonderfully impractical people like Cole Palen of Rhinebeck, New York, jet-age youngsters can still see how man first cajoled a machine into taking him for a ride through the clouds.

Cole Palen puts on air shows with a flair for the people in the Kingston, New York, area every Sunday, weather permitting. Palen's "theater" is an abandoned farm, his "actors" are ancient airplanes, and the "stage" is the clear blue yonder. He and his pilot friends put the planes through their paces as melodramatically as possible: "good guy" airplanes shoot "bad guy" airplanes out of the sky. The crowds love it.

Here's what Palen has to say about the creation of his unique historical hybrid:

"When I was a kid I used to hang around the town airport. I thought the airplanes were wonderful, and the pilots were my heroes. (Now I know that planes are junk and pilots are all madmen — but that's what comes from growing up.) Anyway, after World War II, I studied aviation mechanics at the old Roosevelt Field here, and I'd eat my lunch in the cockpit of an old Sopwith Snipe, or one of the other obsolete airplanes they had stored in Hangar 63.

"Four years later — 1951 — I heard Roosevelt Field was going to be made into a shopping center, so I decided to find out what would become of the old planes. They were for sale, so I offered my life savings (which wasn't much), and I got six airplanes.

"We laid out this aerodrome in 1958 on an abandoned farm. Right now we have thirty airplanes, I think. On Sundays we're flying five World War I'ers, one Pioneer from 1909, and about six of the Lindbergh Era. This is the first living airplane museum in the United States; we've been doing Sunday shows for quite some time. I hate to say this is the first or the biggest or anything, but in this respect, it is.

"Our show is very informal. We ham it up, and we get great crowds. There's the hero, the heroine, the villain, lots of noise, fake crashes, the works . . . melodrama with wings — and people seem to love it."

1844 ◉ 1845

"What hath God wrought!"; Morse sends first telegraph message, Washington to Baltimore — Catholics, Protestants riot in Philadelphia — University of Notre Dame chartered — Texas annexed, admitted to union — Mexico breaks off relations with US — Florida admitted — Mormon leader Joseph Smith killed by mob in Carthage, Ill. — Fremont makes third trek to California — Naval Academy opens — Boston gives first elementary school tests — First bridal suite: New York's Irving House hotel.

Luckenbach, Texas

You may think Orville and Wilbur Wright invented the airplane. They didn't. Jacob Brodbeck did . . . according to the folks who frequent the Luckenbach, Texas, general store and beer parlor. Proprietor Guiche Kooch explains the career of Luckenbach's neglected genius:

"In 1865, a school teacher named Jacob Brodbeck invented a flying machine and flew the first airplane — thirty-eight years before the Wright Brothers. It was a spring-powered machine. He planned it so when one spring unwound, the other would wind up. It didn't work that way, but it did fly. It flew higher, further and longer than the Wrights' did. He crashed on his first flight, though, and lost his financial backing. He couldn't speak much English, and the German people were apparently on the outs with the Reconstruction government which was in power at the time, and so he was never officially recognized. People here remember him taking his models around to the fairs. They say: 'Oh yeah, that old man invented airplanes. But nobody knew anything about airplanes back then.' And when he died, his wife threw all his papers into the creek, because she was so embarrassed that he was crazy enough to try to invent an airplane. But his granddaughter lives over in Fredericksburg, and she still has a lot of his original drawings and calculations (in German). I even came across a notation in my great grandfather's diary about that first flight in 1865."

People's Archaeology

Archaeology? A lot of people still picture somebody in a safari hat — one of a handful of highly-trained scholars, of course — out searching Africa or the Middle East for the world's oldest skeleton. If they see people in casual clothes out sifting through American soil, they figure they must be bottle collectors, arrowhead fanciers or pothunters searching for new trophies.

But there is a new breed of archaeologists out digging up the past (carefully), cataloguing everything they find, and then struggling to put these ancient clues together. They aren't professionals — they're just ordinary curious people — secretaries, truck drivers, students, dentists, grandmothers — who are coming out in ever-increasing numbers to work alongside professional archaeologists. They're rediscovering American history that we've all been walking over for many years.

The Arkansas Archaeological Survey was the first statewide archaeology program to involve amateurs in a formalized training program. And it now may be the most successful state archaeology program of any kind. People from all over the United States, Canada and even Europe join Arkansans in the AAS annual excavations and they all receive expert training from survey heads Bob McGimsey and Hester Davis (and their associates). These many hands don't make light work — instead, they make a big difference in how much work gets done, and how thorough it is: *"In the forty years prior to the survey, the University of Arkansas Museum had recorded fewer than 1,000 archaeological sites in the state. The Survey files now contain records — and generally they are better records — on over 5,000 sites, and they are accumulating at a rate of almost 1,000 a year."*

McGimsey and Davis aren't lukewarm about their operation; they think amateurs are the only answer. Progress —

Hester Davis (above, row 2, at right) and Bob McGimsey are triple-threat people — articulate spokesmen for the cause of participatory archaeology, deft organizers of successful research programs and skilled field workers. Hester's expression says a lot about which part of being an archaeologist she enjoys most.

in the form of traxcavators, steamshovels, concrete dams and man-made lakes — is changing the landscape everywhere. And faster than ever before. There aren't enough pros to touch even one of every hundred sites before they're scraped and mashed. And there's no money to hire personnel — technical or non-technical.

Just like Tom Sawyer (when he had some fence-painting to do), the Arkansas Survey people have had to find volunteers willing to work hard for nothing. Comments made during the 1972 dig hint at why they've had no trouble, why amateur archaeologists keep coming back for more:

Dirk Hood: *"I guess people are just interested in other people's cultures. It's fascinating to me — everybody else here too — just to see how these people lived."*

Joan Kennedy: *"I'm really enjoying it. We excavated a grave right over in the corner of those two squares in Mound B. Four whole pots, and they came right out of here. I think it's neat to let all the amateurs get out and work with supervision. I've heard that now when somebody reports a site that's going to be flooded, bulldozed or something, the Survey people can call upon amateurs to help excavate it before the site is destroyed."*

Mrs Mary Gateley: *"I work as a secretary in Shreveport, but I do this as often as I can. I would say that it's like the training you might get to become a technician in this field of work. Then you can do enough of the work so that the professionals can concentrate on the highest levels."*

A new twist to the Arkansas program involves a certification program for the helpers. Hours worked under professional supervision are recorded and technical competence is acknowledged. An amateur can actually progress to a level at which he is allowed to direct archaeological research projects under the auspices of the Survey — with his own crews of volunteers.

But certification or no, the experience of personally rediscovering history seems to bring a full measure of satisfaction — which is something money never can buy. The Arkansas Society bulletin announcing the 1972 Emmett dig closed with the following list, entitled "What Will You Take Away With You?".

"Memories galore; photographs in abundance; friends by the score from all parts of Arkansas and many other states; pages of notes; some good stories to tell the folks at home; vast amounts of information on how to excavate in a scientific manner, how to record everything you see and do, how to tell what it is you are doing and what you have found. What more do you want?"

The Mystery of Indiana County

A handful of amateur underground history sleuths are out there right now brushing away the dust from a two century old mystery in Indiana County, Pennsylvania. Local people have been debating for years whether or not Fergus Moorhead really did build a log fort in 1781 after he returned from being held prisoner by the British; history books say he did, but not one visible piece of the fort is above ground.

Indiana University graduate student Tom Brandon is leading fourteen volunteers in a search for proof positive. It's a first for most of the diggers, but they're learning fast as they go down toward an answer. The first few weeks' work revealed five post-holes, which gave the Brandon bunch cause for optimism.

They're digging near a stucco-covered building which revealed itself several years ago to be an eighteenth century stone structure long disguised. The researchers believe this building was a house built not long after the fort; but if they don't find that fort, the stone building will retain its claim as the oldest Anglo-built structure in Indiana County.

A "once and for all" answer to the fort mystery is not the only reason to dig. All artifacts removed from the site are labeled and catalogued, and with the help of local antique dealers will tell stories about an era in Indiana County which has always been shadowy speculation. And, of course, everybody's learning — because archaeological research, though not difficult, is something you just can't learn to do from reading a book. Who'd want to do it that way, anyway? Archaeology means discovery and puzzle-pondering — and in Indiana, Pennsylvania, as elsewhere, the fun is in the doing.

The Arkansas and Indiana County projects involve prehistoric as well as historic artifacts — and prehistoric archaeology requires a certain amount of experience and expertise on the part of the project leader. Purely *Historic Archaeology* — such as Roland Robbins is involved in — is something you can do yourself, right now. Turn to page 170 for some ideas.

Roland Robbins is not a popular man among elitist archaeologists. Not only do they consider him personally unqualified to be carrying out archaeological research (he left school at the age of sixteen to work as an office boy, and has learned archaeological methods and theory through independent reading and research), but the fact that he dares advocate that others follow his example and begin digging up American history too — well, that's dreadful. Not to mention the fact that he is interested in artifacts of recent times (seventeenth century forward) instead of esoteric remains of prehistoric ages.

But Roland Robbins' achievements — and his students and friends, who number in the thousands — speak loud in favor of his unorthodox methods. Robbins perhaps has uncovered more buried historic treasure than any man alive or dead: he located Henry David Thoreau's cabin site at Walden Pond; he located and excavated the foundations of pilgrim John Alden's first house; he supervised the uncovering of America's first successful ironworks (Saugus, Massachusetts, 1646); he carried out research on "Shadwell" — Thomas Jefferson's birthplace; he has helped discover and restore a 1683 Dutch trading post on the Hudson; and much more.

Robbins writes books and speaks to women's clubs, college audiences, eighth grade science classes and corporation presidents when he's not busy digging. He stresses his belief that history under the ground belongs to *every* American, and anyone has a right to do first-hand research (if he obtains permission from the landowner). Of course, Robbins insists that amateur archaeologists fulfill their responsibilities to society, too — orderly, careful work; complete cataloguing; excavation for the sake of knowledge and *not* to collect trinkets. But he wants people out digging. He believes that unless ordinary people take it upon themselves to supplement the work of professionals, United States history will be filled with blank pages:

"Times are ever changing. That's the way it should be. But the changing of time shouldn't be at the expense of the past. The records of the past should be kept in order for the future. Careful study should be given to all property that must be altered for progress. Each generation makes its own contribution to the growth and the prosperity of the American way of life. But the contributions of some generations will be forgotten — irreparably crumpled — if responsible communities don't undertake to accurately record the story of their early and their contemporary history."

Robbins teaches a research method which involves digging far more quickly than is normal in archaeology. This does lead to a certain loss of information at a site dug in this manner. But historic archaeology doesn't depend on extensive interpretations as does prehistoric archaeology, because in most cases much is known already about historic cultures under study — and objects found are relatively easy to classify according to date and function.

The Roland Robbins "get off your behind or it'll be gone forever" philosophy of archaeology is getting a great variety of Americans turned on to history. He has a lot of faith in his converts — that they won't be greedy or impatient — and so far the results say his faith in people is justified, and the maledictions of his critics is uncalled for: amateur research has turned up some priceless information. (Oh yes — those of you who are thinking people's archaeology is for young people might be interested to know that Roland Robbins is young . . . sixty-six years young, and going like a house afire.)

Marking Time

In the area around the southern New York community of Pecksville, Reverend Floyd Fisher is making a very personal contribution to the rediscovery of American history. Reverend Fisher locates forgotten graveyards, and resurrects headstones which have long lain hidden. He does it all himself — research (generally informal), discovery, cleaning and restoration, and the recording of the names of the deceased on a list for each cemetery, including a list of War Veterans.

"I start out by locating an old farm; almost every farm had their own burying ground. If not on any maps or records, I start by looking for a high elevation near the farm. Cemeteries were usually on land on a hill, away from the water supply. Then I walk in a circle, small radius, then expanding out until I find the old cemetery. Stones are usually down or overgrown. Care has to be taken not to break them. All the soil has to be removed before standing them up. A strong solution of baking soda and a brush will clean them — never use strong soap or (scouring) powder on them."

"I do it to help people find their forefathers and early settlers of this area."

Brooklyn, New York

Brooklyn, New York, is maybe the last place you'd expect to find archaeologists at work. But the earth beneath city buildings is filled with information about the past, and in some cases the information is more accurate than information printed in newspapers.

In early 1968, three men — James Hurley, a former U.S. vice-consul in Pakistan; Michael Cohn, an archaeologist previously concerned with pre-Columbian civilizations; and William T. Harley, a disabled World War I veteran and lifetime student of the heritage of his Bedford-Stuyvesant neighborhood — began talking about a search into the Brooklyn earth for the truth about Weeksville, a nineteenth century settlement of black freemen: the few references to the nature of life in Weeksville that they'd found in old periodicals characterized the village as full of illiterate, unstable and degenerate people. But Harley's own collection of relics — such as a family Bible containing a neatly-written genealogy in the front — suggested otherwise.

Their chance came in 1969 when construction crews began chewing up a city block of Bedford-Stuyvesant preparatory to building a housing project; the block being cleared was at the heart of the old settlement. They asked for, and received, permission to investigate. But of course these three people — each of whom had other responsibilities — wouldn't have gotten much done alone.

The Bedford-Stuyvesant people rallied 'round their heritage. Boy Scout troops and college students gave up weekends and afternoons to search out the truth. People who saw the work from their windows came down to help. Passersby would ask what was going on, go change clothes, and return with digging tools. Even the construction crewmen caught the fever — in fact, 'dozer operator Jessie Simpkins spotted what director Hurley called "the most important document we have," the constitution and by-laws of the Abyssinian Benevolent Daughters of Esther, printed by a black printer in 1853.

That constitution proves the existence of a literate and socially-aware element in the settlement, and many other finds similarly support a re-evaluation of Weeksville society. An 1873 newspaper article that called Weeksville "goat-ridden" has been discredited by the discovery of peach tree roots and peach pits (goats destroy peach trees). The article also called the residents "shiftless drunkards," but only one fragment of a liquor bottle has been uncovered (while many soda and medicine bottles have been turned up). A small pre-Civil War marble bust of Venus found seems to indicate prosperity and aesthetic concern; children's marbles show that families spent money for children's toys; and a square-toed child's shoe negates assertions that Weeksville children ran around barefooted.

The truth was there all the time — that Weeksville actually was a peaceful, well-knit community — but it took a few special people and many willing hands to bring it to light. People's archaeology is big in Brooklyn. Who knows where next?

1846 ⊙ 1847

War with Mexico over disputed Texas land — Oregon boundary settled in treaty with Britain — Iowa admitted — Bear Flag revolt in California — Brigham Young leads first Mormons from Illinois to Salt Lake — Elias Howe patents first eye-point needle sewing machine — First adhesive postage stamps sold — Smithsonian Institute dedicated — Richard Hoe invents rotary printing press — New York Nine dumps Knickerbockers, 23-1, in first pro baseball game.

Fredericksburg, Texas
The Best Is Good Enough

The cooks in Fredericksburg are artists (page 94), but they're not the only ones in town. This may be a town that loves to eat, but it also knows how to work. There are people around Fredericksburg who are experts in a wide variety of crafts. There is Henry Borchers in his cabinet shop, making exquisite furniture despite an accident which cost him one of his hands; and Emil "Shiney" Schandua, a tinsmith with a golden smile; and the Holy Ghost Lutheran Church Quilting Club working on extraordinary quilts. This little town doesn't boast a huge population, but it's full of life — and part of its vitality lies in its strong ties with traditional ways of doing things.

The Holy Ghost Lutheran Church Quilting Club

The Holy Ghost Lutheran Church Quilting Club has been going for over sixty-five years. The ladies in it quilt for individuals and are paid by the amount of thread they put into the quilt. To quilt, they sit around the frame. Each works toward the center of the quilt. It is rolled under as a side is completed. This four-corner work keeps the quilt taut and smooth. They use dacron rather than cotton for the filler. The bottom cloth is stitched to the cloth on the frame. The filler is next, and then the top piece. Here, they are working on a pattern called "Grandmother's Flower Garden." They were using a size 7 needle and cotton quilting thread. Last year they quilted 153 quilts! That's about three quilts every week.

Henry Borchers

In my younger days I was a highliner, I built electric lines. After I got older I didn't want to climb them high poles any more, so I began this woodwork-cabinet making-furniture reproduction shop as a hobby. Everyone said I'd never make it, but I said I'd try. So with the help of my wife I made a success out of it. I was determined to do it, and that's what it takes. If you want to do something, make up your mind what you want to do and do it. Now I'm teaching my son Bob. He's a real cabinet maker, very particular. After I lost my arm in the combine accident, it took a lot of will power to resume my work — to practice, to do things. I would try to tie my shoelaces — I would sit there and tie and it wouldn't work, but I was determined.

Emil Schandua

Emil "Shiney" Schandua is a tinsmith. "My dad bought into the shop in 1918. He taught me the trade in part, and then I went to school to get the patterns right, in San Antonio. I've made safari stoves, standing seam tin roofs, boats, perch traps, tool cases, tin pants. Nothing in the shop has been changed since my daddy left it."

Many of the chairs I work on are made from China berry. I grew the wood — the tree grew it, rather — in Daddy's back yard. You have to cut it at the right time, before it has come to the peak of its growth. After that, it starts to deteriorate. I work in whatever woods come around. My favorites are oak, walnut, maple, mahogany. We use pine here, some of the real old pine. People ask me about the design of my furniture. Oh, you can take measurements, but my pattern is in my head. Of course, some I do have to make according to pattern, like that spinning wheel. I want to get those spokes fairly much alike. The design is the knowledge I have of what is fitting. You have to have an idea. You must know how a piece of furniture is going to look like before you start it; if you don't it's like being put on a strange road. You go down the road but you do not know where you have to turn or all that. I always knew, not that I want to brag. I had to look before I started, and it worked for me. The best is good enough. In my business I say, if I please you, tell others; if I don't, tell me. I make it for my own satisfaction, and then hope the customer is satisfied.

Zoar, Ohio

Looking for the Clay Pits

It's one thing to carry on the traditional crafts when you are lucky enough to have a teacher; and it's another thing to try to learn about a traditional process when the only clue you have about it is the article that some craftsman produced years ago. That is what Mrs June Knaack is doing in Zoar, Ohio — trying to reconstruct the pottery making process of the German settlers who founded the town in the early 1800's. About all she has to go on is the old utility ware: elegant and beautifully colored jugs, pitchers, crocks, collanders, bowls, and a ceramic horn which was used to call workers from the fields. So now June spends her weekends tramping the fields near town where old timers say the pottery was located, and she is collecting clay samples and trying a variety of glazes on her pots, searching for the one which will produce the characteristic and unique orange-to-ochre Zoar glaze.

June is married to Charles Knaack, who is the (unpaid but official) Mayor of Zoar. They moved to the little Ohio town — whose name means "refuge" — several years ago to find an alternative to city living. They were intrigued by Zoar's history, and encouraged by the way townspeople were working to preserve that history, in the form of Zoar's beautiful old gardens and buildings. The town is the legacy of the German religious society, the Separatists, who founded the town in search of religious freedom. It was a communal settlement which prospered for over three quarters of a century — from 1817 to 1898. When the Society disbanded, many people stayed in Zoar. "Historical preservation" was a part of normal remodeling, since people were still living and working in the old buildings. And the Ohio Historical Society got to work as early as the 1940's fixing up the unused sites.

Work is still going on to preserve Zoar's beauty, and it is now a State Memorial. Visitors come to look around, to learn about Zoar's colorful history, and that history is still a part of the place, a part of the lives of Zoar's people. June Knaack works diligently to learn the secrets of Zoar's pottery, which could be the keystone in a whole program of reactivating the crafts and cottage industries which flourished in the 1800's. College students spend summers in town, working in a living "restoration laboratory."

June assumed that the Zoar pottery had been built near the clay source, and that if she could locate the foundation stones for the building, she would find the clay pits nearby. Late in the fall of 1972, she had a bit of good luck. The following is from a letter she wrote in October:

"I was fortunate to meet a man doing clay stripping behind Zoar and he gave me a tour of the areas he is stripping now. He felt that the clay bed they are in could possibly be an extension of the clay pits I am searching for. He is introducing me to the engineer who will take me to the research plant and work with me analyzing the clay properties and glazes. I've been unbelievably lucky to meet him. We have come to a few sketchy conclusions: Glazes — all colors were the same glaze. The firing temperatures, being rather erratic, varied; thus, the light orange is underfired, the dark tangerine overfired.

Clay — the yellow clay body was not used on the orange glazed pieces. That ware seems to be about half shale and half clay. The flecks of dark in the glaze are actually impurities in the clay which burned through. The Zoarites apparently dug shallow, near creek beds, and their clay was full of impurities. Usually above this type of clay there is a two-foot coal bed. Zoar clay was coal fired. How like them it would have been to use the clay found beneath a coal bed and to use that coal to fire it!"

But mostly Zoar is a town for its people, who like the way it feels, and want to keep that feeling alive. Young folks like the Knaacks are finding ways to re-make the old traditions into the stuff of which a decent life can be made in the present, and they are finding pleasure in doing it. Zoar's traditional role as a place of refuge — like any good home — is still being successfully explored, providing new interests for people of the twentieth century.

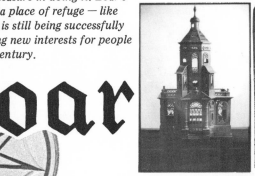

1848 ⊙ 1849

War with Mexico ends; Texas, California, Utah, New Mexico territories ceded — The rush is on: James W. Marshall finds gold at Sutter's Mill — President Polk offers Spain $100 million for Cuba — Wisconsin admitted, pop. 300,000 — Dickens writes "David Copperfield" — Associated Press organizes — In vogue: spiritualism and the seance — Bigelow invents power carpet loom — Walter Hunt patents safety pin — John B. Curtis makes first chewing gum.

Delhi, New York
Morristown, New York

Who Is Hank the Sturgeon, Anyway?

Delhi, New York

There's no stopping the Delaware Rural Crafts Guild! They've bought looms and spinning wheels; they are collecting wool from local sheepherders and dyeing it with natural materials; their exhibit, "From Fleece to Fabric," has won prizes and converts to handiwork all over the area. . . and it has all happened in less than two years time.

It all started in 1971. Peggy Shultz got to work by contacting local craft clubs by letter, and the general community by newspaper articles. She wanted to see if people in the small town of Delhi would be interested in learning some of the traditional crafts of New England. The response was widespread and enthusiastic, so the Crafts Guild found rooms in a local college where they could hold meetings and hired John Davis to set up a definite program. The first class studied textile work — tapestry, stitchery, weaving. That was the beginning.

Now, the course of study has been expanded to include macrame, batik, quilting and banner making, and classes are held every season except winter (when most prospective students are snowed in!). Peggy says: "Our students include teenagers, men and women from all walks of life. Some of the women represent the various craft or community groups, planning to conduct a 'learn and return' type of program. Several of the members are involved in sheep raising projects now, and hope to use their own wool in the courses." The Delaware Rural Crafts Guild is a real community project — all students come from the twenty miles around the little town — and the whole community is completely involved in seeing the old ways in a new light, the light of practical use for today's needs.

Morristown, New York

The Red Barn Museum project started as an outgrowth of the celebration of the 150th anniversary of the founding of Morristown. Townspeople originally wanted to make the anniversary celebration a craft fair which would import people from all over the East Coast, but then they decided that it would be more exciting to work with local craftsmen and local artifacts in the museum to illustrate the heritage of the area. They were right, because the fair turned out to be the beginning of an area-wide rediscovery of historic craftsmanship. Virtually everyone in town is either a "doer" or a "watcher" now, and school children come from adjacent districts to see Morristown's skilled hands in action. Even tourists from nearby Thousand Island State Park are beginning to investigate the town's goings-on. The word — like the action — is spreading.

You never know what you'll find when you visit a Crafts Fair — maybe a braid doll like the one your grandmother made for you — maybe even Hank the Sturgeon. Or you might even discover that a neighbor you've chatted with for years just happens to be an expert traditional weaver — and you never even knew!

"Hank" the Sturgeon Caught in the St Lawrence River in 1970. Weight 35 lbs. Age about 40 yrs

1850 ⊙ 1851

Henry Clay's Compromise; California admitted as free state, pop. 92,597 — Second Fugitive Slave Law OKd; free states retaliate with "personal liberty laws" — Sioux lose Iowa, Minnesota lands — Cholera epidemic strikes Midwest — Zachary Taylor dies in office; Millard Fillmore steps in — First New York Times hits the streets — Melville publishes "Moby Dick" — Singer patents sewing machine — James T. King invents washing machine — Gail Borden makes first evaporated milk — Total US pop. 23,191,876.

Baldwinsville, New York
A Hands-On Approach

Malcolm MacPherson and some of his fellow teachers have hit on a freewheeling approach to letting people know how much fun it is to do something with your hands. They have built a mobile craftswagon — the Trade Guild Trailer — which they take around to fairs and schools so you can see and hear and smell nineteenth century America at work — the fine arts of cabinet making, blacksmithing, harness making, tinsmithing, printing, bookbinding and gunsmithing. Mr MacPherson and his friends aren't experts yet; they just have a passion for tools and tinkering. They started the crafts wagon in their spare time, and, since they are all school teachers, they got their students involved. So while the kids got experience in constructing the Trailer, they also got exposure to some of the old trades, and now both students and teachers are eager to get as many people turned on to the Trailer as possible.

"I think one of the things we see in children today is that they never remember a time when there wasn't television and rockets. There's a lack of identity with any cultural things in our schools as much as anywhere. The kids are living in a vacuum. Here's a television; they don't have any idea how it works. They don't have any idea about its social or political significance or its technological significance because they don't know what came before it. Nobody has ever taken the time to stop and go back and show them how they got there."

Since people have always been fascinated by traveling demonstrations — remember the success of the old time medicine shows — the Trade Guild Trailer seems like a sure-fire way to spread old worlds to new folks.

Malcolm MacPherson continues: *"We held a 'Day Before Yesterday' show for years, and every year it got to be more trouble to assemble all the tools and set it up. So we got*

the idea of working with the school to build a mobile crafts wagon that would go around to different places. We have adults teaching now, but we'd like to have a group of kids develop the skills so they can take it around. We're not interested in having an organization of a hundred kids. All we want is twenty interested kids, distributed through the grades so we can keep a kid long enough that he can really develop skills. If we have a senior that is skillful in wood working, he can very easily show a freshman that is coming in about it. And then he also has the advantage of some teaching experience.

"But it doesn't work to just tell them about it. They have to have some way to experience it. And a crafts wagon like this is just about the best way to show and sell history. This is strictly a 'hands-on' approach. We don't have anything here that can't be used. The purpose of the thing is, if a kid asks, 'Can I pound on that?', the answer is yes. Even when there's a competent teacher, you can't make a kid a finished or expert blacksmith or gunsmith in just six or eight lessons, but once you tell them where the material is and give them the basics to start with and a studio to work in . . . then you've got them! Then it gets in their blood, and they are hooked. And they love it!"

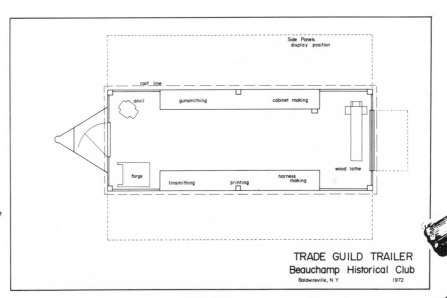

TRADE GUILD TRAILER
Beauchamp Historical Club
Baldwinsville, N.Y.   1972

The Baldwinsville Crafts Wagon seems like such an ingenious and useful idea that we've included complete plans for construction. Turn to pages 175-176 and Do It Yourself!

Lumpkin, Georgia

"You've got
to be a lover
of such things."

Down deep in Georgia there is a little town called Lumpkin. The people there have gotten together and started another town nearby. Lumpkin, which itself is a place of only a few hundred souls, doesn't need to grow. But it did need a boost. Now it has one. Westville is its name and it's a place on the edge of town where the traditional crafts of the South are being kept alive in a collection of traditional old buildings that have been assembled on the site for that purpose. So far, Westville has avoided the sober primness of most historic village reconstructions. The village has the lively temper and open, folksy feel of the townspeople who run it. What really makes it work is the superb assembly of local people who do their work and are delighted to share it. But, as Gus Daniel says, "You've got to be a lover of such things." And that makes all the difference in the world.

The Weaver: Kathy McGlaun

"I didn't know how to weave until I came down here to Westville. I knew book-learning from Georgia State; I was in the Folklore Department. But after I came down here, Westville hired a girl from the mountains to come down here and teach me. That's how I learned most of it.

"I can make repairs myself on the loom. This one is part of the West collection, Colonel West's mother's loom. It was made in 1860 and doesn't have a nail in it. I am using store-bought yarns, since it takes at least ten spinners to keep up with one weaver. I weave barefooted because it's easier to feel the treadles.

"What people mostly wove around here in 1850 was these wool and cotton coverlets and solid white cotton counterpains in what's called a honeycomb pattern. And rag rugs and a lot of plain cloth called jeans for clothing.

"Each one of the heddles (strings through which the yarn warp is passed) is like a needle with an eye in the middle and one and only one white thread has to run through the right one of these little string heddles. It takes about a month to string a loom. And then you can weave about a yard an hour, for plain cloth anyway."

The Blacksmith: George Cobb

"I been in the blacksmithing business all my life. My Daddy been blacksmithing forty-five years ahead of me. I come up a little boy shoeing horses and mules, building wagons, anything. I've been in business fifty-two years myself. (He's sixty-one.) I came up to the shop as a kid, worked the bellows, striking with the sledge hammer, work like that. We used to overhaul anything. We worked for the public. We built anything that nobody else would build and fixed everything that nobody else could fix. There are mighty few blacksmiths now that are really blacksmiths. I'm pretty tired right now, but I can still make anything that I ever could."

The Cook: Mary Ward

Mary just learned the basics of fire-cooking two years ago, and started out by making ash cakes. At first she hadn't learned how to control the heat and she burned everything. "But now it comes out perfect." She makes gingerbread in the Dutch oven. "You heat the lid by moving a few hot coals out onto the hearth and placing the lid over them. Grease the oven slightly. Then you pour in the batter into the oven, and put the lid on and place the oven over hot coals and put more hot coals on the lid. I learned all this by myself. I like to make stews, cracklin' bread, chicken and dumplings, greens, beans, corn, cornbread, biscuits, peach cobblers. I'm sixty-six, and I do it because I just like cooking."

The Quilter: Pearl Ware

"Thread your needle. Put some wax on your thread to make it strong and keep it from getting twisted. You come through somewhere off of where you're going to quilt. Pull your knot through, then put your needle against your thimble and put your other hand under the bottom and you go down til you feel that needle underneath and you push up and that makes like a little hill. You want to be sure you go through. Then you put your thumb down and head the needle up, then you go back, close to where you came through — now Grandmama said, don't make long stitches 'cause if you go to bed barefooted you'll stick your toenails on it — so you're supposed to make short stitches, and it's neater and prettier that way. When you get where you're going, you take up two, three tiny little threads and pull it tight and that locks it. You can't hardly ever get it out, and it won't come out in the wash. Then you put your needle back up where you came and cut it off. My first hobby is playing in the dirt, planting flowers, and quilting quilts. My next one is teaching school. My next one is just loving folks."

The Basket Maker: Gus Daniel

"We go to the woods and get the white oak and we cut it down, bring it here and put it in the wedge and break it half open, then quarter. Then into strips you can work with. The trees can be cut any-time. Some people say there is a certain time to do it, but I always just did it when I had the time, and I been doing it for fifty years. After the wood is busted up, you get the heart out of it. Take a draw knife with a mallet (you hit the knife) and get the heart out. Then the piece of timber you have left you halve with your draw knife, halve it again and again until you get it to the width of two ribs, where you can handle it with a pocket knife. Then you get out the ribs and splits and get everything ready to make the basket.

"There are sixteen ribs in this basket. You lay out eight ribs to start, and it's important how they are laid. Then you lay out another round. Then you split one so you have seventeen ribs. It's important to have an odd number of ribs. Then after you make the last rib, you knock a split in with a pad-dler as you weave. You hold the ribs down in the center with your knee while you weave the first split around. If you don't knock it tight, you got a basket that you can see the sun rise and set in.

"You run the bottom around as many times as you want — depending on how big a basket you want. When a split runs out, a new one is inserted on top, underneath a rib, and both the old and new splits are trimmed with a pocket knife. Then leave it in the sun for about an hour, and then knock it up. Take something to drive it up good and tight — push the slits close together. I have a special piece of iron I do it with. Then you turn it down. One in-side, one outside, with the ribs. When you get that done you put the rims to it. The inside rim goes in first, then the outside. Then you wrap it, and it's finished. If it's a double wrap, it won't split. A basket takes me about six hours to complete. A good basket has good stout ribs and good stout rims.

"I used to make about two hundred baskets a year, and bottom caned one or two hundred chairs too. I worked this county over. Probably ain't nobody around here that don't know my work, 'cause I been doing it for so long. I used to have twenty or more chairs at my house that didn't belong to me. When it was too wet to plow in the fields I made bas-kets and bottomed chairs at night. I used to never go to bed, never took a night's rest like a man should. I used to bottom two chairs before I went to bed, then get up the next morning and bottom two more before I caught the mules to go to the field. You got to first be a lover of such things to be a good father. . . . I just love to sit down and do this work. I can tell any chair I bottomed. I'd know it if I saw it on Broadway in New York. Everybody has their own way of doing things — I can even tell my splits from the other men's."

Blakely, Georgia   I Jus' Learn'd It

Mary Whitehead helped start the Early County Historical Society partly as a way to give people like the quilters above and Harvey Davis below a reason for going on with their traditional crafts. The Society has already sponsored a festi-val and plans teaching programs. Harvey Davis has been making baskets most of his seventy years — and says, "I jus' learn'd it from my daddy" — but he has resisted making baskets again. Mary Whitehead says he's "mostly can-tankerous." Maybe when he sees this picture he'll consent to demonstrate his considerable skill for the eager audiences in Early County.

Harriet Beecher Stowe writes "Uncle Tom's Cabin" — Skyscraper ad-vance: Otis develops safe hydraulic elevator — First steam fire engine runs in Cincinnati — Massachusetts passes first mandatory school attend-ance law — Japan receives Commodore Perry — Gadsden purchase com-pletes Mexican border at Rio Grande — 5,000 die in New Orleans Yellow Fever epidemic — Washington territory formed — Steinway and Sons build first pianos — William Wells Brown's "Clotel," first novel by American Negro.

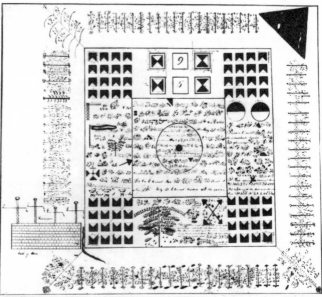

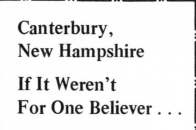

Canterbury, New Hampshire

If It Weren't For One Believer . . .

Charles Thompson is a believer. He is other things as well: folk singer, collector, teacher, museum curator, father. But mostly he is a believer, and he has been devoting his faith and energy to keeping alive the multitudinous crafts of the Shakers — who were and are, like Charles Thompson, believers in the essential goodness of mankind and the worthiness of his acts.

About fifteen years ago, Thompson came to the Shaker village of Canterbury, New Hampshire, to find out about Shaker music — particularly the system of notation that was invented by the Shakers and used for a period of time in the nineteenth century. What he found was an antique village and a handful of elderly people clinging to their beliefs and to the past.

He also found that the power that built nineteen Shaker communities and made converts of almost 18,000 souls was still at work. Charles Thompson stayed. Not as a convert; he stayed as a student, as a friend, and eventually as the curator of the Shaker museum at Canterbury.

Thompson has a solid grasp of Shaker history, but what makes him so impressive is his ability to communicate a sense of Shaker life and spirit that is both comprehensive and relevant. One way he does this is through his astounding knowledge of the "when and how" of Shaker crafts. As he hops from item to item in the colony museum, he talks, explains, demonstrates, praises the Shaker methods of printing, bookbinding, textile production, knitting, spinning, tailoring, silk production, fabric dyeing, various milling operations, mirror design, coppering, box making, basketry,

Here is a room in one of the Canterbury village buildings that Charles Thompson is restoring. Shakers were designing built-in furniture like the bureau drawers in the wall before the turn of the century. Below, the Thompson family poses on the steps of their house in the village. Thompson devotes most of his time to the task of trying to maintain the village against inevitable deterioration. He has some, but not nearly enough, assistance from volunteers.

furniture making, cabinet making, tool design and production, mineralogy, animal husbandry, cooking, candy making, seed sowing, brick making, stone carving, blacksmithing, herbal medicine preparation. He understands the practical elements of Shaker life perhaps as well as the Shakers did themselves.

And he wants somehow to pass along this body of experience which he safeguards. Charles Thompson hopes one day to have a museum that functions as a workshop and a school. He would like to see Canterbury Village become a place where young people come to help with the restoration and maintenance of the buildings in return for being taught Shaker methods of craftsmanship.

Whether or not Thompson will be able to create the museum/school where it belongs — in Canterbury, on Shaker soil — depends on a group of trust attorneys who will administer the colony properties. Though he has spent fourteen years in service to the people and traditions of Canterbury Village, there's no guarantee that Thompson will continue after his Shaker friends are gone. But it is a certainty that wherever Charles Thompson and his Shaker crafts collection end up, there will be the beginning of the living history of a remarkable group of people. And the life and vitality of this history will have been made possible during our time by an equally remarkable man.

Tivoli, New York, is a little town north of Poughkeepsie, small enough that most tourists miss it. But were they to find their way to the main street, they would be rewarded by a sight unique to twentieth century vision: the player piano shop of L. Gadley Broadmoore, Esq. It is the only shop in town painted green and yellow, and it is filled with as many pianos, victrolas and mechanical music devices as you will ever see in one place. They are presided over by a young man who, at the age of twenty-two, is one of the foremost authorities on the restoration and repair of apparatus for the mechanical production of music. His interest in this field, an interest which began during his college days, has now broadened into a desire to return to the nineteenth century — in dress, living and business habits. He dislikes being in the presence of a television set, and talks about "moving in" to an earlier period. He is a truly dedicated young man with a different view of historical involvement, a uniquely personal view.

Mr Broadmoore, a native of Ohio and a former student at Bard College, moved his large collection of antiques into his present shop in January of 1971. He said then, in a letter:

"For several years I have been studying the past with a practical view to eventually moving in. I am totally committed to the late nineteenth and early twentieth century. I am keenly aware of the nature of those aspects of modern life which conspire to prevent an individual from forswearing change and conformity, both materially and culturally, and it is only by absolute refusal to accept the lures of the modern world that I have succeeded to the meager extent that I have in recapturing the serenity, common sense philosophy of living, and relative sanity which the past has to offer. No modern suburbanite, or even businessman-farmer, can fully appreciate his loss of independence, or of the feeling which I experience chopping wood for cooking and heating, and pumping water from my own well and cistern, knowing I have no one to answer to for these utilities, no bill to pay except labor by and for myself."

Broadmoore is now preparing to increase his workshop's scope to that of a nineteenth century-style "manufactory" — so he can make objects and tools that are no longer available, but which are essential to the running of older machines like the music machines or the victrola:

"I plan to find the secrets of tool making, perhaps of ore smelting, of fine cabinet making, of masonry, carpentry, etc., etc., and eventually to build an immense work shop, probably of brick, in which I can make anything, do any repair, duplicate any item, much along the lines of Edison's Menlo Park laboratory."

Broadmoore sees his manufactory as providing a unique service for people who enjoy using old-style items:

"It may be remembered that for many years after Thomas Edison ceased production of cylinder phonographs, he insisted upon supplying his old customers with not only parts for their machines, but also with cylinder records right up until the last day of the existence of the National Phonograph Company. Edison simply refused to bully his old customers into buying new machines. The fact of supply and demand is not basically evil, it simply inconveniences a few. If only industry were a little human, as Edison

was, or if the country could still boast a scattered number of 'make-anything' craftsmen, as it did as recently as forty years ago, the social pressure could be lessened and the value of independence again realized in the material world."

L. Gadley Broadmoore's way of rediscovering America's past is certainly an unusual one. But it is working for him; and, if his manufactory becomes a reality, he will have an opportunity to impart his special crafts knowledge to other young people. They probably won't choose to forsake the twentieth century as Mr Broadmoore has, but after a time in his presence they probably won't forget what the world was like back in the nineteenth century either.

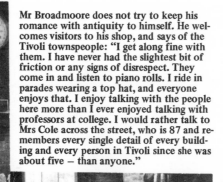

Mr Broadmoore does not try to keep his romance with antiquity to himself. He welcomes visitors to his shop, and says of the Tivoli townspeople: "I get along fine with them. I have never had the slightest bit of friction or any signs of disrespect. They come in and listen to piano rolls. I ride in parades wearing a top hat, and everyone enjoys that. I enjoy talking with the people here more than I ever enjoyed talking with professors at college. I would rather talk to Mrs Cole across the street, who is 87 and remembers every single detail of every building and every person in Tivoli since she was about five — than anyone."

When asked by a visitor, *"Isn't it true that as you retire into the nineteenth century you are in danger of ignoring problems which can't be dealth with from there?"*, L. Gadley Broadmoore replied: *"I would agree entirely. I am entirely incapacitated by my complete involvement with the nineteenth century. I could not possibly cope with modern problems in any way. I can't even stand to be in the presence of a television set or a radio. I refuse to use ball point pens. It is just a kind of distaste. I can't describe it. Every little detail has to be right. I have succeeded to a tremendous extent, but there are still numerous things that I am trying to eliminate."*

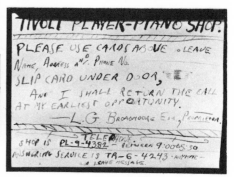

1854 ◉ 1855

Kansas-Nebraska Act: voters to settle slave-state issue — Perry-Toda treaty opens Japan-US trade — Modern Republican party forms at Ripon, Wis.; vows to end slavery — Boston's Jim Crow school system abolished — First black to win elected office: John Mercer Langston clerk of Brownhelm Township, Ohio — Kansas adopts anti-slavery constitution — New York prohibition goes into effect — Immigration on the rise; 400,000 a year — Thoreau writes "Walden," Whitman pens "Leaves of Grass," Dickens publishes "Hard Times."

Mrs Patricia Fitzmaurice — suburban mother and garden club member — is the person largely responsible for saving the old Schwamb Mill, the last manufactory of Victorian-style hand-turned wooden oval and round picture frames in America. She didn't just save the building; she saved the entire factory, inventory and all. And in doing so, she has had to become a real estate speculator, a business-woman, a nineteenth century wood-worker and a community organizer.

For years, the old mill sat down by the brook, just a couple of blocks off Massachusetts Avenue, while the twentieth century roared by all around it. When Mrs Fitzmaurice discovered the building (as she and other members of the Arlington Conservation Commission were on a surveying hike), owner Elmer Schwamb was just about to close down the one hundred year old operation. Mrs Fitzmaurice and several other members of the Conservation Commission wasted no time: they formed a private trust, hoping to buy the mill and operate it as a working industrial museum. But Schwamb sold instead to four brothers named Larsen who immediately scheduled demolition of the building.

That could have been the end of the mill, but the Arlington newspaper just happened to be changing hands at that time, and the new editor ran a front page picture and story about the mill — telling how the trust was trying to save an important historic asset, but that the developers who'd bought the property wouldn't even speak to them. Shortly after that, the Larsen brothers agreed to sell a piece of their new property — the part

The moral of this story might be: the next time you walk down side streets, back alleys or snoop around creek beds, watch out! The old building you discover might be your next career.

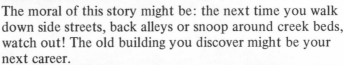

In order to help meet costs and expand support for the mill, Mrs Fitzmaurice has also started an arts center in the building, and rents space to craftsmen. Extra space is occupied by a fine instrument maker and two groups of potters.

———◆———

with the main mill building—for $30,000 (which is what the whole thing had cost them) and they gave the trust sixty days to come up with the money.

Mrs Fitzmaurice's group made the deadline by raising $17,000 locally, and putting themselves personally into hock for the rest. So they bought their mill. Then what? Mrs Fitzmaurice says, "My God, you know what you have to do when you save a mill? You have to run it!" At which point the trust members found out they didn't even own the machinery inside the place. Price: $5,000. And the heating plant: $125 a month rent, plus coal. Mrs Fitzmaurice says, "We decided that the only way we'd make it was to put the mill back into business."

By then, Elmer Schwamb and his last employees had taken a new interest in the future of the mill. They gave the trust the names of all the former customers around the country, and work commenced . . . with Mrs Fitzmaurice as head craftslady.

Why would a nice lady like Mrs Fitzmaurice ever want to get herself into all this? "Our town desperately needed something to be proud of. This was the beginning of other good things that have happened since. Now people aren't so afraid to join unpopular causes. I thought this would be a terribly interesting place for adults, as well as children. And why should it disappear if there isn't another place like it? Why destroy it? It was right here. We didn't have to build a Disneyland. That's enough of a reason, isn't it?"

———◆———

Nadine Hurst, one of several potters who work at Schwamb, stands at the back door of her studio in the main building. In the foreground is the roof of the kiln she built to fire her work. Mill Creek, near-by, is the path Mrs Fitzmaurice took (in hip boots!) to look for environmental "assets" to the community that led to the saving of the mill.

1856 ◉ 1857

Pro-slavery forces sack Lawrence, Kan. — John Brown leads anti-slavery fight against Missourians — Dred Scott Decision: Supreme Court denies black citizenship — Massachusetts requires voter literacy test — First train crosses Mississippi at Rock Island, Ill. — Western Union forms, consolidates telegraph lines — Olmstead lays out Central Park — Lyman Blake invents shoe-sewing machine — Cyrus Chambers introduces print-paper folding machine — Watertown, Wis. offers first kindergarten.

Time was, kids used to learn about the past from their grandparents because they lived in the house. And it seems like things didn't change so fast, somehow, anyway. Now, a lot of young people only see their elders in a rush on holidays, and everything is so different that there's hardly time to understand the changes. But in some towns kids are trying to get information about the way it used to be before it's too late. Here's what's happening in three towns.

Weare, New Hampshire

Bill Herman, Bruce Martin and Richard Frazier are high school students who are crazy about history. Their enthusiasm has infected other students, and is now spreading through the entire population of the town of Weare, New Hampshire. It all began about two years ago when the three talked about twenty of their classmates into celebrating the anniversary of the Pine Tree Riot of 1771. They wanted to find a way to keep the old spirit of Yankee independence alive and well. They're doing it. In 1971 they started the Weare Junior Historical Society under the sponsorship of the Weare Historical Society, and went to work. *"We were on our own to do what we wanted,"* said President Bill Herman.

They completed their first project last year. It is a book which tells about the Pine Tree Riot. They published it at a cost of $1,300. The whole thing was financed by ads sold to the community. It is a lively and compact account of a famous incident in the town's history, and, in Weare, it's a best seller.

Why did they choose the Pine Tree Riot? It sprang from a local situation: the residents of New Hampshire were prohibited from using the valuable and useful white pine tree because the British wanted the wood for ships' masts. The situation became the focus for a vigorous struggle which united the local people and ultimately reinforced the violent feelings and spirited protests which led to the American Revolution. The little book says, *"The only reason why the 'Rebellion' at Portsmouth and the 'Boston Tea Party' are better known than the Pine Tree Riot is because they have had better historians."* Now that the Weare Junior Historical Society has gotten to work, that's no longer the case!

The book not only describes the riot, but also details other aspects of Weare's colorful history. There is an article by Jeff Eaton on "The Churches of Weare — Past and Present"; "Weare's Schools," by Bill Herman; and the following article by Bruce Martin.

THE MODERN CAMP OF H.E. GRANT WHERE THIS SYRUP IS MADE.

My Great Grandfather's Sugar Camp

One of the early industries in Weare was the making of maple syrup and sugar. It states in the Town History that in 1870 the farmers made two thousand four hundred seventeen pounds of sugar and two hundred sixty two gallons of syrup for home use and market. The sap was boiled down in heavy iron kettles over open fires. Later, sugar houses were built, and the boiling was done over brick arches topped by huge metal pans.

There are very few of the old original sugar houses still in existence. One is the Hiram Grant sugar house on Mt. Dearborn Road, built in the early 1900's.

Grant cut down trees on his property and had them sawed into boards. He and a neighbor, Bert Farmer, built the sugar house on the foundation of the old Andrew Philbrick place, which had previously burned. The double floor was made of three-inch thick planks which came from a condemned town bridge. It was originally roofed with hand-made shingles, but was changed to tin when it started to burn. A big arch and a smaller one were installed. A large kerosene lamp was hung from the ceiling for light, because boiling continued through the night. A small deacon's bench sat near the big arch for the comfort of neighbors who came to visit. The sap was gathered in a huge gathering tank placed on a wooden sled pulled by a team of oxen.

The booklet is the result of seven months work by a group of high school students willing to give up some of their time towards the preservation of Weare's history. It was done under the steam of these youths, who compose the Weare Junior Historical Society, with the aid of adult supervision. They went out and sold ads, researched and wrote the articles, and took the time to help type, proofread and edit the booklet. We hope that this sort of work will inspire more people to take an active part in preserving the local history of the town of Weare. (*Pine Tree Riot* Reader's Note)

THE WEARE JUNIOR HISTORICAL SOCIETY

Pine Tree Riot   April 14, 1772

Many gallons of syrup and boxes of sugar were sold locally or packed in wooden crates and shipped to other states. Hiram's wife, Jessie, made the sugar on a black iron stove in the farm kitchen. It was poured into molds or made into soft sugar and packed in metal buckets. Hiram's sons also helped out. The following was taken from an old newspaper clipping. "Masters Maurice and Leon Grant of South Weare, New Hampshire, are two young farmers who are getting into the agricultural harness early in life. In the spring of 1908, they gathered all the sap from two hundred maple trees. This was done with their two pair of Holstein and Hereford oxen. Master Maurice was eleven years old. Master Leon eight."

Leon carried on his father's syrup business until about 1929. Since that time, the sugar house has stood vacant. The old oil lamp and the deacon's bench were stolen, and the arches were sold. Vandals smashed the window frames and the little iron sink. Time and weather left the sugar house an empty shell except for several tons of lime that had been stored there years ago. The bags had deteriorated, adding one more touch of desolation to the old building.

Last summer, Brad Wood and I were looking at the old place and decided it would probably not be standing after another winter, and it seemed too bad that our great-grandfather's sugar camp should disappear like so many of the others.

Murray Wood, Brad's father, agreed to help us on the project, which turned out to be more work than any of us had expected. The lime had to be removed, the building straightened up with the help of a wrecker and "come-along." Next the old floor had to be ripped up, and a cement floor was poured with the help of Bill Adams and Eddie Palmer. A difficult search finally turned up old, small-pane windows. Don Putnam contributed a little black iron sink to be used with the original iron hand pump. This led to the next step, cleaning out the well.

After hours of work, the building was ready for making syrup; but the equipment is very expensive and we had only a small arch and some buckets. As usual, good neighbors came to our rescue. Mr Hood had a big arch and plastic pipe line. It was decided that we would use Ralph's equipment, and Bob Colburn would help with the gathering and boiling. Bob brought up his saw rig, and we filled the shed with wood. Mr Rand showed us how to use the plastic lines. When the season starts, we should be ready to make syrup again.

Plastic pipe lines and a gathering tank drawn by a four-wheel vehicle won't be as picturesque as in our great-grandfather's day, but at least it's a little step towards keeping Weare like it was in "the good old days."

If you would like more information about the Junior Historical Society, or if you want to order *The Pine Tree Riot* ($2.25 postpaid) or *The Flood and Hurricane of '38* ($3.35 postpaid), write to The Weare Junior Historical Society, P. O. Box 54, Weare, New Hampshire 03281.

Huntington Beach, California

Huntington Beach is on the coast of Southern California. It's said to be the fastest-growing city in the United States. It is also the site of hundreds of oil wells. Subdividers and developers had free rein until 1972, and would have transformed the little beach town into a suburban nightmare, if a group of conservationists and people who liked the Huntington Beach of the early days hadn't stepped in. They convinced the town to impose a building moratorium until the effects of large-scale building were given more consideration. And a teacher named Dolores Welty decided to get her students involved in the local history of Huntington Beach before the people who knew it first hand were all gone.

Ms Welty is teaching Marina High School students a class in Historical Research. The class discusses how to conduct interviews; they practice on each other; they study what might constitute "history" and what kind of judgment, if any, can be made about the historical value of objects. Then the students go right out into the field — interviewing and taping. They increase their personal knowledge of their town while they investigate the little-explored field of Southern California oral history.

Scott Romanowski is one of Dolores Welty's students. He interviewed seventy-five year old J. Sherman Denny, who was the general manager of the big local oil interest company (Huntington Beach Corporation) for thirty-six years. Scott loved talking about stamps, coins and music with Mr Denny, and Mr Denny appreciated getting a chance to explain some of the changes he has seen during his years in town.

The Life and Times of Hoosick Falls

In Hoosick Falls, New York, a lady named Christina Stevens has gone back to school. She's evidently a lady who knows the value of a good memory and has set about making sure that her town doesn't forget anything. She works with kids in school history clubs and with the area's old timers. The old timers tell the stories. Recordings are made. The kids take pictures and help with making transcriptions from the tapes. It's a productive partnership. The object is to fill a one hundred year gap in the town's recorded history. Until 1872, there are written annals that were kept by a local judge. After that, no one bothered until Miss Stevens came along.

The project started at the Hoosick Falls Area Senior Center. Its director, Rose Waytkus, writes: "We set up classifications for topics such as industries, inventions and inventors, the political scene, major fires, recreations. The students are doing photography work and compiling those photos into scrapbooks along with old photos, articles, newsclippings. They have permission to sift through garages and attics for more material. As we work, other student groups will write up the information into leaflets, plays and stories. Some have expressed interest in film."

Miss Stevens says: "Once completed, the project will be made available to everyone and will be a record of our life and times."

Like most good ideas, it works because there is something nice in it for everyone.

Knox County, Kentucky
Fight Like Hell for the Living

The sign on the wall of a patched-together office in Barbourville, Kentucky, says, "Pray for the Dead and Fight Like Hell for the Living." The building is headquarters for a part of one of the most effective anti-poverty programs in America, the Knox County Economic Opportunity Council, Inc., and "fight like hell for the living" is exactly what has been going on for the last five years.

Knox County has 24,000 residents, and 19,000 of them are members of families with an income of less than $3,600 a year. More than 600 families have *zero* cash income. So we're not talking about a few ne'er-do-wells — there just isn't any money to speak of in the county. The hills and hollers are all steep-sloped and rocky, and don't support any economic activity except for strip mining. The mining contributes to the poverty of the area. The owners are all absentee corporations. The work is done by machinery. The machinery eliminates topsoil, ruining natural drainage, muddying streams, creating washouts and encouraging erosion.

As a result, traditional subsistence farming is difficult. Paying work is scarce, and even though the area population has been declining in recent years, unemployment for able-bodied men is still over fifty per cent. Food and fuel costs, rent and taxes go up every year; incomes in Knox County do not.

But the people of Knox County make the best of what they have. The crafts of Knox County were born out of survival needs, with equal parts of desperation, ingenuity and love. So it's fitting that the OEO people should give aid in return for handcrafts and other labors, rather than insulting the mountain people with handouts. Hollis West, the OEO Director, and his staff are helping keep mountain heritage *and* mountain people alive at the same time.

The Kentucky Krafts Store is right on Highway 25E in Barbourville. It is an outlet for locally-made crafts. The

This is Roark the younger. His mother had just finished telling Betty Hollinde about making hickory brooms. Though most of the people in Coalport Hollow live in shacks without plumbing or electricity, smiles like this one aren't hard to come by. The mountain people of Knox County are beginning to restore their traditional crafts, legends, and most important, their faith in themselves.

people of Knox County contributed 100% of the materials and labor for the store's construction. The store now does a good enough business to be self-sufficient and is an outlet for hundreds of hand-crafted items, ranging from miniatures to furniture. Next door, the Hill Country Hickory House Restaurant employs local labor, serves local specialties and uses local produce as much as possible.

The Charge Card Store is located in a ramshackle church renovated by local people. It's filled with used clothing, tools, household goods, furniture and other items donated by people in and outside of Knox County. Local residents may charge up to $20 worth of merchandise a month. They pay off their accounts by doing ten hours of volunteer work during the month, such as taking care of invalids, helping on community construction crews, making crafted items, teaching craft skills and working in the store's garden. No cash involved.

The Charge Card Store is run by the Emergency Fund and Service, Inc., which solicits cash donations, and spends the money on necessities for the destitute. It's not a hand-out system: loan recipients are required to repay either in cash, hours of work or (mostly) with craft objects they make — these are sold in the Krafts Store.

The Knox County Oral History project doesn't materially aid poor families — but it reminds the mountain people that they are important, that their traditional ways of doing things have meaning for everyone. Stories of Knox County past and present which have been recorded include the experiences of a lady who was a granny midwife for many years, reminiscences of an eighty-six-year old gentleman who was brought up in Stinking Creek (one of the more populous areas of the county) and still resides there, and tales from a retired schoolteacher who taught in a one-room schoolhouse when school was in session only five months in the year. Al Downey and Betty Hollinde, who are doing this work in addition to their other OEO tasks, hope to see movies made of stir-offs (molasses making), hog killing, nut picking, house building, moonshining and hunting with dogs.

Since their inception these programs have helped desperate people survive, and done it in the spirit of diligence, compassion and ingenuity that is characteristic of the people who live in Knox County. But despite the work — and results that nobody can argue with — future federal support for the program was, at the time this book went to press, very uncertain.

This is Tina Collins, who lives in a cabin up Coalport Hollow outside of town. *"I started sewing when I was a kid, about 6 or 7. I wasn't big enough to sit down. I had to stand up in front of the machine and push. That's the truth."* Tina is encouraged to practice her traditional craft, which she is very good at, by the Knox County OEO, instead of being handed money and then ignored.

Louis "Shorty" Calleb says he started whittlin' while he was working in an oil field at the age of nineteen. Shorty tells a story about when a friend entered him in a whittlin' contest in Knoxville, Tennessee. Shorty didn't want to compete but went along with his friend. He was seated between two ladies. After a while the two ladies stopped their whittlin' to watch Shorty, "Cuz he whittled such fine shavings." He won the contest.

There's an old Appalachian play-party tune called, "what're we gonna do with the baby-o?". The Federal Government may give a final answer to this question in their efforts to improve the lot of Americans by reducing spending — in Knox County they're just about ready to throw the baby out with the bath water.

If the current judicial challenge to the Nixon Administration's decision to terminate the OEO Program fails, the Knox County Program will lose its official status and federal support. You can help — with donations of clothing, food, appliances, toys, and if you can spare it, money for medical aid and winter fuel. Send your contributions to: Emergency Fund and Service, Inc., Box 135, Barbourville, Kentucky 40906.

1858 ⊙ 1859

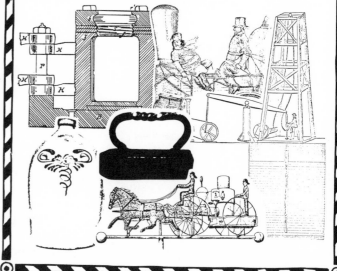

Lincoln-Douglas debates in Illinois Senate campaign — Slaves in arms: John Brown raids Harper's Ferry arsenal — Last slave ship arrives in Mobile Bay — Edwin Drake taps first successful oil well in Titusville, Pa. — Comstock Lode silver strike — Cyrus Field's first Atlantic cable fails — First Pullman cars tested — Minnesota, Oregon admitted — First cross-country mail delivery: 23 days, 4 hours — MIT established — First electric lights in a home: Moses G. Farmer of Salem, Mass.

If our churches, government officials and anyone interested in the betterment of our nation would come down and see the utter poverty that is rampant in this county and how hard and constructively the people try to work out of poverty, this problem would not long exist. Humans would no longer have to live in inhuman need. Our visitors would also be impressed with the goodness of our people and the fineness of the families — and would be anxious to work toward the goal that all people are entitled to the opportunity of reaching their potential, in a constructive, dignified manner.

These families prefer a loan to a handout, wouldn't you? Some when they can pay, pay back with cash. Most of the loans are paid back by crafts made in the home — we give "A" for effort. People appreciate the opportunity to earn at least some of their needs.

The dire malnutrition rate, even with help, is over 25%.

Another father who makes only $1.60 an hour, had saved $200 in case his wife had complications in delivering her second child and would need to deliver in the hospital. There were no complications. The arrival of a beautiful baby delighted the parents. In appreciation and love, they sent EFSI the hard-earned — by the sweat of the brow — the savings of $200! If we only all had this same wondrous trust.

Last month's report mentioned a doctor from the State Health Department who did not believe the atrocious poverty facts concerning families without income and very poor families without medical resources. He came back and, in essence, apologized. He is no longer as ignorant as most of his counterparts. Now, what is he going to do with his newly found knowledge — shove it back in his recesses — hope it will go away — send us a little cash for medical needs or work on whoever up there in Frankfurt — until these horrible statistics actually do go away?

There are at least 1,200 children who live in families who have no income, earned or unearned. Food Stamps cannot pay rent, heat, etc. Imagine living in such a household! You may not ever, but your grandchildren just might — if we as a society continue the irresponsible uncaring that we are guilty of now.

EFSI doesn't give handouts. Handouts are demoralizing! EFSI makes loans that can be repaid by assigned work — and most of them are. Most of our people do far more work than the loan is worth and appreciate the opportunity to earn at least some of their needs.

Social Service Report
August, September 1971

❖

Al Downey is visiting Mrs Roark in her hillside garden, and he's brought along a tape recorder. As the wax beans, corn, tomatoes, potatoes, radishes and cabbages soak up the morning sun, Mrs Roark discusses traditions and tribulations that have long been a part of life in Coalport Hollow. Mrs Roark's description of how hill people make scrub brooms is representative of the unique and valuable information being gathered by Al and his fellow workers.

WHITTLED HICKORY SCRUB BROOM

"You first find a hickory 2 to 3 inches round. The tree should be straight with no knots in it. It's hard to find good hickory trees now without knots. You skin the bark off while the tree is in the ground, then cut it down with a bow saw which costs $4.50. Then with a butcher knife or a dirt knife you catch the pieces — starting from the cut end — and peel it up so far. You keep doin' this till you got the broom part, the sweeper. Then you get to peel another layer on the top there, you come down on it to shape the broom stick and make it more slender to hold. That's all you do. You have a broom then. You take your draw knife and whittle it down to however long you want your handle."

OLD HOMESTEAD OR KENTUCKY WONDER POLE BEAN

Martin Townsley, who lives near Stinking Creek, is one of the people that the Knox County Oral History project has recorded. This is what he had to say about lights in the dark: *"It was hard to get hold of kerosene even to make a light, you see, and people who went out walking, why they'd get these rich pine knots and make a 'torch to walk by,' they called it. Now I seen that. But my kids now wouldn't know what to think to see a man coming up the road with a big fire burning in his hand like that."*

Martin Townsley tells about molasses making: *"That old horse would go around and around and that would feed the cane in this mill. Then you build what they call a furnace to set this here pan on that you boil these molasses in. And then you take this juice over and pour it in this pan and fry it up. Then they's a foam comes off this molasses, and you have to skim 'em off. Don't let 'em turn so dark — that makes 'em taste strong. You take this foam off until it becomes a good white foam and then you go to leave it. And you test 'em just like you be making jelly. When you think they're thick enough, you pull 'em off. Then you put them in cans. Now my daddy . . . I've seen my daddy sell many a gallon of molasses for 50 cents. That was along in the '30's. Well, the other day I gave four dollars and a half for a gallon (laughs)."*

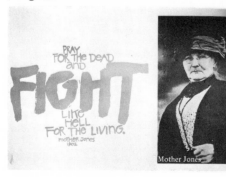

FIGHT
PRAY FOR THE DEAD and FIGHT LIKE HELL FOR THE LIVING.
Mother Jones 1902

Mother Jones

1860 ⊙ 1861

Lincoln elected — South Carolina steps out; state troops seize US arsenal — Confederacy forms — Jefferson Davis sworn in — War begins at Fort Sumter — Congress passes income tax to support army — Lincoln calls for volunteers, blockades ports — South wins at Bull Run, Wilson's Creek, Ball's Bluff — Darwin's "Origin of Species" hits US — Pony Express links California and Missouri — Government printing office established — Kansas admitted, pop. 108,000 — First Ph.D. in US: Yale — Total US pop. 31,443,321.

Central and Union PACIFIC RAIL ROAD LINE

A whistlin' woman an' a crowin' hen air shore to come to some bad end.

A live snake put in a barrel of cider will keep hit from spilin'.

On cold days when the grate fire sputters and cracks, hit's a callin' fer snow, an hit'll kindly snow for three days.

Hit's a sin to burn sass'frass wood. If'n you do, the devil will sit on the roof o' yer house.

I ain't one to lay right flat down. I wanta work.

His nerves are striped right down to the bone.

Honey, I'm right down to nothin' with nary a spoonful.

Whitesburg, Kentucky
The Appalachian Film Workshop

"Every day we lose a few more old coal miners, hunters, dirt farmers, mountain women and the mountaineers who make Kentucky long rifles by hand. The old coal towns are disappearing, too, and, believe it or not, they were great to live in once. Our culture is passing us by. We'll have to hustle to catch it, because we'll never be able to do it again." — Gary Wright

Gary Wright of McRoberts, Kentucky, is one of a group of young people from Appalachia who are busy catching pieces of their culture on film. The Appalachian Film Workshop — APPALSHOP — started in 1969 as a federally-funded program to train poverty-area youths in film production — exactly the sort of enterprise that some hard-headed people consider a "waste of taxes."

APPALSHOP just happens to be paying big dividends. It has, in five years, grown into a self-supporting operation which has to its credit more than a dozen excellent and popular short films dealing with Appalachian culture. And it's keeping bright youngsters like Diana Ott from deserting for the city: *"Like many of my friends, I wanted to leave as soon as I could. But I began to really love the country after dealing with it in the Workshop. I'm proud to live here now and I plan to stay."*

APPALSHOP gives everyone a chance to see a brave and productive culture. The Workshop's catalogue is available from P.O. Box 743, Whitesburg, Kentucky 41858.

The Ozark Gunsmith

by Arthur B. Cozzens

In the year 1925 Carl Hammar, gunsmith, had his shop in a sheep pasture near the small town of Steelville in the Ozark Hills of south central Missouri. Mr Hammar, aged 82 at the time, was using in his work traditional methods of pioneer gunsmithing, having inherited his shop, his tools and his knowhow from a relative belonging to an even older generation. The writer had the pleasure of observing Mr Hammar at his work and he was taught by him to re-rifle muzzleloading rifles.

On the occasion of the writer's first visit to Mr Hammar, he brought to him for re-rifling four cap-and-ball rifles. However, Mr Hammar, because of his advanced age, was unwilling to perform the hard work required for reboring, but instead he demonstrated how each operation should be executed and allowed the writer to prepare his own barrels.

At this point it would be well to explain that in the days of muzzle-loading rifles, the reboring of barrels was a common practice. Guns were relatively expensive and calibers were not standardized. Therefore, when the bore of a rifle became rusty or worn it was customary either to smooth the lands (ridges in the rifling) with a lead plug smeared with emery flour and oil or, if the bore was very bad, to ream out the barrel to a larger size and cut new rifling.

The gunshop of Mr Hammar was primitive and none too well kept. The building, about 10 by 14 feet, was of unpainted, rough-sawed oak boards set vertically and not lapped or matched. Above the door hung the sign of the trade: a wooden replica of a muzzleloader about 8 feet long.

On the inside of the shop the walls were sheathed with corrugated iron (a relatively recent addition) and work benches with shelves above them lined two walls. Machinery consisted of an ancient foot-powered screwcutting metal lathe with wooden pulleys and a hand-operated drill press with a large fly wheel and a ratchet feed which clicked pleasantly when the press was in operation. The benches were littered with a conglomeration of gun parts, tools and baking powder tins containing random assortments of small nuts and bolts. Certainly in this jumble of oddments no one could be expected to

find anything that he needed; however, that did not bother Mr Hammar. He knew exactly where everything was and could, without hesitation, reach under a pile of odds and ends and produce the gun part that he needed for the job in hand.

The tools and equipment required for re-rifling may be listed as follows: (1) Hand-operated reamers of assorted sizes for use in cutting out the old rifling. (2) A light bow consisting of a small branch cut from a nearby willow tree and a silk thread. This was used to check for bent barrels. (3) A sledge hammer and large anvil for straightening bent barrels. (4) A crude rifling bench (described below). (5) Several lead plugs turned on the lathe to the size of the new bore and used in checking for tight spots, for eliminating such spots and for smoothing the lands.

The rifling bench deserves special attention. It consisted basically of a piece of rough-sawed oak 2-by-6 about 15 feet long to which two rifle barrels were attached by ordinary carpenter's "C" clamps. These barrels of approximately the same length were arranged in line with each other and about four feet apart lengthwise. One was the barrel being re-rifled and the other was a master which was used as a guide because it had good rifling. Prior to use, the master was placed on end and poured full of melted babbitt metal to form a plug which, when cool, moved freely in and out of the barrel and imparted the desired twist to the cutter. Rods were inserted in each end of the babbit plug, one bearing a swivelled cross-handle and the other a chuck for holding the steel rifling rod. This rod, about four feet long and small enough to pass through the bore, hooked into a cutting plug of hand-whittled hickory. On one side of this plug was a small rectangular slot elongated parallel to the length of the plug to receive a so-called saw for cutting the grooves of the rifling. The saw had been made of a piece of old file which had been annealed, cut with teeth by the use of a triangular file and retempered.

This article is reprinted from the January 1972 issue of *Pioneer America*.

★★★★★★★★★★★★★★★★★★★★★
★ Williamsville,
★ New York
★
★ The Rocking Chair
★ Deserters
★★★★★★★★★★★★★★★★★★★★★

These proud people have just finished a class called "Retrospect, Recollections and Remembrances." They've been painting favorite scenes from their own personal histories, and they've been having a great time doing it. Actually, the class has done quite a bit more than provide instruction and pleasure for Margaret, Julia, Charles, Winnie and company. It's also introduced them to townspeople of all ages, put the Senior Center in the spotlight as a place where interesting things are happening, and it's given the artists — who helped shape the town of Williamsville in their younger days — a chance to share their best memories in a dramatic way.

Many people stopped to talk with the artists on the days when they were working outdoors. The talk ranged from stories about what was going on in town thirty and forty years ago, to conversation about the arts, to impromptu lessons in drawing and painting. Curious school children got a taste of the history of the town they're growing up in. Senior Center Director Mrs Lucille Kinne thought the whole experience was valuable: "A relationship between generations was established. It was difficult for the artists to haul their equipment to all the various locations, so younger friends helped. Although only twelve people participated in this program, they completed a total of thirty-three canvases."

When the classes were finished, the paintings were hung in the Rotunda of the Town Hall. A tea given later on celebrated the summer's activities.

Here are some of the people who participated in painting their "retrospections, recollections and remembrances." Their assignment was to paint something from their own personal history — a favorite place or memory — and they look pretty pleased about the results. The class also provided a meeting place for the older people to meet other members of the community, and to spread the word about Senior Center Activities. Seated, from left, are Margaret Gary, Julia Lyman, Charles Provenzano, Winnie Rosenow, Elsie Carol Burall. Standing, from left, are Thomas Finnell, Mary Driscoll and Instructor Dennis Insalaco.

"Retrospect, Recollections and Remembrances" turned out to be an exciting way to work with town history. The canvases all sparkle with the same vitality that you hear in the voices of long-time residents when they talk about the early days. The new enthusiasm for history in Williamsville seems to prove the truth of two old sayings: "Seeing is believing," and "One picture is worth a thousand words."

1862 ⊙ 1863

North wins at Roanoke Island, Pea Ridge, New Orleans, Antietam, Gettysburg, Vicksburg, Chattanooga; South wins at Cedar Mt., Second Bull Run, Fredericksburg, Chickamauga — Emancipation proclaimed for slaves in rebellion — Lincoln addresses Gettysburg — Transcontinental telegraph ticks — Homestead Act opens Indian lands to settlement — Sioux uprising in Minnesota — Arizona, Idaho territories formed — West Virginia admitted — National Academy of Sciences chartered — First paper dress patterns printed in Mass.

Prairie Island, Minnesota
The Pipestone Carvers

The new interest that Americans are taking in handiwork as a spare time activity has brought to notice traditional craftsmen who, for one reason or another, kept on making things by hand when everybody else was letting machines do it for them. Amos Owen is one of many master craftsmen among the Dakota Indians of Prairie Island, Minnesota. Mr Owen fashions by hand objects for everyday use, just as his ancestors did five hundred years ago. He is an artist, a teacher and a protector of what is perhaps the most basic element of any culture's history.

Mr Owen carves pipes from reddish-brown pipestone. (Prairie Island is near the only large deposit of pipestone in the United States — in fact, the county is named Pipestone County — and only Indians are allowed to quarry the stone.) He also works with beads and shells. And he paints hides with traditional Dakota designs; some of these hides are then sewn together into the circular wall of the traditional tipi. The Owens are one of several families who choose to live in tipis.

Although his crafts are a strong assertion of Dakota heritage, Amos Owen does not limit his teaching to tribal members. He has participated in numerous Indian art programs on educational television, and has also taught crafts to schoolchildren. In this way, Mr Owen is similar to the great craftsmen of the ages, who have always taken time to pass along their special knowledge.

Fundamentally, Amos Owen is preserving tribal tradition for future generations of Dakotas, but people of many different cultures benefit from his skills. Perhaps that is why crafts are most worthy of attention — they speak across ethnic boundaries in a simple but elegant language, and they speak of earlier times in this world when people of all cultures fashioned necessities and luxuries for themselves and for their neighbors slowly, carefully and according to tradition, using their own two hands.

Joe Liles and the Lumbee Indian Record

This disc won't be a smash best seller, but in terms of American culture and heritage it's one of the important recordings of the year.

The group is called "Lumbee and Friends," and the singers are mostly members of North Carolina's Lumbee Tribe. The purpose — besides enjoying the singing — is to strengthen the tribe's identity as a unit and as Indian people. Lumbee and Friends don't just sing their own tribe's songs; they collect them from tribes all over the country. So actually they are saving a healthy part of a great and unique oral tradition.

Recently, "Lumbee and Friends" made an L.P. recording of many of the songs. Group founder Joe Liles explains the nature of the songs:

"Our songs come from tribes all over the United States. Many of the songs are old. They refer back to the old days of fighting among the tribes, fighting the white man, rounding up horses. Other songs were composed in modern times, some even with English verses. Indian singing is very rigid and complicated, and takes a lot of work to do well. There are two types of Indian songs: 'vocable' (syllable) songs and 'word' songs. The vocable songs are just composed of Indian syllables and have no meaning. They are still sung with much enthusiasm. White people generally have a hard time understanding about singing songs that have no meaning. The Indians usually don't try to explain themselves on this. They sing and dance for their own spiritual satisfaction (excluding the dancing that is done for tourists — for money!).

Joe Liles is the only Caucasian member of Lumbee and Friends; it was his prior experience with Southwestern Indian tribes that catalyzed the project. Thanks to Joe — and especially to the spirit and dedication of the young Lumbee tribe members — many old and wonderful songs have returned to the land of the living.

"Our singing activities are heightening the pride associated with American Indian cultural activities in the Lumbee community. I can already see it working! And, thanks to the album, our singing is also telling other people (non-Indian and Indian) about the Lumbee Tribe."

Wadesboro, North Carolina
Ysleta, Texas

Singing the Ancient Songs

Three hundred years ago a small group of Tigua Indians left the New Mexico settlement of their tribe and migrated to Texas. They settled in Ysleta del Sur — near the modern city of El Paso — in close proximity with Spanish and Mexican cultures. Over the years the Tiguas gradually lost their identity as a people, though they retained many ancient customs.

In the mid-1960's, a local attorney named Tom Diamond became curious about a local legend in which a little band of captive Indians migrated from New Mexico to Texas in the custody of an equally small band of Spanish soldiers. Diamond's own personal historical research led him to identify the modern descendants of this splinter group, and in turn led the Ysleta Tiguas to a great and joyous reunion with their New Mexico brethren.

Now there is a new Tigua Indian Center at Ysleta, which was built by the Indians, using traditional methods, financed by the state of Texas. The Center's purpose is to help Tiguas re-establish their culture and find a badly-needed economic base for their community. Indians from the New Mexico branch of the tribe are conducting classes in traditional dances and music as well as crafts and language.

Diamond's work also led to recognition of the tribe by the State of Texas and the possibility that the City of El Paso may occupy land that legally belongs to this group of almost-forgotten Indians.

What started as one man's amateur interest in history has spawned one of the most productive self-help projects for native Americans anywhere, and may have saved another fragment of that culture from extinction.

Tiguas of Ysleta gather after a dancing demonstration. The young people are learning tribal traditions from their elders and from the New Mexico Tiguas who have come to help.

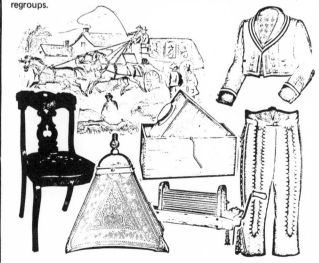

1864 ⊙ 1865

South wins at Olustee, Fort Pillow, Cold Harbor, Petersburg; North wins at Spotsylvania, Cedar Creek, Atlanta, Savannah, Fort Fisher, Columbia, Five Forks — Grant takes Richmond — Lee surrenders at Appamattox — A not-so-civil war ends: North loses 359,528 lives; South loses 258,000 — First assassination: Lincoln dead at 56 — Montana territory formed, Nevada admitted — Pullmans roll on first night trains — 13th Amendment outlaws slavery — Freedman's Bureau set to aid slaves — KKK secretly regroups.

THE FIRST
HOMETOWN HISTORY PRIMER

Making a space for your past in the present.

INTRODUCTION

Until lately, history has been a subject for schools. Now people are beginning to realize that history is a part of the fabric of life. Reduced to its simplest terms, history is what you had for breakfast this morning. And if you can't remember it, you may be the poorer for it.

The rest of this book is written for people who want to explore the history in their own lives. It is a series of suggestions for things to do.

"What has my grandfather got to do with saving the local landmark?" you ask. Plenty! The people who save landmarks and other treasures are usually people who are personally committed to history in general, including their own. How else could you account for all that hard work?

Most of them are not people who want to hide in the nineteenth century, though they've often been accused of that. They just believe that you can't know where you're going if you don't know where you've been. And we think they're right.

CONTENTS

The Pack Rat Principle

The Pack Rat is a creature with limited discrimination. Basically he is a hoarder. No one is sure (perhaps even the rat himself) why he does it. Something inside just says, "better pick it up, rat." There is speculation by observers that the animal selects his treasure on the basis of reflectivity—the brighter the better. But no one knows for sure. All we know (those of us who have come upon his trove) is that an odder assortment of stuff could not be assembled on purpose—a miniature madman's junkyard.

We'd like to propose that the Pack Rat's methods are not altogether mad. There is a certain utility in the fanciful hoarding of trinkets. Very few of us can look at our daily lives with any knowing sense of history and predict what will be important later. One never knows what trinket time will put great value on. We would do well to consider the ways of the pack rat. It might be much better to risk a bit of madness than to come through life with nothing to show for it but an orderly closet.

THE SELF HELP HISTORY TEST

Rate yourself. Score two points for every correct answer. One point for each answer partially correct. No fair cheating. Answers must come from memory. Above 38 points, excellent. Between 24 and 37 points, passable. Below 23 points, dismal, better get to work.

1. Where was your father born? (Town and state)

2. When was he born? (Date and year)

3. Where was your mother born? (Town and state)

4. When was she born? (Date and year)

5. Where and when was your father's father born? (State and year)

6. Where and when was your father's mother born? (State and year)

7. Where and when was your mother's father born? (State and year)

8. Where and when was your mother's mother born? (State and year)

9. What was the chief occupation of your father's father? Your father's mother?

10. What was the chief occupation of your mother's father? Your mother's mother?

11. What is the origin of your family name? Has it been changed?

12. What is the country of your father's family's origin?

13. What is the country of your mother's family's origin?

14. When did your family first come to this country?

15. Where did they land? (Port of entry)

16. Where did they settle? (Town and state)

17. Are there still relatives in that place?

18. Did your family migrate after arriving in this country?

19. How many states were home before the present one?

20. When was the town or city nearest you founded?

21. Who founded it and for what reason?

22. Were Indians living there? What nation or tribe?

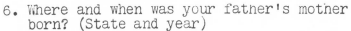

1866 ☉ 1867

Atlantic cable success after 12 years of trying — Congress passes Civil Rights Act, New Freedman's Bureau over Johnson veto — Reconstruction begins — Martial law in South until states ratify 14th-15th Amendments — Nebraska admitted — Alaska purchased at 2 cents an acre — First typewriter patented — First elevated railroad in NY — First 5-cent piece minted — 1,500 buildings lost in Portland, Me. fire — Carroll's "Alice in Wonderland" reaches America.

The Pen-In-Hand Principle

If the central notion contained in the Pack Rat Principle is "pick it up," the main idea here is "write it down." Elsewhere in this Primer there is talk about the merits of various methods of keeping personal or family records. Here what concerns us is the fundamental question of why keep them at all. There are at least three good reasons.

First, if you don't keep some track of your own existence, it is likely that no one else will do it for you. Few of us qualify with the kind of lives that naturally attract biographers. Second, it is also quite likely that those events we fail to mark with some record, however simple or primitive, are apt to be resurrected only through memory, if at all. And that's too bad, because much of what we live becomes more precious with passing time. And that's important cargo to trust to memory. Third (and maybe most important), making a record of an event or some experience is an act which invests the thing itself with greater meaning, as though taking the time and expending the energy to say or write about something is just enough reflection to make the experience assume its true importance.

Probably the biggest obstacle to keeping any kind of consistent personal record is sloth. But once *you* convince yourself that you have something to gain, and find a method for doing it that doesn't monopolize your life, you'll find the process and (eventually) the product very worth the effort.

THE BEST BIRTHDAY PRESENT I EVER SAW

was one of those little dollar blank books (they sell them at most stationery stores) that someone had filled up with a wonderful collection of event scraps for a whole year and given to his wife. What's an event scrap? You know the kind of thing—all the nice stuff that people get but usually don't keep very long: the nicest letters from friends, the funny tags from Christmas presents, the kid's poem from school about the family dog, the matchbook from that special restaurant, etc.

1868 ◦ 1869

Senate attempts presidential impeachment; Johnson acquitted — 14th Amendment passes: blacks gain citizenship — Congress OKs 8-hour federal workday — Central and Union Pacifics linked at Promontory Point — Suez Canal opens — Powell surveys Grand Canyon — Westinghouse invents railroad air brake — First open-hearth furnace fired in Trenton, N.J. — Wyoming territory passes first women's vote — Edison invents electric voting machine — Famous Lost Words: "The only good Indian is a dead Indian." Gen. Philip H. Sheridan.

DIARY IS A DIRTY WORD

To most of us the thought of keeping a diary is about as appealing as keeping an "every-penny-accounted-for" budget. It brings to mind hours of tedious and unrewarding work or unbearable guilt when we procrastinate and miss a day. The point is that when you do miss a day it is really missing. In a week it will be hard to recall what you did on that day, in a month it will be impossible. Keeping the diary is the only way to preserve a record of daily events but it seems as if only lovestruck teen-age girls and direct descendants of Thomas Jefferson are able to sustain the effort. The trick for the rest of us may be to keep the diary but call it something else. Call it: an appointment book; a collection of days; a do it today book; a calendar of events; a life itemizer. The idea is to keep a simple record of your life in a way which will not impose on it. What it looks like doesn't matter as long as it gives you a keepable and retrievable record day by day. Here are some non-traditional diaries that have been successful:

*A desk calendar makes a good one; it has dates and you may already come in contact with it daily.
*One of those pocket appointment calendars is just right.
*A composition book kept by your bed is fine. Be sure to tie a pen to it and keep the pages dated as you go.
*A 3x5 card carried in your pocket or purse can be used to make notes about the day. At the end of the day these go into a small file box.
*Pin a large sheet of paper on the wall of your room and write and date a comment each day.

What Else Happened on your Birthday?

Your contribution to history started at a definite point in time. Having some idea about what was happening in the rest of the world while you and your mother were occupied with your birth will help define the boundaries of your place in time. Since your recollection of that day can be expected to be dim, this project will involve some simple research. You will probably be able to get all the information you need at your local library and from chats with people you know who were interested in the event. Here are some of the events you should try to include:

Family History

Where was your father? What can he remember about that day?

Local News

What was happening close to home? The library will have a copy of the hometown newspaper.

National and World Events

A big city newspaper will be helpful here.

This project would make a fine birthday present for a friend.

Special Note: One may also order a reproduction of the front page of *The New York Times* for any day by sending $2.37 to Front Pages, c/o *The New York Times*, 229 W. 43rd Street, New York, NY 10036, Attention: Library Services, Room 960. Specify the exact date (month, day, year) desired.

YOUR HISTORY STARTS AT HOME

It may be that your view of history is pretty dim but it's not dark. All of us live among the artifacts of our history. Think of the last time you tried to wrap a pile of dishes in old newspapers. How much time did it take to wrap the dishes? How much of the time did it take to read the history in those old papers? The history in your house goes back farther than last month's newspaper. Look around the house. (Don't forget junk drawers and closets.) What are the oldest things? What is the oldest object? How did they get to be a part of your household? What can you remember about the person who gave it to you? Are there any events in which the object played an important role? Why has it survived? This is a simple project but the rewards could easily outweigh the effort involved. It will show how soon your belongings become part of history and the important role familiar objects play in recalling your own past.

THE EYE OF THE BEHOLDER:

HERE IS A LITTLE PRIVATE GAME TO GET YOU IN THE HABIT OF THINKING OF YOURSELF AS HISTORY IN THE MAKING. LOOK AT YOUR CLOTHING AS THOUGH IT WERE A COLLECTION OF IMPORTANT ARTIFACTS. ASK QUESTIONS LIKE: IS ANYTHING HANDMADE? WHAT SKILLS WERE REQUIRED TO MAKE IT? DID IT ONCE BELONG TO SOMEONE ELSE? HOW DID YOU GET IT? WHEN? WHAT WILL YOU DO WITH THESE "ARTIFACTS" WHEN THEY NO LONGER ARE USEFUL AS CLOTHING? PASS THEM ALONG? THROW THEM AWAY? MAKE THEM INTO SOMETHING ELSE?

TIME CAPSULE

Today may be one of the most important days in your history. One year from now it will be even more important if you have made a record which can help you remember it as a point in time. A personal time capsule does the job. Fill a shoe box or an apple crate or something with the items that will tell the story of your life and time to someone who opens it in the future. Limit the time you allow to fill up the capsule—one day or one week is plenty.

Some things you might include: all your mail (including junk); the receipt for a grocery shopping trip; a newspaper; the things your kids bring home from school; TV Guide; a xerox copy of your paycheck; an hour-by-hour accounting of your time for one day; the contents of your pockets or purse on any given day; a list of friends; a tape of your thoughts, your voice; fifty cent bus station photos of yourself; scraps from your dinner or lunch; the list you made about "what I need to do this week" (dated); shopping lists (dated); a copy of any letters you wrote or business documents you worked on.

Now put the capsule away where it is not likely to get forgotten. When you open it twelve months from now you'll have a vivid, three-dimensional, accurate and complete picture of your life as it appeared at a point in time one year ago. This could be a continuing project. Add to the capsule each year. Try it as part of your birthday celebration.

Remember Miss What's-Her-Name?

At age five, school and teacher suddenly start to compete with home and parents for your attention. For many of us, school won out, but how much of this part of our lives can we remember and how much is gone? Try to reconstruct the history of your education for a "single person-all school reunion." List all the schools you attended, your teachers, find your class pictures, report cards, letter sweaters, dance programs, etc. For most of us it would be difficult to compile a complete record of this large chunk of our past.

1870 ◉ 1871

First Negroes in Congress: Hiram R. Revels in Senate; J.H. Rainey in House — 15th Amendment reinforces voting rights — Indian Appropriation Act: all treaties broken; land lost — Legal Tender Act turns Treasury notes into money — Weather Bureau established — Citizens clean house on Tammany Hall; Tweed twice arrested — Rockefeller founds Standard Oil — Grand Central Station opens — O'Leary cow kicks off $196 million Chicago fire — Rail refrigeration cars roll — Film forerunner: celluloid manufacturing process patented by Hyatts — First curve ball demonstrated in Brooklyn — Total US pop. 39,818,449.

PILGRIM'S PROGRESS

If you call your next trip "home" a pilgrimage you will set the scene for a rewarding contact with your past. The problem with "visiting the folks" is usually that's all you set out to do—visit. Many of us know how quickly such a visit becomes tedious and strained. This is usually because a long separation has reduced the common ground shared between family members. (The kids need haircuts and the old folks seem stodgy.) Too often, family history, the always-present common ground, is overlooked. If the trip is organized as a pilgrimage to rediscover Family History, and a good part of your energy is devoted to that search, you may find the trip more like what you thought a vacation should be.

Plan to visit people and places which are significant to your history. Find out as much as you can about them while you are there. (This keeps everyone's minds off the haircuts.) Be on the lookout for clues leading you to people and places which you didn't know were your history. And always keep a record.

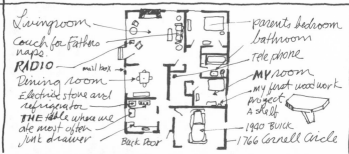

THE STAY-AT-HOME PILGRIMAGE. *When we set about the task of reconstructing our past, we need to do more than just think about it. We need some device which will trigger our recall and help us record the effort. Here is one device which is simple and enjoyable. Try to reconstruct some environment which has played a major role in your history. Draw a plan of your childhood home (for example) as accurately as you can. You will find that some areas are difficult to recall. When that happens, work around them. They will usually be filled in by a process of elimination.*

Make notes on the plan about how the house was used and where important things were, like the radio and toaster. They will help bring the place alive.

GO HOME!
The Basic Pilgrimage

Most of us have a place we think of as being the place where we grew up, our childhood home. A special place in our history. Going there, just to find the house, will be an event which strengthens your ties to the past. It would be a good idea to take someone close to you—your parents, wife, children, good friends—and talk to them about the place. How was it organized? What you did there, the changes you see. As long as you are there, knock on the door. Most people will receive you warmly. Probably because they have been tempted to do the same thing you are doing and because a lot of people are fascinated by the history of their own home.

Some of us can't go home because the house literally is not there any more. It is still an important experience to go find where it was. What is there now? What caused the change? Record this trip. It is a nice little event with specific time boundaries. A tape recorder and camera would be naturals for making a record. Write a letter about the experience and send it to all the people who lived in the house with you.

PILGRIMAGE

Here is a travel project that any member of your family can do. The next time you are traveling, make a record of your trip by sending a picture postcard to yourself at least once a day. Buy the postcards as you go and choose the one which reflects your interest in the place you are visiting. Write a note about the trip on each card. Send as many as you can and try to get each member of the family to join you in the project. When you return home you will have waiting, a practically painless, permanent record of your trip in pictures and words. Bind the cards into book form (rings will do) and put them in the family archives.

1872 ◉ 1873

Guilty of voting: Susan B. Anthony arrested in 14th Amendment test — Muybridge begins motion photo experiments — "Boss" Tweed convicted — Yellowstone lands reserved — Yellow fever, cholera, smallpox sweep South — Bestseller: Jules Verne's "Around the World in 80 Days" — First cable car climbs San Francisco hills — 60 blacks killed in Colfax massacre — Coinage act removes silver currency — Farmers Alliance forms — New parties: National Labor Reform, Prohibition, Liberal Republican — First post card issued.

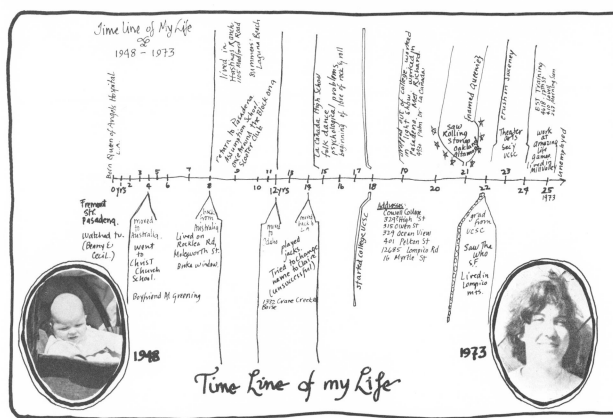

Time Line of my Life

Time Line of My Life
1948 - 1973

Born Queen of Angels Hospital L.A.

Lived in Herthug's Ranch 1105 Medford Road

Summers Laguna Beach

return to Pasadena. Assumption School. Once around the Block on a Scooter Club

La Crada High School folk dance psychological problems beginning of love of rock y roll

dropped out of college, worked on light show, worked in Pasadena. Arco Richard 4320 Palm Dr. - La Canada

Saw Rolling Stones Oakland Altamont

Named Queenie?

Theater Arts Sec'y UCSC

crush on Sweeney

EST Training 4418 12th St. 245 Morning Sun

work at Amazing Life Games. (Lived in Mill Valley)

Unemployed

Fremont str. Pasadena.

Watched tv. (Beany & Cecil.)

moved to Australia. Went to Christ Church School. Boyfriend Al Greening

back from Australia

Lived on Rocklea Rd, Molesworth St. Broke window.

moved to Idaho

played jacks. Tried to change name to Claire (unsuccessful)

1332 Crane Creek Boise

moved back to L.A.

Started college UCSC

Addresses:
Cowell College
329½ High St
315 Owen St
329 Ocean View
401 Pelton St
12685 Lompico Rd
16 Myrtle St

grad from UCSC

Saw The Who S.F.

Lived in Lompico mts.

1948

1973

Put Your Life on the Line

It would seem logical that the one area of history we know most about is the history of our own life. It is possible, however, that we are able to recall as much about the history of Abraham Lincoln as we can about our own. That may be an exaggeration, but for many of us it comes close to being the truth. To find out how truthful it is, try to reconstruct your life on a time line.

HOW TO START A TIME LINE

1. *Draw a horizontal line near the top of a long piece of paper.*

2. *Divide the line into as many years as you need to cover your life. Label the divisions with years.*

3. *In the space below the line write all the events you can recall for each year.*

A simple enough project, but it will very quickly show you where your history has become dim. It will also be an invaluable tool when you start to write your autobiography. This can easily become a "wall size" project and is also suited for starting your family or any group history.

Autobiographies

Race riots in Tennessee, Mississippi, Louisiana — Civil rights act: equal rights in public places — Tweed escapes, flees to Cuba — WCTU established in Cleveland — Potato bugs menace Atlantic coast — Miller, Vincent found Chautauqua movement — National Railroad convention at St. Louis — Aristides wins first Kentucky Derby — Boston first baseman Charles Waite uses first baseball glove — First steel arch bridge spans Mississippi at St. Louis — James Eads dredges delta, opens New Orleans to sea trade — Philadelphia: first public zoo.

THOMAS JEFFERSON, AMELIA EARHART AND YOU

This project deals with the thing you have in common with every other person. Famous or not, everyone has a self-history. Most people would call this Autobiography and wouldn't touch it. In the first place, we have a feeling that we are not important enough to have an autobiography, or that there would be no one interested in the story of our life. It wouldn't be worth the energy required to generate a book of our life.

In reality, self-history is not that bad. In fact, it can be fun and all of us has a history that is or will be important and interesting to someone. The book is not the only form of self-history. We have already talked about slide show history, life line and oral history. All of them are great for self-history but writing does have advantages. It requires no special equipment. Most important, it doesn't depend on any prior preparation. Your memory and whatever records you have available are all you need to get your self-history project started. Begin with a life line (see "Put your Life on the Line") or some similar outline. Then fill in the details as accurately and completely as you can.

I've seen long ones and short, serious and funny. They are all good and important, and worthwhile. I wish more people in my family had made the effort to record their history. Our history would be the richer for it.

Collecting and Collectors

(or, Pack Rats, arise!)

You name it, and someone collects it. There probably isn't an artifact known to man that isn't the object of someone's passion. Collecting is a process that by definition provides some relationship with the past. And collectors are more often than not colorful people who know a great deal about at least one subject. At one end of the spectrum are the individuals whose collections appear to the rest of us to be the product of some quirk—like the man who made the papers with his string collection. He had saved a ball of string so large that he kept it in his front yard and had to move it with an automobile jack. At the other end are those whose collections are so valuable and rare that protection from theft, the elements or devaluation become life pursuits. In between there is a lot of territory for the rest of us to roam.

There is no point in trying to explain a collection (I know a man who says he has the world's largest collection of potato mashers—and I believe him) any more than there is trying to explain why one climbs a mountain. The best collections are very personal matters—often queer, always in some way a source of pleasure. If you don't already have one, here are some ideas for collections that are simple, interesting and inexpensive.

But don't stop here. Invent your own.

BONNIE
THE
BADGER

Here are pictures of parts of Bonnie Russell's badge collection. Most second-hand shops have little cut glass dishes or felt-lined boxes filled with miscellany.... including old political and other badges. Some of the oldest ones bring fancy prices of $10, sometimes more, but mostly they can be had for $1 or less. The catch-phrases of the 19th and 20th century America are to be found printed on celluloid discs... representing fad, scandal, political ambition, and the celebration of heroes great + small. Within the field of badge collecting, there are even specialties. Collecting mementos like these is one good way to nibble at the past. (does anyone remember Kilroy?)

Something Old

Everyone knows about stamps, coins, dolls, toys and all the other standards. Here are a few others that you don't hear about so often but require little if any investment and can lead to many other historical places.

Recipes. If you like to cook, begin collecting old-time or traditional recipes. Start with dishes that are native to your area (every part of the country has them) and try to find out as much as you can about original methods of preparation, foodstuffs and serving styles. Don't worry too much at first about authenticity. As you learn more, you'll get better at selecting.

Kitchen tools and products. While you're in the kitchen, think about all those nifty little hand tools that Sunbeam and General Electric have replaced with newfangled appliances. Some of the old ones are still being made. Like the apple pealer-corer shown here, made by White Mountain. (They also make a terrific line of hand-crank ice cream freezers.) Don't worry about the term antique. Use old-fashioned, instead. Watch junk shops. Stay out of antique stores unless you have a lot of money to spend. Check back issues of *Yankee Magazine* for ideas.

Vegetable Strainer.

1876 ⊙ 1877

Reconstruction ends — Carpetbaggers, Union troops vacate South — Bell's telephone talks — Edison invents phonograph, mimeograph — Battle of Little Big Horn — Chief Joseph, Nez Perce defeated — Colorado admitted — Twain publishes "Tom Sawyer" — Wild Bill Hickok shot — Asaph Hall discovers moons of Mars — John W. Draper first to photograph solar spectrum — Army quells rail strikes — Desert Land Act promotes irrigation — Central Park opens.

1878 ⊙ 1879

Edison forms first electric power company in NY — Dakota land boom — Powell reports on Grand Canyon lands — First bicycle made in US — Albert A. Michelson determines velocity of light — US Geologic Survey established — Ute Indians exiled to Utah — National Guard formed — Massachusetts passes first effective child labor law — James Ritty invents cash register — First "five-and-ten" opens in Utica, NY — Edison perfects incandescent light bulb — Famous lost words: "The public be damned" William H. Vanderbilt.

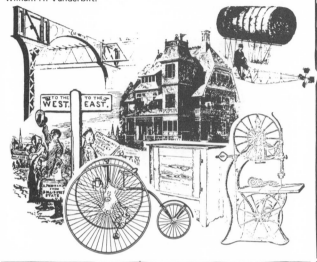

Silver Images

The California Gold Rush was the first national news event to be covered by the camera. That was in 1849. Ever since that time, American culture has been under the constant scrutiny of the quiet eye of the camera. Its images are an eloquent record of the history of the last century and a quarter, and make fascinating and inexpensive collecting. Almost every second hand shop or antique store sells post card photographs (not the lithographed ones, but actual photographs), and every estate sale turns up at least one and often several family albums. Tintypes and paper prints are usually cheap—anywhere from ten cents to a dollar each. Daguerreotypes, or images produced by other early and short-lived processes, are more rare and more expensive. Our collection isn't a large one, but it provides a good excuse to stop at any and all shops to explore.

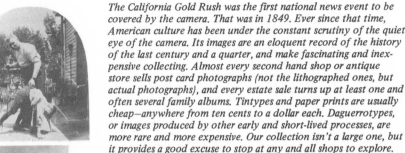

The Newsprint Museum of Life and Times

The morning newspaper is accompanied by a pair of scissors. What seems to be curious, funny (there isn't a whole lot of that these days) or typical of our time is clipped out and pasted into an album. Pictures, headlines, articles, sometimes advertisements. The resulting collection of historical information is no longer newspaper, but a personally selected view of the present-becoming-past (particularly if annotated) and as individual and interesting as the imagination of the curator who puts it together. And all for the price of a daily paper . . . or for free if you don't mind using yesterday's papers.

One Last Word....

Before passing over the subject of collections and going on to something else, let us suggest that you may already have a collection or the start of one, but just call it by another name. The verb "to collect" may seem a little too single-minded and compulsive to suit some tempers. Another way to think about it is to say from time to time,"That's a very fine___, I think I'd like to have it." That's called "picking up," not collecting, and though the net effect may be similar, there is a world of difference in the approach. Think "Pack Rat."

spoken antiques

Mrs Mary Whitehead writes about a basketmaker in Blakely, Georgia, Harvey Davis, who is getting too old to go out in the woods and drag back the white oak logs he needs for his craft. When a friend brought back four good-sized logs for him, Davis rejected them, calling them too "brickly." One of Mrs Whitehead's pastimes is old words. She had never heard this one before, so she looked it up and "found it in the unabridged dictionary in good standing." (Check it yourself to see what was wrong with Harvey's white oak logs.) There are many places in America, and especially in the South, where ancient Anglo-Saxon words are still used without any knowledge that they are antiques.

In Knox County, social worker Betty Hollinde is systematically assembling a lexicon of old-timey words used by the mountain people with whom she works. She's also collecting traditional stories in order to build up an archive. Which takes us to oral histories, which is another subject (see page 168).

Brickly

DOOR JAMB HISTORY

We'd almost forgotten that in the house we grew up in, the frame around the door between the kitchen and the dining room was all marked up with the history of growing children.

It's true that people move around so much nowadays that there isn't time to accumulate much history in any one place. But for anyone who's settled in, and has little ones, it's a nice old tradition.

Make the measuring and marking a for-sure annual occasion. The best time, of course, is on the birthday of each child.

PS: If you happen to have the family archive in a closet, locate your growing post on that door jamb.

Growing Post

• 72
• 70
• 68   Eddie December 1970
• 66

MAKE YOUR FAMILY THIS FINE MEASURING STICK. 1 X 6 REDWOOD OR FIR. PAINT OR WOODBURN THE INCHES. MAKE AN ENTRY AT EACH BIRTHDAY. GLUE, OR HAVE THE KIDS DRAW THEIR PICTURES TO GO WITH EACH ENTRY. MAKES AN EXCELLANT PRESENT. HANGS IN ANY DOORJAMB.

Lace Makers, Hide Tanners and Knot Tiers

Family Craftsmen

My grandmother knew how to make lace, my father can tan hide with the hair on, and I just made a knot board with seventy-five knots I learned when I was a kid. Crafts and skills are a part of every family history and are among the first things to be lost if an effort is not made to preserve them. The first step would be to ask around. Find out who knew or knows how to do what. It is important not to be too particular about what you define as a craft. Making a willow whistle can be just as important as making a patchwork quilt. The second step would be to preserve an example of each craft in the family archive along with all the information you can find concerning the object. Who did it? When? How and why did they learn it?

Pass It On

The best way to keep the craft part of your family history alive is to perpetuate it. Learn or teach a craft. Encourage everyone in the family who has skills to instruct someone else.

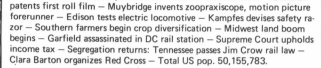

1880 ◉ 1881

MAKING A FAMILY ALBUM

Scrapbooks are things our funny ancestors made because they didn't have anything better to do with their spare time. Somehow television and radio and campers and a thousand other things can more than fill any time we have to spare. The vision of spending hours with a pile of scraps and a pot of library paste doesn't go over well any more, but if you have ever had a chance to leaf through one of those old scrapbooks and see the scraps turn into a picture of life as it was experienced by its keeper, you know the value of that kind of document. Records such as scrapbooks contribute a richness to your family which cannot be obtained elsewhere.

It's easy to be convinced of the value of keeping a family scrapbook. Overcoming the barriers which keep us from making the effort is the real problem. Here are some suggestions that could help:

Tell everyone. Make sure everyone who can contribute knows why the scrapbook is being started. *Make it easy.* Keep the book in a well-exposed place with the "sticky stuff" close by. The only rule is to stick it in as you go. Waiting to do it all at one time makes keeping the scrapbook a job. *Sticky stuff.* The messy days of slow-drying smelly paste are over. Clear tape, spray cement and glue sticks have come to the rescue. Provide the easiest stuff you can find. *Share the load.* Try to make it a family affair. The book will grow faster. *Remember:* The first year is the hardest. The older it gets, the better it looks.

Make A People Index

Mrs Marian D. Baldwin added a new and active dimension to the Vancouver (Washington) Library by enlisting people in the community with skills to share their knowledge with others. Each volunteer fills out a 3x5 card with name, address and phone number, an explanation of what skill he or she is willing to share, what level of skill he or she possesses (beginning, average or expert) and what hours he or she is available. Library visitors flip through the Index to find a lawyer versed in patent law, a retiree who is an expert fly-tier, or a young man who has mastered the art of chair caning. The file is not for commercial purposes—all persons listed offer their services for free. The extent of involvement is up to the user and the donor. And it's being heavily used by students, retirees, housewives—not just because it's a novelty. Mrs Baldwin's People Index is the best way we've heard of to implement the sharing of skills within a community. (We read about this good idea in the Small Towns Institute newsjournal.)

1882 ⊙ 1883

First hydroelectric plant opens in Appleton, Wis. — Electric firsts: Wheeler's fan, Seely's iron, Boston Bijou's theater lights — Telsa discovers magnetic field rotation — Koch finds TB germ — Railroads institute standard time zones — Brooklyn Bridge finished — Metropolitan Opera House opens — 85,000 homeless in Mississippi River floods — Pendleton Act creates Civil Service Commission — Rivers and Harbors Act passes over President Arthur's veto — Pulitzer acquires New York World — Idaho gold rush — Buffalo Bill opens Wild West Show.

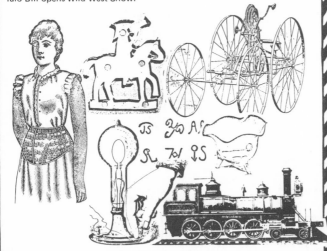

THE PHOTO ALBUM OF THE SILVER SCREEN

FAME AND FORTUNE DO NOT AWAIT THE FAMILY MEMBER WHO WILL UNDERTAKE TO MAKE HIS FAMILY HISTORY INTO A SHOW. NO SIR! BUT AWAITING THAT ENTERPRISING PERSON IS THE PRIDE OF ACCOMPLISHMENT AND THE PRAISE OF ALL WHO BEHOLD THE PRODUCTION. THE IDEA IS TO BRING THE FAMILY PHOTO ALBUM OUT FROM THE BOTTOM DRAWER OF THE BEDROOM DRESSER — AND TO PUT THOSE DIM IMAGES INTO A FORM THAT WILL REVIVE ALL THEIR VITALITY. NOT EVEN THE MOST APATHETIC FAMILY COUSIN WILL BE ABLE TO RESIST THE IMPACT OF A WELL-ORGANIZED SLIDE SHOW LIKE THIS.

Family Maps

If you don't already have one, now is the time to make a family map. Draw a big ink outline of the U.S. showing state boundaries. Then plot the migrations of your family as far back as you can. Mark towns where you have relatives (alive or buried). You may be surprised at the geographic distribution of your clan when it's all done.

Resting Places

The places where our relatives are buried are sacred spots to all of us, yet many of us don't even know where those places are. If that is the case in your family, the time is right to see that the information is preserved. Record names, relationships and places (see Family Bible, page 154). If you decide to work on a family tree project, the information may be vital. Try to visit the graves of as many relatives as you can.

139

THE MYSTERIOUS ADVENTURES OF (YOUR FAMILY!!!)

HEY YOU! YOU'RE A VERY IMPORTANT PERSON

YOU

WHERE DID YOU COME FROM?

I WAS BORN IN SALT LAKE CITY YOUTAH!

SALT LAKE CITY

YOU

NO! I MEAN BEFORE THAT!

HUNDREDS OF YEARS BEFORE THAT!

YOU MEAN A FAMILY TREE?

I'VE ALWAYS THOUGHT THAT WOULD BE FUN TO DO!

ME TOO! MAYBE WE'RE LONG-LOST COUSINS!

YOU

GRANPA SAYS WE'RE DESCENDED FROM GEORGE WASHINGTON!

YOU

I GUESS I'D BETTER GET A PROFESSIONAL TO DO IT...

NONSENSE! IT'S YOUR FAMILY! AND THE REASON YOU DO A FAMILY TREE IS TO LEARN ABOUT YOUR FAMILY!

YOU WON'T LEARN MUCH FROM BUYING A LIST OF NAMES!!

DO IT YOURSELF!

STOP

MAKE IT YOUR FAMILY TREE! YOU CAN DO IT BETTER THAN ANYBODY—CHEAPER THAN ANYBODY— (EXCEPT GYP OUTFITS)! AND HAVE FUN!

3 THINGS YOU PROBABLY NEED TO DO A FAMILY TREE:
- ✓ CURIOSITY
- ✓ A NOTEBOOK FULL OF 8½ × 11 SHEETS
- ✓ PERSEVERANCE

A FAMILY TREE CAN LOOK LIKE ANYTHING YOU WANT IT TO LOOK LIKE! (TWO STANDARD FORMS ARE SHOWN ON PAGES 142-3, BUT WHO WANTS TO JUST FILL IN STANDARD FORMS ?????)

YOU

I DON'T EVEN KNOW WHAT A FAMILY TREE IS SUPPOSED TO LOOK LIKE

START HERE! WRITE DOWN EVERYTHING YOU KNOW ABOUT ALL YOUR RELATIVES!

ONE GENERATION TO A PAGE

OKAY! SO WHERE DO I START?

YOU

AND START YOUR GENERATION PAGES

MAKE NOTES AS TO WHERE YOU GET EACH FACT, AND PUT PAGES OF DETAILS ABOUT THESE RELATIVES IN THE BINDER DIRECTLY BEHIND THIS PAGE

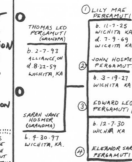

THOMAS LEO PERGAMUTI (GRANPA)
b. 2-7-93 ALLIANCE, OH
d. 8-22-59 WICHITA, KA

SARAH JANE HOSMER (GRANDMA)
b. 4-30-97 WICHITA, KA.

① LILY MAE PERGAMUTI
b. 11-7-25 WICHITA KA
d. 7-9-69 WICHITA KA

② JOHN HOSMER PERGAMUTI
b. 3-19-27 WICHITA KA

③ EDWARD LEO PERGAMUTI (DAD)
b. 12-7-30 WICHITA KA

④ ELEANOR SARAH PERGAMUTI
b. 5-29-32 WICHITA KA

Tested ~ **20** ~ Proven
WAYS TO REDISCOVER YOUR ANCESTORS

WANTED DEAD OR ALIVE (MY FAMILY) CALL 8624175

YOU

NOTE: BECAUSE THIS IS A GENERALIZED SCHEME, YOU MAY HAVE TO ALTER SOME SUGGESTIONS...

FOR INSTANCE, IF YOUR PARENTS AND GRANDPARENTS ARE DECEASED, YOU CAN'T ASK THEM...

BUT THEY MAY HAVE LEFT LETTERS OR ALBUMS WITH ANOTHER MEMBER OF THE FAMILY.

1 GRANDPARENTS

VISIT EACH OF YOUR GRANDPARENTS —

ASK THEM FOR THE FULL NAMES OF EACH OF THEIR PARENTS AND GRANDPARENTS

DATE AND PLACE OF BIRTH · WHERE EACH LIVED · WHAT THEY WERE LIKE WHERE AND WHEN EACH DIED

LET THEM TELL STORIES!

YOU

TAKE NOTES OR YOU MAY FORGET!

COME AGAIN

2 VISIT YOUR GRANDPARENTS AGAIN. ASK ABOUT THEIR BROTHERS AND SISTERS (COUSINS, AUNTS, UNCLES...)

"IT'S PROBABLY BEST TO GIVE FOLKS A REST"

TRYING TO REMEMBER DETAILS IS TIRING, ESPECIALLY FOR ELDERLY PEOPLE... SO DON'T TRY TO GET EVERYTHING AT ONCE!

AND EACH TIME YOU COME BACK, THEY'LL PROBABLY HAVE REMEMBERED SOMETHING THEY FORGOT TO TELL YOU!

BE ON THE LOOKOUT FOR:
- FAMILY PHOTOS
- LETTERS
- CLIPPINGS
- DIARIES
- NOTATED CALENDARS
- ALBUMS
- SCRAPBOOKS
- BORROW ✓ COPY RETURN

3 WHERE OH WHERE?

FIND OUT ADDRESSES OF ALL RELATIVES LIVING AND DEAD, PAST AND PRESENT.

WRITE EACH LIVING RELATIVE A NOTE ABOUT YOUR SEARCH, THEN VISIT THEM IF YOU CAN.

A FAMILY TREE SHOULD BRING A FAMILY CLOSER TOGETHER

4 FRIENDS

VISIT OLD 'FRIENDS OF THE FAMILY'

THEY'LL PROBABLY BE ESPECIALLY GOOD AT TELLING YOU STORIES ABOUT YOUR RELATIVES

5 NO STONE UNTURNED

ACCOMPANY ONE OF YOUR OLDER RELATIVES ON A VISIT TO FAMILY GRAVE SITES

YOU'LL FIND OUT WHERE YOUR ANCESTORS ARE BURIED

AND YOUR RELATIVE MAY REDISCOVER MARKERS OF LONG FORGOTTEN FAMILY MEMBERS!

FAMILY BIBLE

6 IF YOU HAVE A FAMILY BIBLE, IT CAN BE VERY HELPFUL FOR DATES OF BIRTHS MARRIAGES AND DEATHS

YOU — GEE, I THINK GRANDMA GAVE IT TO COUSIN AL

HANDWRITING ANALYSIS TIPS:
IF ALL ENTRIES IN YOUR BIBLE ARE IN THE SAME 'HAND' AND THE SAME INK, THE CHART WAS PROBABLY DONE ALL AT ONCE -- AND IS LESS LIKELY TO BE ACCURATE THAN LISTINGS MADE INDIVIDUALLY AFTER EACH EVENT.

7 KEEPSAKES THAT TALK

WRITTEN RECORDS AREN'T THE ONLY STORYTELLERS IN THE ATTIC!

SAMPLERS SOMETIMES CONTAIN A LIST OF THE STITCHER'S BROTHERS SISTERS

FRIENDSHIP QUILTS OFTEN HAVE NAMES OF FRIENDS AND RELATIVES WRITTEN IN INDIA INK

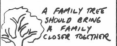

OLD SILVER OFTEN HAS INITIALS OF WEDDED COUPLE

GO AHEAD -

 YIELD TO TEMPTATION—START SEARCHING THAT ATTIC!

ALL IS NOT LOST

8

IF YOU CAN'T FIND IT OUT FROM FAMILY AND FRIENDS —

TRY THE LIBRARY!

IF YOU LIVE IN A LARGE CITY — EITHER THE MAIN LIBRARY OR A UNIVERSITY LIBRARY PROBABLY HAS A GENEALOGICAL SECTION... WHICH OFFERS A LARGE NUMBER OF PRINTED GENEALOGIES — IF YOU TIE INTO ONE, GREAT!

(YOU SHOULD PROBABLY ASK THE LIBRARIAN TO CHECK TO SEE IF ANY OF THE VARIOUS BRANCHES OF YOUR FAMILY HAVE BEEN INCLUDED IN A PREVIOUSLY-PUBLISHED GENEALOGY)

RURAL LIBRARIES SOMETIMES HAVE COLLECTIONS OF LOCAL HISTORIC INFORMATION — TRY THEM!

DON'T FORGET TO CHECK THE TOWN MUSEUM

X

YOUR LIBRARY ALSO MAY HAVE SOME PUBLISHED **INDEXES**

9

SOME LIST ALL FAMILIES TRACED IN A GIVEN SET OF GENEALOGIES

SOME TELL WHERE YOU'LL FIND COLLECTIONS OF GENEALOGIES.

10

LISTS OF GENEALOGIES

THE LIBRARY OF CONGRESS IN WASHINGTON D.C. AND THE LONG ISLAND HISTORICAL SOCIETY IN NEW YORK HAVE LARGE COLLECTIONS OF PUBLISHED AND UNPUBLISHED GENEALOGIES.

THEY HAVE PUBLISHED LISTS OF THEIR COLLECTIONS, AND THESE CAN BE FOUND IN MANY LIBRARIES.

ALSO, SEVERAL PUBLIC LIBRARIES HAVE PUBLISHED LISTINGS OF ALL GENEALOGIES IN THEIR COLLECTIONS.

Geronimo captured: Plains Indian wars end — Dawes Act legally dissolves tribes — Statue of Liberty unveiled — Haymarket riot: workers demonstrate for 8-hour day — AFL forms in Pittsburgh — ICC begins federal regulation of interstate commerce — First Labor Day — Drought in Midwest — Hatch Act sets up experimental agriculture stations — Rail gauges standardized — Lick Observatory opens — Talbert Lanston invents Monotype — Pearl Harbor leased from Hawaii.

VISIT

THE TOWN YOUR PEOPLE CAME FROM!

ENTERING YOUTICA POP. 425

YOU ? / SURE! I REMEMBER THEM

TALK TO OLD RESIDENTS!

11

VISIT THE KEEPER OF THE TOWN RECORDS HE'S OFTEN CALLED THE **TOWN CLERK**

MOST TOWNS BEGAN RECORDING VITAL STATISTICS AROUND **1850**

IT'S PROBABLY NOT HIS FAVORITE PASTIME TO PULL DOWN HEAVY VOLUMES OF DUSTY RECORDS — SO HE MAY BE A BIT GROUCHY...

BUT THEY ARE **PUBLIC RECORDS** —

YOU **DO** HAVE THE **RIGHT TO LOOK!**

12

ALSO IN THE TOWN CLERK'S OFFICE:

→ MORTGAGE RECORDS!

→ TAX LISTS!

→ SCHOOL CENSUSES!

AND ESPECIALLY

→ LAND RECORDS!

13

LOVING HUSBAND OF / BELOVED WIFE OF / INFANT SON

LONG LOST UNCLE

TAKE A WALK THROUGH THE TOWN'S CEMETERIES

YOU MAY HAVE TO CHECK OLD MAPS TO REDISCOVER THE YARDS

(SEE PAGE 108 FOR INFORMATION ON CLEANING OLD MARKERS)

14

XX

OLD-TIME LANGUAGE:
— HEADSTONES —

"CONSORT" MEANS WIFE OF A MAN STILL LIVING

"RELICT" MEANS WIDOW

— CORRESPONDENCE —

"BROTHER", "SISTER" MAY MEAN "BELONGING TO THE SAME CHURCH"

"UNCLE", "AUNTIE" MAY BE JUST A TERM OF AFFECTION INSTEAD OF DENOTING BLOOD RELATION

EACH LOCAL AREA HAS A

15 PROBATE OFFICE

"BEING OF SOUND MIND AND BODY"

USUALLY AT THE COUNTY SEAT

WILLS OFTEN LIST ALL FAMILY MEMBERS

CHECK FOR ADDITIONAL INFORMATION ON **DIVISION** OF **PROPERTY** DOCUMENTS

ALSO LAWSUITS TELL MUCH ABOUT PEOPLE INVOLVED IN THEM

HOME CHURCH / TOWN RECORDS

16

MANY HAVE LISTINGS OF WEDDINGS, BAPTISMS

ALSO MEMBERSHIP LISTS

? IS THE OLD CHURCH CLOSED?

THE RECORDS MAY HAVE BEEN EITHER SENT TO THE DENOMINATION'S STATE OFFICE, OR GIVEN TO A LOCAL HISTORICAL SOCIETY

EARLY AMERICAN FAMILIES

17

THE NATIONAL ARCHIVES HAS A COPY OF THE 1790 CENSUS — AND ALL SUCCEEDING CENSUSES TO 1880. (AFTER THAT THEY'RE STILL CONFIDENTIAL)

• IF YOU KNOW WHO AND WHERE YOUR ANCESTORS WERE, YOU CAN FIND VALUABLE DETAILS IN THE CENSUS.

NATIONAL ARCHIVES: CENTRAL REFERENCE DIVISION · WASHINGTON D.C. 20408

USING THE NATIONAL ARCHIVES

YOU / THEY BELONG TO YOU AND ME / ME

BEST WAY: VISIT WASHINGTON D.C. AND CARRY OUT YOUR RESEARCH IN PERSON

OTHERWISE: WRITE THE NATIONAL ARCHIVES AND THEY WILL SEND YOU A LIST OF ORGANIZATIONS WHICH LIST THE NAMES OF PEOPLE WHO WILL DO THE RESEARCH FOR YOU — FOR A FEE. **$**

THE SUPERINTENDENT OF DOCUMENTS (U.S. GOVERNMENT PRINTING OFFICE) PUBLISHED A BOOKLET ENTITLED "GENEALOGICAL RECORDS IN THE NATIONAL ARCHIVES" IN 1964. YOUR LIBRARY MAY HAVE A COPY OF IT.

WAS HE A SOLDIER? **18**

BANG

THE NATIONAL ARCHIVES HAS PENSION RECORDS OF REVOLUTIONARY WAR SOLDIERS

OTHER MILITARY RECORDS — HONOR ROLLS — ESPECIALLY LOCAL — CAN HELP YOU, TOO!

THE DAUGHTERS OF THE AMERICAN REVOLUTION 1776 "D" ST. N.W. WASHINGTON D.C. HAVE INFO ON MANY REVOLUTIONARY SOLDIERS' LINES OF DESCENT.

YOUR ANCESTORS WERE IMMIGRANTS?

19

Start at home - try to find out exactly when and where your family entered the United States. If you know the name of the ship, the date, and the port of entry, you'll probably have no trouble finding their names on a passenger list in the National Archives. If you know the name of the ship but not the date of arrival, check The Morton Allan Directory of European Passenger Steamship Arrivals (it's in most large libraries.) Once you find your family on the passenger list, you will have sufficient data to contact the Immigration and Naturalization Service for a copy of the naturalization petition. Their address is 119 D Street N.E. Washington D.C. They will send you "Application Form N-585." You then must fill in this form and send it to the nearest regional office of the I & NS — except for information about naturalization which took place between 1906 and 1956. These requests must be sent to the Washington D.C. office. There is a $3 non-refundable search fee, for which you receive a copy of the first page of your ancestor's naturalization petition. But the 3 additional pages of the petition should contain a wealth of family information - yours for 75¢ extra!

BACK TO THE OLD COUNTRY

20 YOU

IT'S POSSIBLE TO FIND RECORDS OF YOUR FAMILY BEFORE THEY CAME TO AMERICA. YOU SHOULD WRITE TO THE RECORDS CLERK IN YOUR ANCESTRAL VILLAGE... ALSO WRITE TO THE LOCAL CHURCH OFFICIALS. THEY WILL OFTEN SEARCH THEIR RECORDS FOR A FEE.

SOME NATIONS HAVE PUBLISHED "GUIDES TO LOCATING YOUR ANCESTORS"

WRITE THE CONSUL GENERAL'S OFFICE AND ASK WHAT AIDS ARE AVAILABLE.

WHEN IT'S DONE...

21 IT'S NEVER DONE!

YOU'LL ALWAYS HAVE NEW AND OLD STORIES TO ADD -- PICTURES --

NOT TO MENTION **NEW FAMILY MEMBERS!**

BUT WHEN YOU'VE GOT IT FAIRLY COMPLETE, YOU CAN SEND COPIES TO RELATIVES... THE LOCAL LIBRARY... THE LIBRARY NEAR YOUR FAMILY HOME... A NATIONAL GENEALOGICAL SOCIETY.

GET GOING!

WELL, UH, GOSH, I'M UH AWFULLY BUSY GUY AND UH WELL MAYBE... / YOU

WHEN AN ELDERLY RELATIVE DIES, A WEALTH OF INFORMATION IS LOST TO YOUR FAMILY FOREVER!

MORE DETAILS

NEXT PAGE!

John B. Dunlop invents pneumatic tire — Photo advances: Eastman develops box camera, movie film — Adding machine, induction motor patented — Electrocution becomes New York capital punishment — Louisville first to use Australian secret ballot — Great blizzard blankets East; 400 lost in New York City — Oklahoma land rush — Montana, North and South Dakota, Washington admitted — Sioux lose 9 million acres — Mayo Clinic founded — Walter Camp picks first All-American grid squad.

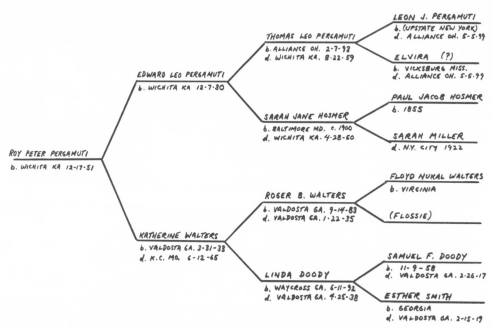

This is an example of a multi-generational lineage chart. It reads from right to left and gives vital information about the ancestry of the fictitious Roy Peter Pergamuti. It does not include any information about the brothers and sisters of Roy or any of his forebears. Single-generation pages (such as the one shown in the ninth panel of The Mysterious Adventures of your Family—page 140) are able to include brothers and sisters, and their families, too.

your tree should be ALIVE

Are you among the many who prefer to dip into an assortment of pictures, anecdotes, keepsakes, sketches, clippings and correspondence rather than spend time decoding sheaves of figures, footnotes and small print? If so, why not put in the good stuff when you start your family tree? The opposite page shows one very simple way of making a lineage chart into an interesting visual experience. And below this paragraph is a list of other suggestions to put pzazz into your family tree. But it really depends on your approach—if you decide you want a lively family tree, you'll find a way . . . suggestions or no suggestions.

1. Use pictures of everything—pictures of family members (of course), pictures of houses the family has lived in, pictures of where they have gone to school, pictures of trips, pictures of pet turtles.

2. Make maps showing where branches of the family have migrated.

3. Save family correspondence, newspaper articles and other written artifacts. Write your own headline for each one.

4. Tape record the voice of each family member telling some story of interest to the family.

5. Make a series of posters which show the different occupations of family breadwinners.

6. Write a history of family pets, family friends or favorite vacation spots. Or family investments or family parties . . . .

Sherman Anti-Trust Act goes into effect — "Ghost Dance" war: Sioux lose 11 million acres more — Sitting Bull captured and killed — Oklahoma territory carved from reservations — US illiteracy rate 13.3 percent — Idaho, Wyoming admitted — Edison patents motion picture camera, projector, radio device — George Hale takes first photos of sun — Castle Garden closes as immigration depot — Carnegie Hall opens — New Orleans jazz begins to emerge — Naismith introduces basketball — Total US pop. 62,947,714.

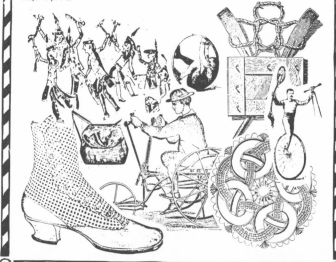

On the previous page, we showed you an example of one way to draw a multi-generational chart. To the right 👉 you will see another example using family portraits to create an interesting, visually pleasing Family Tree.

1. Roy Peter Pergamuti
2. Edward Leo Pergamuti
3. Katherine Walters
4. Thomas Leo Pergamuti
5. Sarah Jane Hosmer
6. Roger B. Walters
7. Linda Doody
8. Leon J. Pergamuti
9. Elvira ?
10. Paul Jacob Hosmer
11. Sarah Miller
12. Floyd N. Waters
13. Flossie ?
14. Samuel F. Doody
15. Esther Smith

NAME CALLING

One of the most personal elements of your own history is your family name. You use it every day, but how much do you know about it? Do you know where it came from? Or what it means? Have you wondered why you even have a family name?

Let's suppose you have only one name—the name your parents gave you at birth, such as Keith (or Mary, or Bill). And you live in a village which has a population of one thousand people, including nineteen males named Keith. How would people identify you to avoid confusion? Maybe by adding something descriptive. Keith Redhead. Which helps considerably. Except that not everybody would call you Redhead. Some might refer to you as Keith who lives by the hill; some might call you Keith the carpenter. Imagine

all the conversations which died due to inconsistent identifications: "You mean Keith by the Hill?" "No, I'm talking about Keith the Carpenter." Anyway, you probably would step in at some point and announce that henceforth you would answer to Keith Redhead. Great!

Your brother, Bill, faces a similar problem. His solution is a bit different, though, since he doesn't have red hair, He calls himself Bill-Simon's son, identifying himself through your father. And in that way each family member would decide on his or her own identifier.

But maybe somewhere along the line your family might decide that it's inconvenient to have fifteen assorted grandparents, parents and children in the family each having different surnames.

Or you might see a successful family who all use the same surname and follow their example of consistency. (Or maybe you are forced to conform to a royal edict that all families pick a surname and stick with it.)

Your ancestors probably went through that about 400 years ago. That was sixteen generations back, and your 16,384* male ancestors of that generation each selected a family name. How many of those approximately 16,384 surnames belonging to you and your ancestors do you know?

Back to that big decision—What surname to choose (or be stuck with). Most names fall into one of four classes: (1) relation to father (or other relative), such as Simonson, Johnson, McElroy, Christensen, Posewicz, Fernandez and O'Reilly; (2) relation to town or

geographical features such as Hill, Lake, Robles (oaks), Stone, Rivers, Lester (from Leicester), Frankfurter and Madrid; (3) description of occupation such as Smith, Wright, Cook, Chandler, Myers (from the old French word, *mire*, meaning "doctor"), Weaver and Boatman; (4) nicknames—colors, names of animals or personal attributes such as Goodspeed, Wolf, Finch, Brown and Loud.

Do you know where your family name came from? Seems like it deserves some attention. After all, it made it all the way to your generation—and it had to beat out 16,000 other names to do it!

*The number 16,384 represents the name of your father plus the name of your maternal grandfather plus the name of your maternal great grandfather and your maternal paternal grandfather and so on (doubling each generation) back through a total of sixteen generations.

If you look closely at the old photographs of parlor interiors from, say, 1880 until well into this century, you may be struck, as I was, at the incredible clutter, particularly on the walls. Apparently, walls were not sacrosanct then, and since windows were a good deal smaller, the visual salad that adorned the interior must have been put there in part as food for the eye. Well, friends, this is the page on which we propose an excursion back to the busy wall for the purpose of mounting

The Family Gallery.

The proposal isn't really all that extreme. There are already lots of people who put family photographs on the wall rather than on the mantle. We're just suggesting that in order to get the flavor of the family saga, you go somewhat beyond the portrait level. Not all at once, mind you.

First of all, it should probably be a family project. Anyone in the family should be permitted to add anything he chooses so long as it does not subvert the true purpose of the wall. (Which, by the way, is to provide a collective record of family history.) Once an item has been added to the wall, it should stay there, unless there is some consensus that it is inappropriate or for some other reason should be taken down. In other words, although the wall is in fact a source of family enjoyment, it has a serious aspect. If you establish a few simple rules, it will be more fun because it is taken seriously.

There are any number of ways to organize the wall, depending on how many people are involved, and how much wall is at your disposal. Try an arrangement where family members occupy the vertical dimension, for example, and time the horizontal. Designate one wall, or part of a wall, at first. If the project works, you can always expand it.

The idea is for the wall to become, over time, an operating graphic museum of family history. Start with as many photographs, over as long a period as possible, of family members. Let each member be responsible for choosing what he wants to be displayed in his "zone." (Later on, it should be open territory for all.) Pictures of events, trips, outings, celebrations. Put up small trinkets, memorabilia, anything that has significance to the family group or its members.

If you stick with it a while, it'll amaze you in time. The nice thing about this "scrapbook wall" is that it's all there at once. And seeing it all together is very different from hauling it out and turning the pages on special occasions. For one thing, it is a reminder of change—a physical expression of passing time, and a device that helps important events to be fully appreciated. It will fascinate your visitors. And, oddly enough, if you put it in a place that isn't in the main flow of traffic, you won't get tired of looking at it.

This is composer Robert Hughes and his scrapbook wall. He describes it as "randomly organized" which is a polite description. It is one of the few of its kind that occupies the entire end of a living room. Hughes says he doesn't tire of it, because it's always changing, and also because someone is forever pointing out some aspect of it that hadn't occurred to him. This wall is not strictly speaking historical, either, though it has much historical content. Hughes puts up what he likes, and is known on occasion to permit his good friends to contribute.

Whatever your style, if you can once overcome the resistance to clutter, and keep it going a while, you'll find this family project a constant source of pleasure and amusement.

Household Yarns—or, Oral History Starts At Home

Most of the greatest legends and tales had humble origins. They grew out of someone's life. Every household has its legends and myths—some altogether fabricated, some a hybrid of fact and fancy. They are part of what knits us together. Preserve them. Write them down in a book, or album (get the family artist to do illustrations), or record them on tape. You won't ever regret it. Here is a check list of family story genres that might help you track down your own indigenous literature:

The mythologies of children. Every child has a fantasy life that abounds with characters that are worth reading about. One of my cousins was close friends with a Mr Peabead, an invisible yet infinitely real gentleman friend who used to join the family at the dinner table from time to time, but always at the very last minute, sometimes with his pal Homly-Gomly. He was the spinner of yarns. My brother and I had a land-in-the-sky we used to travel to each night, in our beds, after the lights were turned out.

Famous family jokes. Usually involving one or more family members, the telling of which is often painfully embarrassing to the members in question.

Famous family adventures. Generally involving danger. The night we stayed up all night on the summer camp kitchen roof in order to try to shoot the marauding bear (which we missed anyway).

Family romances. How my mother at first spurned my father's first entreaties to marry, and how my father bought a sporty roadster and sulked.

No one realizes how rich the family literature is until they start to remember all the famous stories.

Keeping Tracks

One good way to develop the habit of keeping family records is to establish a journal for vacations or other family travel. Either make one person the keeper-of-the-journal, and everyone suggests entries, or rotate the duty each day to another family member.

Often it is easier to begin records of this kind simply because the normal daily routine is broken anyway. The intervals in the car, or waiting for meals, can be occupied with journal rather than back-seat hassling. And it just might be that the effort will be enough fun that the habit will stick.

In addition to the standard topics of where we stayed and what we ate and how far we got Saturday, write down stuff like: the funniest thing we saw; the prettiest thing we saw; what we found out that we didn't know before, etc. Save room for snapshots and be sure the kids draw pictures of the things that interested them most.

This is another part of family history that is worth recording. In this case, let the kids do the work, and take the credit. First of all, they'll probably do it better than anyone else could, and besides, it's good experience, and helps establish the habit of keeping track of those important things in life.

Charles "Chuck" McClain
1971
Author: My Dog Shag

MY DOG SHAG!

This is Shag when he was 3 months old.

A
My Dog

My Dog was born in 1960. He was bought for my brother Bob. His birthday May 16, is what we changed it to because our birthdays are the 16th. He was born Boise Idaho. When he was a year old he took a train to Pasadena, California. Then he came to La Canada to live. When Shag was two years old, Chuck was born to be his Master. He was pleased eating cookies from the playpen.

One of Shags adventures was running away from home. When we

THE STATION, THE TOWN PROPERTY, A HUNDRED MINES, PLUS. GOOD WATER PIPED FIVE MILES. SHE'S REALLY SPECIAL. SOMEONE COULD DO A BWUNXV FAT BOOK--LIKE LON TAYLOR. SHE SAYS THAT RHYOLITE WAS A WOOD TOWN, THAT PEOPLE WOULD TOTE THE HOUSES AWAY TO LOS ANGELES. IT SEEMS WOW WHEN YOU SEE THE PANARAMA PHOTO OF RHYOLITE IN 1907.

EVAN THOMPSON, 34 YEAR GRANDSON OF THOMASON OL TIMER AT BOTTLE HOUSE TALKED ABOUT HIS NEW FOUND WISDOM, SOLITUDE, BEING DIFFERENT, LOST LOVE ETC. I LIKED HIM. LOTS OF FUNKIE RUSTY JUNKS SURROUNDING BOTTLE HOUSE. FENCE OF OLD CARS, REFRIGERATORS, COGS ETC ETC ALONG 'N ALONG 'N ALONG
FENCE OF STRUNG VIOLET BOTTLENECKS

Here are two pages from Richard Wilson's hiking journal. It's a pretty good interpretation of this idea, so we show you a piece of it here. Maybe you can't draw as well as Richard, but we'll bet you can spell better.

MON 25

A LONG BEAUTIFUL ONE-WAY DIRT ROAD NEAR RHYOLITE SOUTH TOWARDS D.V. REMOVE THE NASTY REAR VIEW MIRROR. TWISTY RED PASS DOWN TO LEADVILLE (SCATTERED CORRUGATED SHACKS & A COUPLE HOLES IN THE MT. WHICH A SUCCESSFULL PROMOTER BLASTED FIVE FAKED MINES, SPRINKLED ORE ON THE PILES OF EARTH, LIED, LIED IN ADS TO LURE INVESTORS. WE COOKED LEFTOVER DOG DEHYDRATED TREATS FEATURING ASPHALT STEW IN GUTTER WATER, SET OUT OUR SISSY RENTED COTS (THE KEY IS RED CROSS ABOUT SNAKES), COUNTED STARS. IT RAINED LAST NIGHT AND WE SPENT THE EARLY AM IN THE CAR. SNOWED ON THE PEAKS ABOVE. COLD WINDY NIGHT BUT WE SCORED OK. WE BRAVELY EXPLORED ONE

1892 ⊙ 1893

Duryea builds first gas driven auto in US — Dr. Rudolf Diesel patents engine — Ford road tests his first auto — Tesla develops first AC electric motor — Edison makes movies in West Orange studio — Bell's phone patent expires; small companies move in — First successful heart operation in Chicago — 18 die in Carnegie Steel strike riots — Ellis Island opens as immigration depot — Crow Indian lands open to Montana settlers — Boll Weevil first seen in Texas — George W.G. Ferris invents Ferris Wheel.

Fig. 120
Fig. 121
Fig. 122

CLINTON STREET RAILWAY

MAKE YOUR OWN

Mom's Pie / Apple Book

Did you ever wish you could make a pie that duplicated the sweet tooth memory of good ol' mom's? Here's a way to preserve the family tradition of fine cooking. If you're the cook and your family raves about your manicotti or fresh peach cobbler, give the kids a present for tomorrow. Begin now to write down all the family favorites in one of those hard cover unlined books. You can get them at stationery stores. Prepare one for each child in the family as a "leaving home" present. You could include traditional holiday menus, styles of holiday celebration. Also include any folk remedies that you may practice for making the young ones feel better when they're ailing. If you take the time to write it down now as you think of it, you'll have a wonderful collection by the time the kids are grown. Who knows, maybe they'll follow suit and pass the family kitchen craft on to their kids. You will have started a tradition.

1894 ⊙ 1895

THE FAMILY ARCHIVE

1. CLOSET ARCHIVE: MOST BIG STATIONERY STORES SELL LETTER-SIZE "LIBRARY BOXES" LIKE THESE THAT ARE OPEN AT ONE END AND ARE GOOD FOR STORING DOCUMENTS, SMALL PUBLICATIONS, LETTERS AND PICTURES.
ABOUT $2.00 EA.

—OR—

CORRUGATED CARDBOARD FILE BOXES LIKE THIS ONE DESIGNED FOR STORAGE IN OFFICES. GOOD FOR LARGER ITEMS.
ABOUT $4.00 EA.

—OR—

OTHERWISE COLLECT A BUNCH OF 2 PIECE (TELESCOPING) APPLE CARTONS LIKE THE ONE

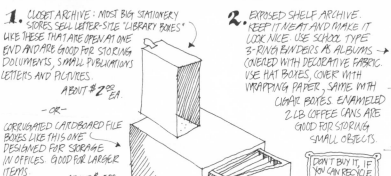

2. EXPOSED SHELF ARCHIVE. KEEP IT NEAT AND MAKE IT LOOK NICE. USE SCHOOL TYPE 3-RING BINDERS AS ALBUMS COVERED WITH DECORATIVE FABRIC. USE HAT BOXES, COVER WITH WRAPPING PAPER, SAME WITH CIGAR BOXES. ENAMELED 2 LB COFFEE CANS ARE GOOD FOR STORING SMALL OBJECTS.

DON'T BUY IT, IF YOU CAN RECYCLE AND REDECORATE IT. LOOK AROUND THE HOUSE FOR IDEAS.

3. THE ARCHIVE-IN-A-TRUNK. OFTEN TO BE FOUND AT LOW PRICES IN 2ND HAND SHOPS, RESTORED, THEY MAKE GOOD STORAGE. SURPLUS STORES ALSO SELL ARMY FOOT LOCKERS YOU CAN REPAINT. USUALLY HAVE LIFT-OUT TRAYS.

The family archive is a special place to keep family treasure like:

★ the boxes of artwork the children did we couldn't bear to throw out

★ anything else we couldn't bear to throw out

★ special occasion heirlooms like great grandma's lace antimacassars and the stove pipe hat no one knows where it came from

★ your mother's college photo album

★ your father's baby book

★ his teddy bear (your teddy bear)

★ your brother's HO gauge Lionel electric train set

SHOWN HERE. THEY ARE STRONG, A GOOD SIZE WILL CLOSE TIGHT, AND THE PRICE IS RIGHT— ABOUT NOTHING EA.

It might be an attic. But that's better reserved for dead storage. The archive should be in a place that has more of a part in your life. Like a closet in the hall. Or a shelf or cabinet in a corner of the living room. And the reason for that is that the archive is something you *use.* Maybe not every day, but every so often. If your family is like ours, you may have to learn how to live with the past, in order to feel its effects. It's pretty hard to get a feel for what's stashed away in the attic under layers of dust.

Resist That Urge To Purge. *The next time you trip over that carton of old clippings, summer camp memorabilia and school pictures—or the family archive comes out of the closet to meet you—don't leap to the conclusion that your accumulated history is getting the upper hand. It might just need a little reorganization.*

If you must thin it out, sit down some rainy afternoon with a calm attitude, and preferably with the other members of your family. Decide what should be kept (and where). If you let the whiskbroom decide what, if any, of the family history is to be saved from oblivion, you'll surely regret it later.

More Door Jamb History

If you've tried diaries and family scrapbooks and the like and none of it works, here's a way to keep track of the daily family history that might be just right for you. The secret of this method is location—we're talking about a way-station, and in order to work it has to be in your traffic pattern. It should be on a wall, or on some small table (like a telephone table), and if your house is anything like ours you'll have to chain a pencil or pen to the wall or table so it will be there when you need it.

The best way to organize this is to post one of those rather large daily calendars where it will be easy to get at and write on. Then use it. Write family notes there. Put telephone messages, shopping lists, appointments, anything you think needs writing down. At the end of the year, along with the social history of your family you'll find other interesting historical stuff, and what's more you may have initiated the habit of recording family history. Save the old calendar and try to expand the effort into something even more ambitious.

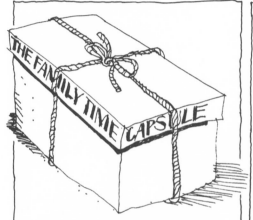

A Fine New Year's Day Project:

Get each member of the clan to choose one item each that represents the year best for them. Then, together, decide on what was the most important family event or events (if you just can't settle on one)—and find something to symbolize that choice. Then get a current photo of the family or each member. Add that to the pile—plus any writing or drawing that seems appropriate— and put it all in a shoebox, seal it and tie with twine. It is not to be opened until next New Year's (or even longer if you can wait). No exceptions, no peeking.

The Family Totem

You won't find one of these in every suburban patio, that's for sure. Making a family totem isn't for everyone, but if you're game, it's great fun and the result is always impressive. Start with a 12 foot long (at least) 4 x 4 post. Put 4 feet of it into the ground, and then start collecting "stuff" for the rest. Anything goes, so it's impossible to make suggestions. The only thing we can recommend is that you allow each family member to select the parts he wants to represent himself. The result is always junk sculpture of the highest order.

If you're timid about exposing your collective genius to neighborhood scrutiny, try the same thing collage-style indoors on a room-high strip of wrapping paper. Use old family photographs, fabric scraps, bits of colored paper, anything you can glue. (PS: try taking your cues from your kids. They'll be a lot less inhibited than you.)

The indoor version makes a nifty gift for art-loving grandparents.

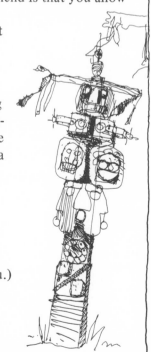

HERE IS A GOOD WAY TO PRESERVE SOME OF THE NATURAL HISTORY OF YOUR BACKYARD. ❀ OR FAVORITE ROADSIDE BOWER. ❀ COLLECT SAMPLES OF WHATEVER BLOOMS IN YOUR GARDEN AND CAN BE PRESSED. IF YOU LIVE IN A CITY AND ARE GREAT AMERICAN BACKYARD, COLLECT ON YOUR SPRING THE COUNTRY. ❀ IS THE BEST TIME WHERE WINTER FIND WILDFLOWERS BEREFT OF THAT TRADITION, THE SOME SAMPLES PILGRIMAGES TO MARCH OR APRIL IN MOST PLACES ❀ LINGERS, YOU'LL AS LATE AS THE END OF MAY. YOU DON'T NEED MANY. COLLECT HALF A DOZEN OF THE NICEST OF EACH KIND OF FLOWER AND PRESS THEM BETWEEN SHEETS OF WAXED PAPER, UNDER WEIGHT. THEN PICK THE BEST PRESSED ONES, ARRANGE ON A PLAIN BACKGROUND, AND FRAME THEM. BE SURE TO WRITE THE DATE ON THE MOUNT BEFORE FRAMING.

❀ ❀❀

1896 ⊙ 1897

Yukon gold discovered — Grover Cleveland invokes Monroe Doctrine in Venezuela — Guiana border fight — Marconi patents "wireless" in Britain — Emil H. Grube first to use X-ray for cancer treatment — Rural Free Delivery established — Utah admitted — Dorothy Dix writes first "advice to lovelorn" column — 75,000 coal miners strike in Pennsylvania, West Virginia, Ohio — Eugene V. Debs forms Social Democratic Party — First Boston subway runs — Book matches become popular — Congress votes $50,000 relief for Americans in Cuban rebellion.

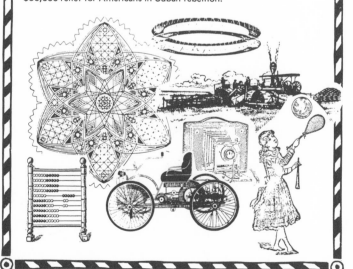

TREE IN THE TRAIL

Tree in the Trail is the name of a delightful book by Holling C. Holling that traces the history of the west through the life of one cottonwood tree. It is a book for kids, but everyone who likes history should read it. We honor Mr Holling by borrowing his title for the name of this idea.

When something very important happens to alter the life of your family, think about commemorating the event by planting a tree. (If you don't have enough yard of your own, try talking the City Park Department into setting aside space in a park for a "people's grove" for this purpose.) There is nothing new about the idea except that it isn't done much any more.

The Shakers, up in Canterbury, New Hampshire, are a celibate religious community. They adopted children. A recent visitor wrote this about their tree planting custom:

". . . On a gently sloping expanse of some of New Hampshire's most beautiful land, they worked, forty abreast—the Shaker men. As they worked, they sang together to maintain the rhythm of their work, the long scythes swinging in unison—forty voices singing joy in their labor. Their song boomed across the fields and must have soared into the summer sky a good long way toward heaven: the Shakers were a gentle, happy people.

"Beyond the haymowers was another line—a twin row of trees, young elms and maples—planted to form a broad avenue from the road back some three hundred feet to the meeting house. It was the Shaker custom that children adopted by the Society were given a young tree to plant and care for. The Shakers cherished the children they took into their midst, and understood that early in his life each child must learn to be responsible for other living things. The trees stand today, firmly rooted in the soil of that New Hampshire hillside. And, though the Shakers are about to become history, this land of magnificent trees will remain to whisper their stories to anyone who pauses long enough to listen."

It's a pretty nice custom.

Recording Your House

Our houses are museums of our work, our things, our lives.

Have you ever looked at a photograph of someone in their home and tried to discover something about them from the objects you can see in the room? It's possible to find out quite a lot. Our homes are the most graphic display of the work we have done, the things we love and the way our families are organized.

Homes are worth recording. Like everything else, they change and can't be brought back. On the next sunny Sunday, with camera in hand, do it. Shoot at least a couple of rolls of film. That many shots will enable you to look at and record every detail . . . even the ones you may think aren't important. Be sure to get the yard, bathroom, kitchen, bedrooms, garage, basement. Whether you make a photo album or slide show, you'll be amazed at how good the old place looks and how valuable that record gets as the years pass.

1898 ⊙ 1899

Spanish-American War: Battleship Maine sunk in Havana — Dewey dumps Spanish fleet in Manila — Marines land at Guantanamo — Toral troops surrender at Santiago — Treaty signed in Paris — Spain gives up Cuba; US acquires Puerto Rico, Guam — Hawaii annexed — Race riots in Georgia, Carolinas — Congress authorizes voting machines in federal elections — John Dewey's "The School & Society" stirs up education — First motor truck collection of mail in Cleveland.

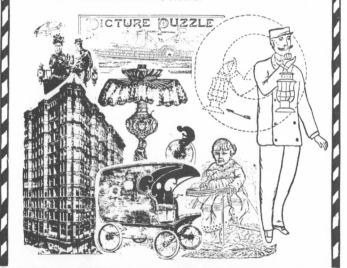

OUR LIVES
MILDRED DEUTSCH
RICHARD DEUTSCH
OUR TREE

PLANTED FOR
LUMA CORTÉZ
BORN JANUARY 10 1973
GROWING STRONG

THIS TREE
IS GROWING IN MEMORY OF
MY GRANDFATHER

THE TREE
OF RICHARD HARRIS
PLANTED ON HIS 13TH BIRTHDAY
A GIFT FROM THE
EARTH

1900 ⊙ 1901

Marconi sends first transatlantic wireless signal — McKinley assassinated — Teddy Roosevelt becomes President — Carry Nation begins anti-saloon hatchet raids — Wright Brothers test full-scale glider — Race riot-fire in New Orleans — Philippine Rebellion ends by proclamation — Commission links mosquito with yellow fever — Spindletop oil strike in Texas — Carnegie sells steel interest, begins life as benefactor — Total US pop. 75,994,575 — 18 million horses and mules, 10 million bicycles, 4 thousand cars.

If You Don't Have a History Group, Start One!
On page 118 is the story of how Bill Herman, high school student, started the Weare Junior Historical Society, an organization which has since published several books on local history and in the process has turned on an entire town.

If Bill Herman can do it, chances are you can too. Any live-wire class or group of concerned and motivated citizens is a splendid nucleus. And don't worry about formalities like rules and officers and minutes and charters and the like. Those things never *make* a group work. They are tools which sometimes (not always) make the management of a group a little more orderly. You'll know when they are needed. What you *will* need is a project. Further on in this section are some suggestions to help you identify the historical resources of your town or neighborhood.

Making A Grand Town Quilt

You may need the help of your local newspaper editor to do this project, because it depends on locating enough workers to do the job.

Ask each worker (or group of workers) to be responsible for one or more "squares" or sections of the quilt. Each will supply the fabric and the design for the section. Sections can be embroidered, appliqued or pieced, or some combination.

All designs should in some way relate to the town, its history and early inhabitants. There should be some preliminary design established so that the finished sections will go together nicely. But the overall layout should be kept simple, so as not to compete with the design of each individual section.

When the section pieces are ready, each group should send delegates to help assemble and quilt the work. The result is almost guaranteed to be a source of great pride in the town and a work of art, and can be displayed in the library, town hall, hospital or other public place where it can be appreciated by all.

Having Dinner on the Town

(Or, How to Make a House Tour That No One Will Forget)

This is an idea to combine two time-honored American traditions: the house tour and the progressive dinner. It might happen in any number of small southern or midwestern towns on a balmy spring or fall evening, the cicadas singing, a smell of freshly cut lawns in the air . . . etc.

It works for a modest sized crowd. But not a big one. And of course it needs the utmost cooperation of the people who own the homes you plan to visit.

Each home is an old one, with some historic significance in the town. At each one, the owner or someone else in your group has provided part of an authentic old-time dinner: a rum or wine punch at the first; appetizers at the second; soup at a third; salad at the fourth; an entre at the fifth; dessert at the sixth; and coffee and sweets at the last. If you have more people and enough houses, you could have two houses offering each course and let people choose.

It's a good way to launch a campaign to awaken interest in history . . . via the stomach. It's also a good fund raiser.

The Annual Photograph

In the days before "pocket" cameras, photography was a science, and the making of a likeness a very special event. Exposures were long (a minute or more) and in some photographic "salons" the apparatus for holding the subject still during the exposure was not unlike medieval torture equipment in appearance. Until the turn of the century, cameras were not available to record daily life. Pictures were taken only rarely—once a year, if then—and kept in a velvet-covered album in the parlor.

The Annual Portrait is still a good idea. If you arrange your family in more or less the same manner each year, and make sure that it is a full-length picture, you will in time have a remarkable graphic recording of the history of your family. Be sure to include the family pets.

Reclamation Act: public domain lands reserved — Wright's lift off from Kitty Hawk — Henry organizes Ford Motor Co. — First transcontinental auto trip: 57 days from San Francisco to NY — Cuban Republic forms; US occupation ends — Panama declares independence; US gains control of canal strip — First transpacific cable: Roosevelt sends round-the-world message — Charles Stiles discovers hookworm — Militia quiets Pennsylvania coal strike trouble — Michigan dumps Stanford in first Rose Bowl — Boston beats Pittsburgh in first World Series — Poultry price: spring chicken, 7 cents lb.

The Gentle Chain

This is one of the nicest family history projects we know about. Like most other good ideas, it's been around a long time, but we don't know very many people these days who try it.

Family chain letters were a device for keeping all the members of large families informed without writing to everyone separately. It was a labor-saving device, actually. And it's time it made its comeback, but for different reasons. Here's our plan for the

Old Glory Circular Album.

Get a plain school-type three ring binder and cover it in a nice fabric—something you can glue easily over the blue cloth that's already on it. (Or, if you've got the time, make your own cover—just so it is of loose-leaf design.) Make up the circulation list, names and addresses, of each member of the family and glue that to the inside cover. Then start.

Each member gets the binder and inserts his own news, pictures, recipes, whatever he thinks will be of interest to others. Then he sends it on to the next member, who adds his news, and so forth. It's important to keep the binder moving—two or three weeks in each household ought to be maximum. When the binder gets full, the pages can be pulled out and bound permanently in book form. The completed book can circulate on a slower cycle, while the new binder makes its rounds.

We've seen one or two of these books and even to an outsider they are beautiful and very interesting. Try it with your family, or friends. It's one of those good old ideas that really works.

MAKING A PHOTO TIMELINE

If you or your children went to schools that provided individual portraits each year, you have a unique bit of historical documentation at your command. Spend some time collecting the ones you have and arrange them in chronological order. Make a photographic timeline for each person. Looking at individual histories this way is remarkable. Aside from looking at them, or startling the subject with his life all laid out in pictures, here are some other things you could do with them.

See how many people in your family can arrange the photographs in the correct chronological sequence. It's not as easy as it sounds. Make an endless magic picture book, like this:

Glue to covers →   Seam glued to extend book →

pictures, one for each year, with anecdotes, drawings, comments.

Or arrange the pictures into a grid and have them framed.

Cave Paintings—or, Graffiti Made Easy

Sometimes what seems least important when it happens becomes the history you remember. There ought to be a place in your life where the vernacular resides. Maybe the basement?

If you have a spare one, designate a wall as the place where it's okay to write and draw. A basement wall of concrete or plaster is perfect. Just a bare light bulb and the wall. That's all you need. Technique should be up to the discretion of the user. Pocket knives, crayons, enamel, anything goes. Let the kids know that's the place they can let off steam. It's a perfect way to air grievances, or make semi-public pronouncements. It has the aura of the illicit—the promise of anonymity, and absolute freedom. That's heady stuff.

We guarantee you, the history in your basement will be some of the richest folklore in your family.

THE TRAVELING TALKING MACHINE

This is a space-age variation on the family chain letter. Using audio tape cassettes instead of paper. Although tape has some of the same characteristics as telephone conversations (listen, but don't look), it is less expensive over long distances and you can play it back as many times as you like. Most machines are designed so as to record only one half of the tape in each direction. This is handy for simple two-party exchanges. If you are corresponding with your brother in Memphis, for instance, you can use Side A each time, and he Side B until the tape is used up.

1904 ⊙ 1905

Panama Canal Commission established — Gorgas begins yellow fever study; 400 die as disease hits New Orleans again — IWW forms in Chicago — First all concrete building: Wright's Unity Temple in Chicago — Cellist Pablo Casals makes US debut — Travel Time: New York to Chicago via Pennsylvania RR: 18 hours — Registered autos in US: 77,988 — New York speed limit: 10 mph — Subway opens in Manhattan — Famous lost words: "Sensible and Responsible women do not want to vote." Grover Cleveland — Football legalizes the forward pass.

His Master's Voice

If you already have a tape recorder in the family, give some thought to setting up a family history that you listen to. Tape is a versatile and relatively inexpensive way to store information. What's more, it's possible to record the important events as they happen, which is sometimes an important advantage.

The biggest problem with tape is getting too much of it. If you aren't selective enough, you'll build up an unwieldy collection of reels or cassettes and there will be great temptation (usually irresistible) to erase and record over them when you run short of blank tape. You can avoid that problem by keeping history tapes in a special place, carefully marked, and by recording selectively in the first place.

Somewhere in our family, there is a scratchy old recording (disc) of my sister singing her first song, "Mother's Making Gingerbread," coached along by my father. It would never make the hit parade, but it's a treasure

You might think about organizing your tape library so that you have one set of cassettes for each child, or all the children, one set for family celebrations and another for miscellaneous events.

Aug. 1874

The Family Reunion

In rural parts, where there are families that have not been pulled apart by migrations, or distracted by the complications of urban life, there is still quite a bit of the fabric of the old-time family life still intact. The people in rural Texas and Ohio know what we're talking about. Family gatherings are still pretty large and the people can still be counted on to come a fair distance to be there simply because it's worth the trip.

The rest of us are going to have to learn all over again what a family reunion can be like. It's been that long. And the best way to find out about family reunions is to have one. Our idea for the family reunion is that it be an excuse to delve into the family history with a vengeance, and to make a little history while you're at it.

Our plan calls for a weekend reunion, to take place at some location which has historic significance to the family. It could be an old homestead, the town your grandfather came from, etc. The reunion we have in mind takes place in a camptown—in a state or county park with camping facilities. Everyone brings a tent, all the kids and the makings for an old time family dinner on Saturday night. Saturday is spent getting re-acquainted. There would be contests and games in the afternoon for the kids. A tug-of-war. A watermelon eating contest. Sack races. And, of course, the old timers softball game. Saturday night is the big family dinner. Everyone has brought a family recipe to trade, along with old family photos and the accompanying stories.

Somewhere along the line, the Grand Family Photograph is taken, and perhaps there is music, or skits, or dancing, or all three. And before you know it, a bit of history is alive right before your eyes.

Once Upon A Christmas

If you have begun to chafe at the cost and hypocrisy of Christmas, here is an idea that will help restore Christmas to its proper place in your life and also give you a taste of the past.

Make a pact in your family that the Christmas celebration will be entirely handmade next year. That means Christmas cards, decorations, gifts and all of the other necessities, even to the firewood in the fireplace you gather and split by hand, and the decorations on the tree.

One word of caution: it's even more work than it sounds like, and it can become a first-class nightmare if you **don't** plan it pretty carefully. If you wait until the last minute, you won't enjoy it.

Here are a few suggestions to consider. But a trip to the library will supply you with a lot of ideas for other ingredients.

The Big Baby Book

Another custom that seems to have fallen on hard times is the Baby Book. Time was, when every new mother got a pink and blue volume with Gerber-faced drawings of cherubim adorning the pages, the titles of which were things like "baby's first bath," "baby's first step" and so forth.

Those books were nice, but they seldom had space for very much past one or two years, which is too bad because that's about the time things get interesting.

Here is another use for the little blank book (those hardcover books with unlined pages that stationers have, and that are good for a million uses). Do one book for each child. And don't stop at age two. You can include all the "firsts" that you want, but leave room for quotes, pictures, snapshots and other mementos. When you fill up volume one, go on to volume two. You may get complaints as years go by, but there will come a time when those books will be like solid gold. (Us family historians have to take the long view. Don't watch the clock!)

A Family Affair

There are traditions in every family. If you think there aren't any in yours, it's probably because you call them something else & don't think of them as traditions. And that's easy to remedy. Sometime when you don't have anything better to do, sit down with a note pad & write down anything you think could be called a tradition. If your parents are around, get them to contribute to the list. If the list doesn't satisfy you, think about starting a tradition or two. That's a little hard to do, but it's worth a try. Traditions are normally things that happen on some cycle because they are important. And they usually evolve around an already-established event. So if you think about inventing traditions, begin with holidays or other important family anniversaries.

The Family Museum

This is a variation on a couple of suggestions made elsewhere in this section. It is based on the idea that family artifacts, regardless of any negotiable value outside the family, have enormous symbolic value to family members. This value is only realized, however, if the meaning of the article in question is understood.

The nicest family treasures usually have stories attached. That is what makes them valuable. Take the time to identify the treasures in your household. Write the stories down somewhere where they won't get lost.

This is the teapot that Nancy Burrows brought with her when the family came by wagon from New Hampshire to Kansas in 1832. It is English china and it was old then. Nancy had gotten it from her great grandmother Claire. She was so afraid that it would break on the trip that she carried it on her lap the whole way. It is said that President Zachary Taylor had a cup of tea made in this pot when he passed through Salina.

Not everyone will be able to boast that the family teapot once made tea that touched the lips of a President. But there will be other stories just as interesting. Make the identification of your family treasures, and the setting down of their stories, a family project. And don't forget to add your own contemporary artifacts when you think they have significance. After all, heirlooms are being created every day.

Keep the treasures in a safe place, but not so safe that you can't haul them all out once in a while or put them on display on some special family occasion.

Presents From the Past

If you want to begin nibbling at history without turning your routine upside down, here is one nice idea we've heard about. All it requires is an agreement in the family about giving birthday, anniversary or other gifts. Decide that you will give only old or old-time gifts. That doesn't mean expensive antiques or nonsense joke gifts from the second hand store either. It could mean passing on a family treasure. It could mean some article of folk art. If you know a book lover, scour the used book stores for the most interesting old editions you can find. The same with old costume jewelry. Or clothing. Don't be apologetic about doing your gift shopping at the flea market.

1906 ⊙ 1907

Lusitania arrives in NY on maiden voyage — Currency Panic of 1907 — Standard Oil of Indiana, railroads nabbed in freight rebate fraud — Sinclair's "The Jungle" exposes meat packers — Pure Food & Drug Act passed — DeForest perfects vacuum radio tube — Race riots in Georgia, Texas — Oklahoma admitted — Earthquakes shatter San Francisco, Formosa — Roosevelt appoints Inland Waterways Commission, establishes first national monument — Michelson first US winner of Nobel Prize.

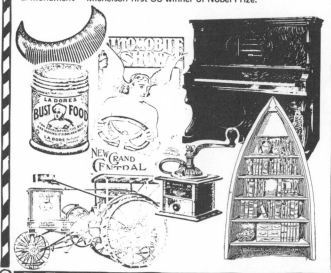

Dates of Births and Deaths in the Family

The basic material from which all family histories are made is the information relating to critical family events: births, deaths, weddings. In the old days, this information was considered to be of such great import that it was recorded in the Family Bible, the safest and most sacred spot in the household. The Family Bible tradition has faded but there remains a need to keep a record of family events in a safe place. One of the most rewarding projects you can undertake is that of reviving the Family Bible. The essence of this project is to update, reconstruct, initiate or maintain a record of family events. The Bible may no longer be the ideal form for the record but its substitute should have similar qualities; should be a permanent and respected part of the household and easily accessible. Here are some steps you could take to establish the record:

Try to locate the real Family Bible. Fill in any missing information.

Start a new record with names and dates you know or can find out.

Keep the record current.

1908 ◦ 1909

Ford introduces mass-produced Model-T for $850 — First modern skyscraper: 47-story Singer Building in NY — NAACP forms after race riot in Springfield, Ill. — "Gentlemen's Agreement" restricts Japanese immigration — Matthew Henson, Admiral Peary first to reach North Pole — President Taft conserves 3 million acres — Idaho, Montana, Washington open 700,000 acres to settlement — First cartoon: Gertie the Dinosaur by Winsor McCay — NY law: no smoking by women in public.

We Are All *Licensed Historians*

Institutions spend a lot of time recording history for us in accurate and sometimes beautiful ways. The number of certificates, licenses, permits, awards and diplomas one receives in a lifetime is an incredible record of our activities. The problem is that only the very special ones are thought important enough to save. As we learn more about history we come to understand that the diploma from Sunday school is as valuable as the college sheepskin.

Keep them all, frame them, put them on a wall.

No matter where you live or how old the building is, your home is a vital part of your history. Knowing something of its history will make living in it a more whole experience. On the other hand, living in a place while knowing nothing of its past is a nagging reminder of the speed with which our knowledge of our heritage fades. Take heart if the history of your house seems dim. There are plenty of clues which will help you brighten it.

It only takes some detective work to find them and fit them into a picture of the past. Part of the fascination in this search is the discovery of sources for clues. The more you look, the more you find. Here are a few places to start looking.

Your house is the primary document. *Look for inscriptions and dates placed on it by the builder, or on building materials or hardware—ash bin doors, furnaces, inside cabinets are likely places. Sometimes there is a dated note inside the porcelain toilet tank if it is the original fixture. Look for names or dates written on the walls or on the paving. Look for anything which seems to be original to the house and could be dated. If you own the house, reading your deed and all the papers you have can be a help.*

Ask neighbors. *Although you must take this kind of resource with a grain of salt, it can be very useful. Positive statements like "I was thirteen when they built your house in my father's apple orchard" are most useful. Statements prefaced with "I think" or "As I recall" and the like are less useful but can give leads.*

Libraries. *Libraries often have documents concerning town growth, subdivision, maps, guide books, bird's-eye views and old photographs. All are potentially helpful.*

Title companies *have records of all transactions involving the changes in ownership of the property. This can be a very valuable source of information but could also be expensive, since they are profit-oriented enterprises.*

Utilities. *Most utilities have records which show the date service was hooked up in your house.*

City Hall *has a wealth of information. Everything—building permits to tax records—is kept there. A trip to a friendly city clerk will be time well spent.*

It's easier to keep it than to rediscover it!

Once you have the history, make a final effort to keep it. The man who built my house wrote all the vital statistics on a shingle, varnished it and nailed it above the basement door. I love him for doing that!

★★★★★★★★★
PARTY TIME
★★★★★★★★★

Parties that celebrate birthdays and anniversaries always seem to be good ones. Problem is the anniversaries we usually celebrate don't always occur when we want to have a party. Here's your chance to introduce a little history into the affair. It will give you some direct knowledge of an event in history and it could turn some party-goers on to the history idea. For instance . . . Give a party celebrating the anniversary of moving into your house; have packing boxes around and borrow dishes to eat from; invite the people who helped you move. Celebrate the anniversary of the local power and light company; turn off the electricity at 8:30 pm. (A candle-light party is great fun.) Celebrate the election of your town's first Mayor. (Could be a costume party.) Great grandfather's birthday party—serve food they would have had. Picnic in the park on its founding day. It would be easy to come up with 360 more.

1910 ◎ 1911

Supreme Court dissolves Standard Oil, American Tobacco — Teddy Roosevelt outlines Square Deal, new nationalism — Mann Elkins Act regulates telegraph, phone and cable companies — Radios required for passenger liners in US ports — C.P. Rodgers makes first transcontinental flight; time in air: 82 hours, 4 minutes — $30 million crop damage in Midwest cold spell — Halley's comet scares earthlings — Combine, air conditioner, auto self-starter invented — Boy Scouts organized — Total US pop. 91,972,266; 4 percent college graduates.

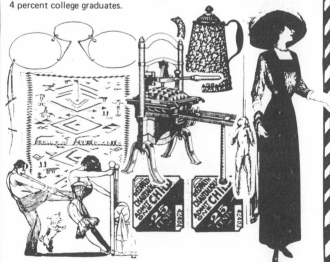

Events flash by and their image is gone. If they are not recorded while they happen, there is no way to reconstruct them. Most of us would like to save those images, but for some reason find it difficult to initiate the process. Here are a few excuses for becoming the historical documentor of events without becoming a historic pest in the process.

1. A gift of wedding pictures and/or tape recordings of the event will be more treasured than a chrome-plated egg cooker. It's a good excuse at birthdays and anniversaries, too.

2. Make a historic photograph. Any gathering of people with common interests or a common purpose qualifies as a historic event. Bill it as such and photograph the group. A copy for everyone is a good idea.

3. One of the best wedding presents I have ever given was an antique picture frame small enough to accommodate a Polaroid photograph. Immediately after the ceremony I had the father of the bride photograph the couple with his Polaroid camera (someone always has one, but if you don't trust people you could bring your own). In sixty seconds I slipped the photo into the frame and handed it to the newlyweds.

4. What's your excuse?

EDNA

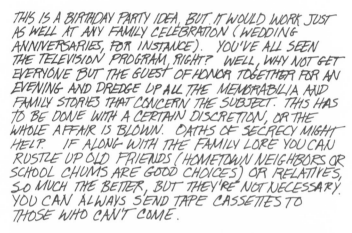

THIS IS A BIRTHDAY PARTY IDEA, BUT IT WOULD WORK JUST AS WELL AT ANY FAMILY CELEBRATION (WEDDING ANNIVERSARIES, FOR INSTANCE). YOU'VE ALL SEEN THE TELEVISION PROGRAM, RIGHT? WELL, WHY NOT GET EVERYONE BUT THE GUEST OF HONOR TOGETHER FOR AN EVENING AND DREDGE UP ALL THE MEMORABILIA AND FAMILY STORIES THAT CONCERN THE SUBJECT. THIS HAS TO BE DONE WITH A CERTAIN DISCRETION, OR THE WHOLE AFFAIR IS BLOWN. OATHS OF SECRECY MIGHT HELP. IF ALONG WITH THE FAMILY LORE YOU CAN RUSTLE UP OLD FRIENDS (HOMETOWN NEIGHBORS OR SCHOOL CHUMS ARE GOOD CHOICES) OR RELATIVES, SO MUCH THE BETTER, BUT THEY'RE NOT NECESSARY. YOU CAN ALWAYS SEND TAPE CASSETTES TO THOSE WHO CAN'T COME.

 THERE MIGHT BE A MASTER OF CEREMONIES, AND EACH MEMBER OF THE GROUP COULD HOLD FORTH WITH HIS OWN STORIES FROM THE PAST. IT WOULD ALSO BE PRETTY IMPRESSIVE IF SOMEONE MADE UP A COMMEMORATIVE PLAQUE, OR KEEPSAKE BOOK, OR SOME SUCH DEVICE IN WHICH THE STORIES, PICTURES, ETC., WERE ASSEMBLED.

TINY TEN PINS

THE "PINS" ARE MADE FROM LITTLE MATCHBOXES THAT YOU COVER WITH PAPER (OR PAINT) AND DECORATE WITH FACES OR NUMBERS. THE BALL IS A MEDIUM SIZED MARBLE. MAKE A NEAT BOX TO KEEP ALL THE PARTS IN, AND YOU'LL HAVE A FINE GIFT TO GIVE TO SOME SMALL BOWLER.

QUOITS (OR RING-TOSS)

MAKE A STAND BY GLUEING TWO BOXES TOGETHER LIKE THIS. CUT A HOLE IN THE TOP FOR THE PAPER TOWEL WHICH SHOULD ALSO BE GLUED INTO PLACE. FOR CORE POST, ONE FOR CORE POST, BE GLUED THE QUOITS YARN OR BRAID HEAVY RAFFIA OR TWINE, LOOP, TIE AND VARNISH.

THE GAME OF ROLY-POLY (OR, BEADS-GO-HOME)

A SET OF THREE BOX-LIDS AND SOME SMALL, FAT BEADS ARE ALL THE INGREDIENTS YOU'LL NEED FOR THIS FINE GAME OF SKILL. THE OBJECT IS TO GET ALL THE BEADS (3, 4, OR 5) TO THE HOME IN THE CENTER BOX. TRY IT.

THE FEATHER-BLOW GAME

TRY TO BLOW THE FEATHER INTO THE TARGET (ARROW). MAKE THE TARGET FROM A SHALLOW BOX LID, CUT A SIX INCH DIAMETER HOLE TO MAKE THE TARGET, MOUNT ON A LARGE BOX FOR A BASE. BE SURE YOUR FEATHER IS A DOWNY ONE.

Some Old Fashioned GAMES YOU CAN MAKE

from household odds and ends

THE ANIMATED SERPENT

DRAW THIS COILED BEAUTY ON STIFF (NOT THICK) CARDBOARD, LIKE BRISTOL BOARD, THEN CUT HIM OUT, TIE A THREAD THROUGH HIS TAIL, PAINT HIM UP AND HANG HIM IN A BREEZE.

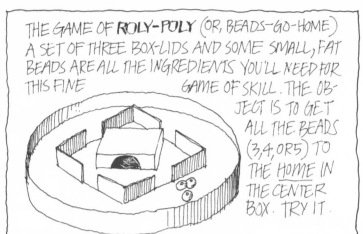

1912 ⊙ 1913

Titanic sinks — Roosevelt leaves Republican Party, forms Bull Moose — Income tax, direct election of Senators legalized — Parcel Post begins — Federal Reserve System set up — New Mexico, Arizona admitted: last of the contiguous states — Capt. Scott reaches South Pole — Overseas RR to Key West finished — Ford sets up first assembly line — A.H. Goss invents refrigerator — 150,000 garment workers walk out.

THE WATER-CUTTER

IS MADE BY CUTTING A ROUND OF TIN OR STIFF CARDBOARD, THEN NOTCHING TO MAKE "TEETH." BORE 2 SMALL HOLES FOR THE STRING, TIE ENDS AND ROTATE THE CUTTER TO TWIST THE STRING. PULL TAUT, THE CUTTER WILL SPIN BACK & FORTH. TRY PAINTING DESIGNS ON IT TOO.

THE SKIPJACK

MOST OF US WILL RECOGNIZE THE SIMPLE TOY AS BEING CONSTRUCTED FROM THE WISHBONE. IN THE DAYS WHEN IT WAS POPULAR THE TOY WAS MADE FROM THE BONE OF A GOOSE CALLED A MERRYTHOUGHT. WIND A LITTLE STICK THROUGH A RUBBER BAND AND TWIST UNTIL TIGHT. PUT A DAB OF BEESWAX ON THE END OF THE STICK. WATCH IT JUMP!

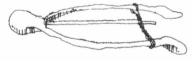

PICKUP TWIGS

JUST LIKE THE GAME YOU PAY MONEY FOR, EXCEPT YOU MAKE IT YOURSELF. STRIP THE BARK OFF SOME DRY HARDWOOD TWIGS, SAND & MAKE A "PICKER" FROM ONE AND A BENT PIN. MAKE A NICE BOX FOR THE SET TOO.

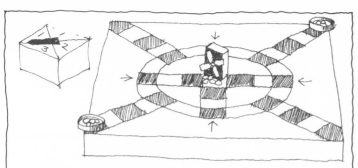

GOING TO THE MILL IS PLAYED WITH WHITE BEANS (SACKS OF FLOUR) A MATCH BOX MILL, A GAME BOARD DIVIDED AND DECORATED, AND A SPINNER. SPINNER TELLS HOW MANY SPACES A PLAYER MAY MOVE. EACH MUST GO ONCE AROUND THE CIRCLE AND MAY ENTER ONLY WHEN THEY LAND AT THE END OF A MOVE AT AN ENTRANCE SPACE (ARROWS). THEN IN FOR A BEAN AND HOME AGAIN, THEN BACK FOR MORE UNTIL THE BEANS ARE GONE. IT'S OK TO OVERTAKE A PLAYER AND TAKE AWAY HIS SACK, BUT WATCH OUT, HE CAN DO THE SAME! PLAYER WITH THE MOST SACKS WINS THE GAME.

1914 ⊙ 1915

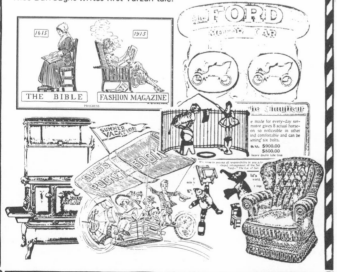

World War I begins in Europe — US claims neutrality — Lusitania sunk by German sub; US protests — Panama Canal opens — Ford produces millionth auto — First taxis into service — First transcontinental call: Bell in NY to Watson in SF — KKK incorporates under Georgia charter — D.W. Griffith's controversial "Birth of a Nation" released — Ty Cobb steals 96 bases — ASCAP organizes in NY — In vogue: the waltz, two-step — Edgar Rice Burroughs writes first Tarzan tale.

THE GAME OF **TRIPLE TIDDLEDY** - OR BUTTON-IN-THE-BOX. MAKE THIS GAME FROM 3 SMALL BOX LIDS AND SOME BUTTONS. SCORE 1 FOR EACH BUTTON IN THE OUTER BOX, 3 FOR EACH IN THE MIDDLE AND 5 FOR THE ONE IN THE CENTER. PAINT THE BOXES BRIGHT COLORS.

THREE-IN-A-ROW IS PLAYED WITH RED AND WHITE BEANS ON A BOX LID THAT HAS BEEN DIVIDED LIKE THIS AND PAINTED AND VARNISHED. OBJECT OF THE GAME IS FOR EACH PLAYER, IN TURN TO TRY TO KEEP HIS OPPONENT FROM PLACING 3 BEANS IN A ROW. FIRST TO SUCCEED, WINS THE GAME.

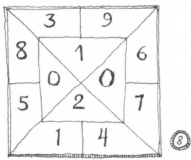

STAND TWO FEET FROM A BOX LID DIVIDED LIKE THIS. TOSS THE BUTTON TO MAKE A HISTORICAL YEAR (1776) EACH PLAYER TOSSES UNTIL HE HAS A YEAR FOR WHICH HE CAN MAKE AN ACCURATE HISTORICAL STATEMENT. FIRST PLAYER TO GET 3 SUCH YEARS WINS THE GAME.

THE BLOW RACE IS PLAYED ON A TABLE TOP WITH "RUNNERS" CUT FROM POSTCARDS. OPPONENTS AT EACH END OF THE TABLE TRY TO CROSS THE FINISH LINE AT THE OPPOSITE END BY BLOWING, BUT NOT SO HARD AS TO TIP THE MEN OVER. A FINE GAME FOR KIDS OF ALL AGES.

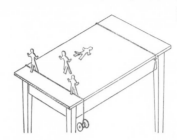

Time was when entertainment was made by hand rather than delivered on a screen. For those who would like a taste of those good old days, we offer on these two pages and the next some authentic turn-of-the-century games, toys and parlor pastimes you can try in your own family. (The games make nifty gifts for Christmas.)

THE FISHING GAME. MAKE A POLE FROM ANY LIGHT STICK, STRING AND BENT PIN. FOLD THE FISH FROM PAPER ABOUT 5 X 7 INCHES. PUT THE FISH IN A BOX ON THE FLOOR. FISHERMAN STANDS ON A STEPLADDER. COLOR THE FISH OR ASSIGN THEM VALUES TO ALTER THE GAME. PLAYERS TAKE TURNS. THE ONE WITH THE MOST FISH WINS THE GAME.

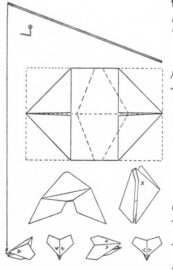

PARLOR PASTIMES

Acting Proverbs

In this game each player may take a part, or if thought preferable, the company may divide themselves into actors and spectators. The actors then fix upon a proverb which is to be represented by every one of them individually. There is to be no connection between them in any way. Each one in turn has simply to act before the rest of the company the proverb he has selected. A player might, for instance, come into the room rolling a ball, a footstool, or anything else that would do to represent a stone. After rolling it about for some time he takes it up and examines it with astonishment, as if something were wanting that he expected to find on it, making it, perhaps, too plainly evident to the company that the proverb he is aiming to depict is the familiar one of "A rolling stone gathers no moss." If really good acting be thrown into this game, it may be made exceedingly interesting.

Blowing Out the Candle

No end of merriment has frequently been created by this simple, innocent game. It is equally interesting to old people and to little children, for in many cases those who have prided themselves on the accuracy of their calculating powers and the clearness of their mental vision have found themselves utterly defeated in it. A lighted candle must be placed on a small table at one end of the room, with plenty of walking space left clear in front of it. One of the company is invited to blow out the flame blindfold. Should any one volunteer, he is placed exactly in front of the candle, while the bandage is being fastened on his eyes, and told to take three steps back, turn round three steps, then take three steps forward and blow out the light. No directions could sound more simple. The opinion that there is nothing in it has often been expressed by those who have never seen the thing done. Not many people, however, are able to manage it—the reason why, you young people will soon find out.

Hiss and Clap

In this game, the gentlemen are all requested to leave the room, when the ladies take their seats leaving a vacant place on the right side of every one for the gentleman of her choice. Each gentleman in turn is then summoned, and asked to guess which lady he imagines has chosen him for her partner. Should he guess rightly he is allowed to take his seat by the lady who has chosen him, while the company loudly clap hands, in proof of their congratulations on his success; but should he guess wrongly, he will be only too glad to disappear from the scene, so loud will be the hisses of his friends.

The Comic Concert

In this performance the company for the time imagine themselves to be a band of musicians. The leader of the band is supposed to furnish each of the performers with a different musical instrument. Consequently, a violin, a harp, a flute, an accordion, a piano, a jew's-harp, and anything else that would add to the noise, are all to be performed upon at the same time. Provided with an instrument of some description himself, the leader begins playing a tune on his imaginary violincello, or whatever else it may be, imitating the real sound as well as he can both in action and voice. The others all do the same, the sight presented being, as well may be imagined, exceedingly ludicrous, and the noise almost deafening. In the midst of it, the leader quite unexpectedly stops playing, and makes an entire change in his attitude and tone of voice, substituting for his own instrument one belonging to someone else. As soon as he does this, the performer who has been thus unceremoniously deprived of his instrument takes that of his leader, and performs on it instead. Thus the game is continued, every one being expected to carefully watch the leader's actions, and to be prepared at any time for making a sudden change.

Dumb Crambo

After dividing the company into two equal parts, one half leaves the room; in their absence the remaining players fix upon a verb, to be guessed by those who have gone out when they return. As soon as the word is chosen, those outside the room are told with what word it rhymes. A consultation ensues, when the absent ones come in and silently act the word they think may be the right one. Supposing the verb thought of should have rhymed with Sell, the others might come in and begin felling imaginary trees with imaginary hatchets, but on no account uttering a single syllable. If Fell were the right word, the spectators, on perceiving what the actors were attempting to do, would clap their hands, as a signal that the word had been discovered. But if Tell or any other word had been thought of, the spectators would begin to hiss loudly, which the actors would know indicated that they were wrong, and that nothing remained for them but to try again. The rule is that, while the acting is going on, the spectators as well as the actors should be speechless. Should any one make a remark, or even utter a single syllable, a forfeit must be paid.

Shouting Proverbs

A game that is much more speedily despatched, and much more boisterous than the ordinary game of Proverbs, is this one. A proverb having been selected, one word of it is given to each of the company, which he must shout clearly and distinctly when told. The person to whom the proverb is unknown then stands as near the company as they will permit him, while he says the words "Charge! Present! Fire!" As soon as he utters the word "Fire!" the party all shout their words together, and from this confusion of sounds he is expected to guess the proverb. Generally the shouting has to be repeated many times before the proverb can be detected.

"Jack's Alive"

No one at all inclined to be slow in their movements need offer to take part in the game of "Jack's Alive," for quickness and promptitude of action are indispensable to its success. A piece of paper, or, better still, a long piece of firewood, is put into the fire until it is in a blazing condition when taken out. The first player, blowing out the flame, passes it to his neighbor, saying, "Jack's alive." It is then passed on to the next, and to all the company in succession, each one trying to get rid of it before the spark has died out. Every one to whom it is offered must take it immediately the words "Jack's alive" are uttered, or a forfeit must be paid; and the one in whose hands Jack really expires must produce a forfeit. In some cases boys have actually been known, when playing at this game, to improve each other's appearance by marking black moustaches and eyebrows, &c.; but as such proceedings have nothing whatever to do with the real "Jack's Alive," we feel sure that none of our readers will ever practice this foolish habit.

"Our Old Grannie Doesn't Like Tea"

After being seated in order, the first player announces that "Our old Grannie doesn't like Tea." The person sitting next inquires what it is the old lady likes in preference, the answer to the question, if right, will name some article in which the letter T does not occur. For instance, if Grannie can't eat potatoes, or carrots, or vegetables, she may still be passionately fond of peas and beans and cauliflowers. Coffee and cocoa, too, she is able to drink, although tea has the effect of giving her indigestion and making her frightfully ill.

Retsch's Outlines

By those at all skilled artistically great fun may be extracted in the following manner: Each person must be provided with a piece of paper and a pencil. Upon every paper the owner then scribbles a crooked or straight line of any description and passes it on to the right-hand neighbor. All are then expected to make the line on their paper the foundation for a little picture of some kind; and although very often the results are exceedingly absurd, it is possible on the other hand for pretty little sketches to be thus produced. The original outline must be drawn very thickly to distinguish it from the rest of the figure.

Think of a Number

Tell your neighbour to think of any number he likes, but not to tell you what it is. Tell him then to double it; when he has done that, let him add an even number to it, which you yourself must give him; after doing this he must halve the whole, then from what is left take away the number he first thought of. When he shall arrive so far, if his calculations have all been made correctly, you will be able to give him the exact remainder, which will simply be the half of the even number you told him to add to his own.

Forfeits

As an evening spent in playing round games would be thought incomplete if at the end of it the forfeits were not redeemed, so our book of amusements would be sadly lacking in interest if a list of forfeits were not provided. Indeed, many young people think that the forfeits are greater fun than the games themselves, and that the best part of the evening begins when forfeit time arrives. Still, although we will give a list of forfeits, it is by no means necessary that in the crying of them none but certain prescribed ones should be used. The person deputed to pronounce judgment on those of his friends who have had to pay the forfeits may either invent something on the spur of the moment, or make use of what he has seen in a book, or may have stored in his memory. Originality in such cases often is the best, simply because the sentence is made to suit, or rather *not to suit*, the victim; and the object of course of all these forfeit penances is to make the performers of them look absurd. For those players, however, who in preference to anything new still feel inclined to adopt the well-known good old-fashioned forfeits, we will supply a list of as many as will meet ordinary requirements.

1. *Kiss the lady you love best without anyone knowing it.* To do this the gentleman must of course kiss all the ladies present, the one he most admires taking her turn among the rest.

2. *Lie down your full length on the floor, and rise with your arms folded the whole time.*

3. *Take one of your friends upstairs, and bring him down upon a feather.* Any one acquainted with this forfeit is sure to choose the stoutest person in the room as his companion to the higher regions. On returning to the room the redeemer of the forfeit will be provided with a soft feather, covered with down, which he will formally present to his stout companion, obeying, therefore, the command to bring him down upon a feather.

4. *Kiss a book inside and outside without opening it.* This is done by first kissing the book in the room, then taking it outside and kissing it there.

5. *Laugh in one corner of the room, sing in another, cry in another, and dance in another.*

6. *Leave the room with two legs, and return with six.* To do this you must go out of the room, and come back bringing a chair with you.

7. *Put four chairs in a row, take off your boots, and jump over them.* This task would no doubt appear rather formidable for a young lady to perform, until she is made to understand that it is not the chairs, but the boots, she is expected to jump over.

8. *The German band.* In this charming little musical entertainment, three or four of the company can at the same time redeem their forfeits. An imaginary musical instrument is given to each one—they themselves must have no choice in the matter—and upon these instruments they must perform as best they can.

9. *Ask a question, the answer to which cannot possibly be answered in the negative.* The question, of course, is "What does y-e-s spell?"

The Anybody Can Make One, Educational and Entertaining, Homemade,

TIME MACHINE

Living in the Past and Loving It

The idea is that if one desires to have a feel for the history of his environment, it would seem logical to create an environment in which history could be felt. What did it feel like when there were no electric lights in your house? What did it feel like to spend a month of evenings at home with no TV or radio? What did it feel like to make butter? The time machine isn't hard to make, and it need only take us back a few years before we reach a place beyond memory. If you do your homework (a little research) you can build a Time Machine that will spark the imagination of all passengers. (If you're going to take a trip into the past, it's more fun to travel in groups.)

The principle of the Time Machine design is to look for the things that have caused changes in the way we live, then think of ways to eliminate some of those things for a short time. An

example—most of us have been forced on a simulated trip into history by a sudden power black-out: the hurried search for candles, then the dark melting into a soft warm orange light and the silence. All the motors and compressors are quiet, even electric time stands still. People talk more quietly. When the bulbs and tubes and motors surge back to life, the event is received with mixed feelings. Here are some simulations which can be a little more planned. Remember to involve as many people as you can in your time travel plans.*

Turn off the electricity for an evening. If you are having a dinner party at the time, so much the better.

If you can't bring yourself to turn the power off, replace *all* the light bulbs with 15 watters (only a little brighter than the old Mazdas). (Later you may not want to put some of those big bulbs back in.)

Unplug all TV's, radios and record machines, and other appliances, for a week.

Plan your life so that you won't use a car for a week.

Fight a cold the way they used to (honey, vinegar and tea).

Beat the heat the way they used to.

Beat the cold the way they used to.

Celebrate grandmother's birthday like she did when she was a kid.

Play croquet.

Make something you need instead of buying it. Make it out of what you can find around the house.

Buy fruit by the lug and spend a weekend making jam or canning.

Make bread, four loaves at a time.

Make cheese.

Make pickles.

Make sausage.

Grow popcorn—have a popcorn party.

Kids can build time machines too. Here are some more:

A class can make butter by putting heavy cream in a jar; give each kid a turn at shaking it.

Smoke corn silk.

Put on a Marble Tournament.

Read a book your grandfather loved. (Mine read *Penrod and Sam* twice a year.)

Next time, take a train, if there still is one.

Invent your own. You can think of better ones, and there are plenty.

1916 ◎ 1917

US enters the war — Wilson cuts German relations — Merchant ships armed — USS Algonquin, Memphis, Illinois, Vigilancia, Healdton sunk — Selective Service conscription OKd — US troops to France — US-Canada sign migratory bird treaty — National Park Service established — NY code allows unlimited heights for setback skyscrapers — Federal Farm Loan Act goes into effect — Race riots in E. St. Louis, Houston.

1918 ◎ 1919

US takes Belleau Wood — Selective Service ruled constitutional — Battles of Marne — Turning point: German line repulsed to Vesle — Battle of Meuse-Argonne — German Chancellor seeks peace — Austrians surrender — Kaiser Wilhelm II abdicated — Germans surrender — Charles Strite invents automatic toaster — Daylight Savings Time approved — Joyce's "Ulysses" banned and burned — Railway Express formed — First air mail delivered — Prohibition ratified — 26 race riots in one summer — Margaret B. Owen sets typing record: 170 wpm, no errors.

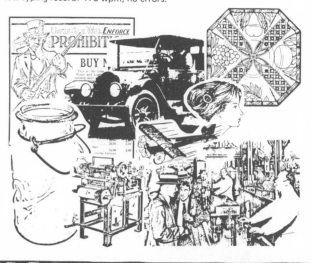

This picture is the result of still another time machine. It is a daguerrotype taken last year in the salon of a photographer in Columbia, California, who has restored the old process to use, and along with it the costumes of the period.

Hunting for History

Odd but true—the physical history of your town or neighborhood is harder for you to see than it would be for someone from out of town. Familiarity breeds contempt. It also makes things invisible.

The all-time classic invisible treasure story is that of the old Schwamb Mill in Arlington, Massachusetts. It had been there since the middle 1800's, and most long-time residents "knew" of it. But it wasn't until a serious effort was made to inventory the town's environmental assets that the Mill was "discovered." And then it was only because the searchers radically changed their point of view. Instead of driving around in cars, they walked. And instead of walking down the sidewalk, they put on hip boots and waded down the town's creek. They experienced the town's backside, so to speak, and if they hadn't been looking from a new point of view, the last manufactory of Victorian picture frames in America might now be an apartment house site. The ironic part of it is that the mill is only half a block off Massachusetts Avenue, one of the town's main streets.

The moral of that story is: if what you're looking at is invisible, it doesn't matter how close you are to it. The trick is to learn how to switch your eyes over.

Even after the Schwamb Mill was found, most people in the town thought it was a pile of junk and eminently deserving of destruction. Patricia Fitzmaurice and her partners in the effort to save it were considered crazy by most of the people in town who were in a position to do something. It was only because people from out of town who knew better (Richard Candee from Sturbridge Village, for example) spoke up that Mrs Fitzmaurice was finally able to raise the money (also from out of town) to save the old relic.

So, you readers who would run out and try to save the local history—watch out. You're not only blind, you're probably crazy too. (But don't let that stop you!)

Whether you plan to make historic preservation your personal mission or not, history hunting is a wonderful way to spend some of your spare time.

The Old Building Collector

Consider being an old building collector. Get in the car some weekend with a good road map, a notebook and, if possible, a camera. Route yourself away from big highways. Choose a route that will take you through small towns.

Take your time. The amount you will see is in direct proportion to the speed you travel. If something catches your eye, stop. Check it out. Obey your impulses. Be inquisitive.

Between towns you might come across old things such as:

stone or other old-style fences

barns

farmhouses

country schoolhouses

churches

grange halls

inns

country stores

old mills

ghost towns

old bridges

railroad stations

old time farm equipment

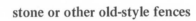

When you spot something interesting—take a picture of it, mark it on your map and make a notebook entry describing what it is, its condition and any comment about its age or features. Inquire about its history and add whatever you can to your notes. You'll find most local people very willing to talk to anyone who demonstrates a genuine interest in the neighborhood. And often, those conversations and the stories that emerge are the best part of the trip.

Leave your notebook and map in the car so it will be handy any time you see something to add to your "collection."

A WEEKEND HISTORY TOUR

Once you've explored around a little and have identified some local treasure, try inviting your friends to join you on a weekend tour. Stop over at an old inn or hotel. Visit a couple of the best antique shops or museums along the way. If you go in the summer or fall, try to time the trip to co-incide with a county fair or a fall harvest festival. If your friends share your interest, get them to "trade" tours, and take you to their favorite places.

Making A Natural Histomap

The U.S. Geological Survey sells topographic maps for almost every inch of the country. These maps are accurate and fascinating in their own right, and they cost very little, generally from $1 to $5, depending on the size and scale. Get one for the place you live, and use it to plot the locations of original or surviving native plant and animal life. Use colored shading for plants and solid dots or little drawings for animals.

In a notebook, collect more detailed information. Drawings or photographs. Descriptions and measurements. Animal feeding or other habits. Each time you find out about another plant or animal to add to your "collection," make both map and notebook entries.

Before There Was History

Before there were settlers there were Indians. And before there were Indians there were native plants and animals. Part of knowing the history of *your* place is finding out about the *before* parts.

Before the Settlers

Most of what preceded white settlements of this continent has become invisible to us. Native American cultures have not been given much room or encouragement. The results are either outright extinction, partial or complete assimilation into other ethnic groups or isolation. Your search for local native American history should be conducted in two parts: one for the traces of now-extinct cultures, the other for what, if any, remains of more recent or surviving groups.

Your state archaeologist will probably be able to tell you what is known about early native cultures. If your state has no archaeologist, try contacting the departments of history and archaeology of the nearest college or university. You should use these sources to direct you to published material that will provide specific information.

Inquiring about surviving native American groups may be a little more difficult. Again, the university or college may be helpful. If groups in your area exist as organized tribes, there is likely to be a county or state official who is directly concerned with their welfare. Be cautious and circumspect in your inquiries about any ethnic group. No one likes to be treated as an object of curiosity.

Before the Indians

Native plants and animals are just as much a part of the history of this country as anything else. And they are just as threatened. If your interest lies in the area of natural history, you probably already know about local sources of information. If you are just getting started, begin at the library. Most county libraries have some locally published material on indigenous plant and animal life. Ask the librarian. If you can't get to a library, contact your county agricultural agent, or a representative of the U.S. Forest Service, or the nearest University Extension service. Any of these sources should be able to put you in touch with local horticultural and zoological people who can help you directly.

Quack

A Note to the Reader... Up to this page, The Hometown History Primer has offered mostly suggestions that are meant for individuals or family use. Starting on this page, the ideas are a little more applicable to groups: a school class; a club; an informal group of friends; a neighborhood association; a historical society; a community organization

Things To Do With and About Quilts

If there is any symbol of American traditions and folk craft, the quilt is now *it*. Simple, useful, comforting, ingenious, colorful and unselfconscious, it represents a good deal of what we seem to be searching for in our past.

How many old time quilts do you think there are in your town or neighborhood? Invite your neighbors to exhibit their quilts (stitchery or other traditional sewn handcrafts) at a quilt fair. Charge admission and use the proceeds to give free classes to teach quilting to interested young people.

The people at the children's museum at Rose Hill Manor in Frederick, Maryland, have a good idea. Each visitor who comes is invited to take a stitch in a big old-fashioned quilt that is on display.

Some of the girls in the Middle School in Mill Valley, California, decided last semester to make a quilt. Each girl did one square (or more) of her own design. They collaborated in the quilting. The finished quilt was called "Get Well Quick Quilt" and they gave it to the nurse to comfort sick kids.

Ask everyone in your town to copy in black ink on a white letter-size piece of paper the design of their favorite old quilt. Ask them to write about the design, what it represents, how it came into the family, etc. Collect these in a book and have the local printer run off copies so everyone can have one.

Our Town in Stitches is the name of a little community project we heard about in Chicago. The kids at the Gads Hill Center settlement house did a big burlap stitchery about their town. It was a good project, and it is a beautiful piece of work.

The Quilting Bee isn't dead either. The ladies of the Holy Ghost Lutheran Church in Fredericksburg, Texas, meet two and sometimes three times a week and quilt for money. They accept finished "tops," mount them on a frame and sew the bottom to the top with the filler in between. They charge by the amount of thread used and have raised a lot of money for their church. (See page 106.)

The Quilters of the First Presbyterian Church of Bellflower, California, are another group of ladies who meet in the church's social hall every Wednesday. If you give them the fabric and a design, these industrious ladies will make the whole quilt from scratch.

Supreme Court upholds woman's vote — Teapot Dome scandal unearthed in Wyoming — Harding dies in office; Coolidge sworn in — First non-stop transcontinental flight — 15 million registered autos — Yankee Stadium opens — Poet e.e. cummings writes "Tulips & Chimneys" — Lewis writes "Babbitt" — Technicolor, sound-on-film, iconoscope TV scanner, electric shaver, and cellophane invented — First mechanical phone switchboard installed in NY — Dr. Alexis Carrel discoveres white corpuscles.

Baby quilts make wonderful new baby presents and are fairly simple to make. Here is an easy design. If you've never tried one, these little quilts are a good way to start.

Materials: 6 yds unbleached muslin; 4 yds cotton prints (1 yd each print); 1 roll cotton or dacron batting.

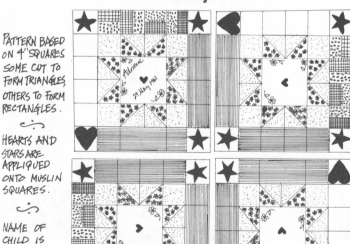

PATTERN BASED ON 4" SQUARES SOME CUT TO FORM TRIANGLES, OTHERS TO FORM RECTANGLES.

HEARTS AND STARS ARE APPLIQUED ONTO MUSLIN SQUARES.

NAME OF CHILD IS EMBROIDERED ON CENTER BLOCK.

The Moveable Feast

In the days before Macdonald's, when people left home for a day in the country, they took lunch along in a big wicker suitcase called a hamper. And what they ate was no 24 cent hamburger, either. If you've never been on a real old-fashioned picnic, we suggest you do a little research on the subject, organize a few of your friends and have one. Not a latter day pale imitation. A real down-home backwoods up-country-for-true picnic. With homemade pickles, mayonnaise that you whip by hand, not dig out of a jar, and no paper plates or napkins.

We recommend the Fourth of July as a perfect time for it. And if you plan ahead, and everyone brings a part of it, and the weather's right, it will be totally unforgettable.

Here is our list of suggestions for a menu—just to whet your appetite and set your own memory and imagination to work. A simple picnic might include: sandwiches (egg salad, chicken salad, cucumber, cream cheese and olive); potato salad; olives, celery, carrot sticks, deviled eggs; fruit; cake; ice cream (made on the spot with an old ice cream maker); and lemonade.

BOX LUNCH SOCIAL

A delicious way to raise funds for your project might be to host a box lunch social picnic. Decorate shoe boxes with colorful wrapping paper. Make the food inside as fancy as you can. You might include fried chicken, home-made bread, pickles, olives, fruit and tarts. The boxes are sold at the picnic along with fresh lemonade or home-made root beer. You might encourage the picnic goers to dress in nineteenth century clothes and play some old-timey games (lawn tennis, croquet or baseball).

1924 ○ 1925

John T. Scopes guilty of teaching evolution in Tennessee — RCA sends first wirephoto — 2.5 million radios in US — Ford's lowest price: $290 retail without self-starter — First national dance craze: the Charleston — Florida land boom peaks — Midwest tornado leaves 15,000 homeless — Rockne's Notre Dame team wins national title — First woman governor: Wyoming's Nellie Taylor Ross — Louisville Courier Journal initiates National Spelling Bee — Scarlet fever antitoxin found — First Guggenheim Fellow: composer Aaron Copland.

Rip Van Winkle

This is a game about a man who oversleeps and wakes up to find the world around him has changed. It can be played by any group of two or more, and at any level of sophistication. Here are two variations:

How Long Did Rip Sleep? *In this version, the player on the spot (Rip) decides for himself when it was he fell asleep but doesn't tell the other players. The object of the game is to guess when it was by asking Rip questions that can be answered with a yes or no. You could limit the number of questions and give a "free" question for each "yes" answer, as in Twenty Questions. Or you could make it easier by requiring that Rip give clues before the questioning.*

Is Rip A Liar? *In this version, Rip announces that he has been asleep 20 (50, 100, 200) years. The "strangers" in the game, always suspicious, challenge him about what it was like then. If Rip gets trapped in an innacurate statement three times, the game starts over with another player as Rip.*

What Was My Line?

This is a past-tense version of the famous TV show in which a single player tries to stump the others with an occupation that is real enough, but is also historic (and perhaps obsolete). Each contestant chooses an occupation from history: blacksmith, cooper, wheelwright, sawyer, tinsmith, cordwainer, tinkerer. Each of the other players takes turns asking questions that will enable him to guess the occupation. Any question is permitted, so long as it can be answered with a yes or no. Questions should be limited in number, and if the "experts" have been unable to guess the occupation, the wheelwright (or whatever he or she is) wins.

Who Was It?

This is a historical version of a standard guessing game. In this one, the player who is "it" takes the identity of some historic person. The game is very much more interesting if the players know something about events in American history. The object is to guess the identity that the player has assumed. Again the questions must be ones which can be answered with yes or no, and are limited in total number.

SIX HISTORY GAMES

We offer here a few suggestions for group games that bring the players into new relationships with history. Some knowledge of history will make the play more interesting, but it is not required.

The Price Was Right

Using one of the old Sears Roebuck catalogues, or some other large source of material, hold a pretend "sale" in which one player displays or describes an article but withholds the price. The other players bid what the original cost of the object was at the time it was first offered for sale. The player who comes closest to the right price "buys" the article. The player with the most goods wins. A variation is to ask each player to maximize the value of his collection by trading with other players during a limited time period after the "sale." The player whose "collection" is the most valuable wins.

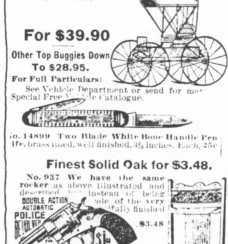

For $39.90

Other Top Buggies Down To $28.95.

For Full Particulars:
See Vehicle Department or send for mar Special Free V——le Catalogue.

No. 14899 Two Blade White Bone Handle Pen Ife, brass lined, well finished, 3⅜ inches. Each, 25c

Finest Solid Oak for $3.48.

No. 937 We have the same rocker as above illustrated and described ——— instead of being DOUBLE ACTION ——— ule of the very AUTOMATIC ———fully finished POLICE REVOLVER $3.48

each........... $0.25

History Darts

For this game, you should have three to six players, a good-sized map of the United States, a set of darts and a good reference book on American history or, better yet, a historical atlas. Each player takes a turn and is allowed to throw three darts at the map. He must then be prepared to describe some historic fact or event that relates to the place where at least one of his darts landed. If he can do it for none, he loses points. Each player gets five turns per game. The player with the most points wins. *If you're not good at darts, you'd better be good at history!*

Hometown History Darts

Here is a nice variation of History Darts for school groups. Each player throws a single dart at a map of a local area. He must then find out as many things as he can about the history of that place, starting with the present and working back. At the end of the week, each must display his findings. The class votes to see whose is best.

1926 ◉ 1927

Transatlantic radio-phone service begins — Network radio inaugurated — Hoover in TV demonstration at White House — Federal Radio Commission established — First talkie: "The Jazz Singer" with Al Jolson — Lindbergh completes first solo flight across Atlantic — Byrd-Bennett first to fly over North Pole — Martha Graham introduces modern dance — Hurricane leaves 18,000 homeless in Florida — Sacco and Vanzetti executed — Ford introduces 40-hour week to check overproduction.

LOOKING FOR YOUR TOWN HISTORY

HERE ARE A FEW WAYS TO SIZE UP THE HISTORY OF THE TOWN OR NEIGHBORHOOD THAT YOU'RE LIVING IN.

Alley Catting

Alley cats are free spirits, paying little attention to a town or city's designated travel routes. They cruise backyards and fences, vacant lots and alleys, riverbanks and edges, fields and train yards without regard to property lines. In searching out the historical remains of your town or city, it will be helpful to adopt the point of view (if not the actual habits) of the alley cat when you:

Look at the Backs of Buildings

Often, particularly in cities, building backs are not remodeled along with the fronts. It will be a clue to the original appearance of the street.

Look Up

Get your eyes above the awnings and the street-level plastic surgery that was done on most old buildings just before or after World War II. In many small town commercial districts, such renovation work is only skin deep and eyeball high. Beneath a layer of aluminum, or plastic, or sheet metal, is brick, stonework, carved wood, fancy plasterwork, all kinds of treasure. Above the first floor level, old buildings often reveal their original lines.

Seeing Through Time

There are probably many time gaps in your town's appearance. Places where the twentieth century has worn thin (or was never applied) and some older era shows. If you keep that notion in your head and look for those places, you will begin to piece together a picture in your mind of what your town used to look like, jigsaw puzzle fashion. A brick or cobble street here (or a part of one showing through the asphalt), an old painted sign there, a lonely hitching post or the concrete block along the curb on which ladies used to step when boarding a carriage. Watch for the fragments. The present isn't nearly so solid as you think.

Make A Neighborhood Time Map

If you live in a city, especially if you live in a big one, try starting with your own neighborhood before you take on the history of the whole shebang. Take your own block, or whatever you define as your "neighborhood." (Actually, putting a line around your neighborhood in a city is a very interesting thing to do. What are the invisible lines that mark your territory? What feels like home ground? Why is the line where you put it and not down at the corner?)

You can easily make a bird's-eye picture of your neighborhood, making a square or rectangle for each building. Then pick some time scale that makes sense to you. It could be twenty or fifty year increments. Or it could be in terms of generations: before you were born, before your father was born, before your grandfather was born. Then date each building. When was it built? What was it originally used for? Try to find out as much as you can. Mark each building with a color representing whatever period is appropriate.

Try to verify your information where possible. Sometimes what looks a lot like a modern building isn't. If you do this kind of "time map" for a big enough area, you will end up with a graphic representation in color of how your neighborhood or town grew.

Beginnings

Towns start for interesting reasons. How about yours? Ours began because it was a source of fine fresh water and whaling ships put in here to take on water, and later other supplies. Railroads started countless numbers of towns. Some started around the country store at a crossroads, others because of a nearby mine, some for odd, even bizarre reasons. There are very few towns that happened by accident. Find out what started yours. What was the first building in the town? Is it still standing? What was it used for originally? Now?

If you can locate one, study an old map that shows how the original town was laid out. Who did the town plan? How much of the original street plan is still in existence? How did the town get its name? Was it always called by its present name? What is its meaning?

1928 ◉ 1929

Philo T. Farnsworth invents TV pickup tube — WGY-TV Schenectady begins first programming — Mickey Mouse debuts in "Plane Crazy" — Sebastiano Lando patents coin-operated vending machine — Byrd flies over South Pole — Franz Boas' "Anthropology & Modern Life" discounts master-race dogmas — Supreme Court upholds Presidential pocket veto — St. Valentine's Day Massacre in Chicago — Kellogg-Briand Peace Pact goes into effect — NY birth control clinic raided after DAR protest — LA dam breaks; 450 lost — October '29 Roar turns to bite: Depression sets in.

Make An Edges Map

Take an edges walk. To do that, you will need to know what the town's approximate first boundaries were. The best source of that information is an old map. The town clerk or county recorder's office may have one. Or you might find one at the library, or in a town history, if one has been published. You'll also need a contemporary map, but that should be pretty easy. (If you can find neither one, you'll have to draw both, but it's probably time someone did in that case.)

Mark the town's original boundaries on your modern map and follow the line as closely as you can. Try to get some idea of what that edge of town might have looked like. Be on the lookout for old buildings that may still exist.

If you are successful in identifying your town's original edges, have some fun and do other folks a favor: Make up an Edges Walk for others to follow. You can do it just by drawing a simple map on a letter-size sheet of paper that shows present streets. Be sure to include what you can about the origins of the town and its name; stories about old town life; interesting facts about town edge landmarks that might still be visible.

Get the town paper to publish the map. Leave copies in the public library. Distribute copies to clubs and to the Chamber of Commerce.

SOME PEOPLE THINK THAT HISTORY IS WHAT COMES IN BOOKS AND THAT IT'S SAVED WHEN IT IS KEPT IN A SAFE PLACE. THAT SEEMS LIKE A PRETTY DRY CONCEPT OF HISTORY. HISTORY IS REALLY ALL BOUND UP IN THE LIVES OF PEOPLE — WHAT IS KEPT IN LIBRARIES AND MUSEUMS IS JUST INFORMATION. HISTORY IS A LIVING THING. IT CAN BE SAVED ONLY WHEN IT IS SHARED AND PASSED ALONG. THE HISTORY OF YOUR PLACE IS A PART OF THE PEOPLE WHO LIVE THERE. IF YOU WANT TO FIND OUT ABOUT IT, THEN YOU'LL HAVE TO TALK TO THE PEOPLE WHO EMBODY IT.

Human Treasure

The Newspaper. Pick long-time residents, of course. But also try to look for people who are in a position to know about other people in the town. Like the editor of your local paper, for instance. If he's an old timer, he'll not only remember a lot of what happened, he'll also remember the people. What's more, his collection of back issues, if they go far enough, will be a great help.

History in the Firehouse. If you live in a small town, stop in at the volunteer fire department and get acquainted. It's one of the best repositories of local historic lore that we know of. Firemen are a special breed—they know the town well; they have a first-hand acquaintance with the chronicle of local disasters; and between occurrences they have the time to sit around and develop their history through palaver.

The Post Office. The man who always seems to know a lot about what happened and where is the retired mail carrier. Often his sense of chronology isn't as keen as someone else's, but his knowledge of the physical history of his territory is terrific.

Ox trainer, Texas   Tinsmith, New York

Instrument maker, Ohio   Blacksmith, Texas

In most places, there is someone around who still does it the way it used to be done. Anything. Makes guns. Baskets. Mandolins. Cheese. Knows how to build a buggy. Plows with a team of mules. Builds shoes from scratch. Makes handmade brooms. Restores dolls. Does wood inlay work, tinsmithing, blacksmithing. They are very special people, though most often they don't think of themselves that way. Where you can do so without imposing, it's important to talk to these people because along with their trade or skill goes a whole attitude about the past and the present that others can learn from. It isn't usually put into words, but it can be seen in other ways.

Sometimes these people are pleased to allow others to observe and document their craft. Don't ever pass up a chance to record on tape and film the work of a local craftsman. Sometimes, the same people can be prevailed upon to participate in a crafts program and teach their skills to young people either as students or apprentices. Maybe you are just the person to organize such a program through the local high school, community arts organization, historical society or church group.

People Who Knew People. Any general practitioner is apt to know a lot about the history of the families who occupied your town or neighborhood. Retired school teachers are apt to have a good sense of history, and with it the kind of education that tends to make them want to keep records. They can tell you what happened to the children. In small communities, the town clerk was often a part-time functionary, and spent most of his time tending store. If he had either post for very long, and is still around, be sure to get to know him. He'll be helpful.

1930 ◉ 1931

Banks close — Gold hoarded — Hawley-Smoot protective tariff steps toward economic nationalism — NY Mayor Walker charged with malfeasance — Rockne killed in plane crash — Wickersham reports prohibition enforcement failing — Bestseller: Pearl Buck's "The Good Earth" — Planet Pluto identified in Lowell Observatory — Radio Astronomy developed by Bell Telephone's J.G. Lansky — First airlines form — Empire State Building, George Washington Bridge completed — Grant Wood finished "American Gothic" — Total US pop. 122,775,046; 13 million unemployed.

TURNING ON THE TOWN

If you are looking for a good way to begin to get your community interested in its own history, here are some ideas to consider. They have this aspect in common: they publicly acknowledge the gifts that time and a good memory bestow on us. They honor the venerable members of your place by putting value on the special contribution each makes. In the process, they hold up a mirror to the rest of the community, in order that it can see a little of its own rich past.

The Craftsman's Social

Acknowledge the skill and value of local craftsmen (those people who still make things the old way) by honoring them at a town picnic. Not a fancy dinner with speeches, but something outdoors that is in keeping with the simplicity of what they do. Ask them to demonstrate or bring an example of their work, but be careful not to make it an ordeal for them. This kind of event would be a perfect way to launch a program of crafts instruction at the local school. Be sure the newspaper does a little story on each guest of honor.

The Town Hall of Fame

Start your own chronicle of local heroes. The criteria for selection should be anyone who has contributed to local history:

★ the old gentleman who tells wonderful tales

★ a local inventor (not necessarily an Edison)

★ the oldest living school teacher

★ the oldest living man or woman

★ the last civil war veteran

★ local craftsman of special excellence

★ revered old-time town doctor or veterinary

We're not speaking of locals who made national history (although you won't be able to leave them out). Just plain folks who somehow deserve to be remembered this way. You'll have to work out your own criteria and selection process.

Put each "hero," his picture and a story about his life and contribution on a page in a big book in the library. Make a photocopy of the finished page, frame it and hang it in the town hall, community center or other public gathering place.

Accept nominations from anyone. Be sure the local paper covers the story of each selection.

1932 ☉ 1933

Prohibition ends; FDR's New Deal begins — CCC, AAA, TVA, NIRA, FERA established — FDR closes banks, suspends the gold standard — Reconstruction Finance Corp. set up to aid failing banks — FM radio, polaroid glass invented — Nobel Prize to Thomas H. Morgan for chromosome discoveries — Amelia Earhart first woman in transatlantic solo flight — Ban on Joyce's "Ulysses" lifted — "Humanist Manifesto" supports evolution, rejects Divine Creation — Mayor Walker resigns under pressure — Average life expectancy: 59 years.

This certifies that

Christopher Swan

is a guest of honor for

OLD TIMERS' NIGHT

Old Timers' Night

Get a local restaurant owner (preferably one who is already interested in history) to have an Old Timers' Night once a month. On that night, the house special should be free to anyone over eighty, and half-price to everyone else.

The idea is kind of a community dinner at which old folks are honored, and encouraged to talk about what is often most important to them—their memories. Be careful not to let the event take on the tone of a state occasion. The first time that happens, your paying customers will evaporate. The idea is for everyone to have a good time. Organize special speaking topics such as:

the best tall tale (audience applause selection);

the best flood (or fire, etc.) story;

the best old time joke;

etc.

Each evening choose a surprise guest of honor simply by having someone tell a little about the guest's life and awarding a certificate. (Be sure to give the "victim" equal time for a response.) Put time limits on speeches. And be sure the master of ceremonies has a good sense of humor.

ORAL HISTORY

"The first house my father built on our farm was a big house—you know, like a farmhouse—six or seven rooms. And every bit of lumber was hauled out there in the rough. And there were two carpenters and they had boxes full of those (he pointed to the old hand tools that were lying around on the top of a work bench) and they made all of the cuts—the window frames, the door frames—they did them all with those hand tools. And their charge for the labor of building the whole house was $138. They worked from mornin's daylight until dark, and it didn't take them but two or three weeks. Now it takes eight or ten men to do the same work."

That's part of what Henry Borchers of Fredericksburg, Texas, remembers about farmhouse construction in the early twentieth century. Mr Borchers, like most of us, has never written down most of his experiences. If it weren't for a portable tape recorder, a friendly interviewer and a few pointed questions, this bit of American history would have faded into silence.

Oral History—spoken accounts of firsthand experiences—is both the oldest and newest technique for passing on information about bygone days. Oldest because the spoken word was almost certainly the primary method for carrying information across time spans in the early days of civilized man; and newest because verbal recollections now may be preserved indefinitely, thanks to the advent of inexpensive tape recording devices.

What this means to the academic historian is that an almost unlimited source of information about events in modern times is available to him. And it is information which the historian cannot afford to let pass. The technological revolution giveth and it also taketh away: the availability of modern communications devices is quite likely responsible for

the fact that Americans of today don't write the voluminous letters that their great grandparents once wrote, and also for the decline in popularity of diary-keeping. Written sources of familiar history have dried up. So without careful recording of oral history, future historians could quite possibly inherit less of this sort of personal information about our times than we inherited about our great grandfathers' times.

But oral history isn't just a pastime for titled scholars. It's something you can be doing. And probably should be doing. Not because it's going to protect grains of truth for future Americans (though it will do this)—but because it's a detective game, a social event and a great learning experience: your enjoyment is unconditionally guaranteed!

The collecting of Oral History can be as large or small a project as you want it to be—and it can be as formal or informal as you wish. Even if you just tape one person one time, your effort can be of significant value. Especially if it's put to good use.

All you need to become a great Oral Historian is a portable tape recorder. Unless you are a hermit, you have potential oral history sources living and breathing all around you. A pencil and note paper are not essential, but they can make future use of your recordings easier.

It's up to you whether you want to research one subject or dig into the memory of one individual. If you want to find out, say, how the Stock Market Crash of 1929 affected wealthy families in your town, you'll want to interview several people, limit individual interviews to this one subject area and be listening for names of other people to interview. (People familiar with an event are the best sources of learning who else·to ask about that event.) However, if you want to search the memories of old Mr McHolm who has lived in town since the railroad came, your project will require a different approach.

In either case, though, you should relax and let your narrator explain events in question. You should not question so as to make the session into an interview. A basic premise of Oral History is that the product is a first-person statement. If you gently direct your narrator toward what you're most interested in, and ask just enough questions to keep him thinking and talking, you'll probably end up with first-rate tapes.

FEED-BACK

Here are ten terrific ways to channel oral history information back into the flow of your community:

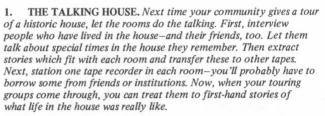

1.   THE TALKING HOUSE. *Next time your community gives a tour of a historic house, let the rooms do the talking. First, interview people who have lived in the house—and their friends, too. Let them talk about special times in the house they remember. Then extract stories which fit with each room and transfer these to other tapes. Next, station one tape recorder in each room—you'll probably have to borrow some from friends or institutions. Now, when your touring groups come through, you can treat them to first-hand stories of what life in the house was really like.*

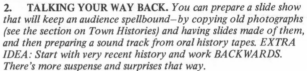

2.   TALKING YOUR WAY BACK. *You can prepare a slide show that will keep an audience spellbound—by copying old photographs (see the section on Town Histories) and having slides made of them, and then preparing a sound track from oral history tapes. EXTRA IDEA: Start with very recent history and work BACKWARDS. There's more suspense and surprises that way.*

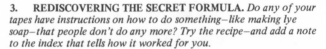

3.   REDISCOVERING THE SECRET FORMULA. *Do any of your tapes have instructions on how to do something—like making lye soap—that people don't do any more? Try the recipe—and add a note to the index that tells how it worked for you.*

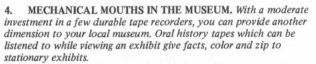

4.   MECHANICAL MOUTHS IN THE MUSEUM. *With a moderate investment in a few durable tape recorders, you can provide another dimension to your local museum. Oral history tapes which can be listened to while viewing an exhibit give facts, color and zip to stationary exhibits.*

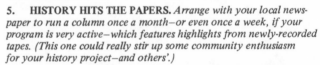

5.   HISTORY HITS THE PAPERS. *Arrange with your local newspaper to run a column once a month—or even once a week, if your program is very active—which features highlights from newly-recorded tapes. (This one could really stir up some community enthusiasm for your history project—and others'.)*

6.   SELL A MILLION. *If you have an especially interesting excerpt of two minutes—and a group of willing and creative musicians—you might want to record a musical background for the anecdote. (All it takes is one stereo tape recorder. Use one channel for a dub of the anecdote, and the other channel for recording the music.) If it works out well, you could have it pressed as a 45 RPM disc and sell it locally to raise money for history projects.*

7.   HISTORY QUIZ SHOW. *One person can excerpt statements from tapes and leave blanks. For example, "The family who lived in the great white house on Oak Street before Mayor Reynolds bought it was named . . ." "I'll never forget the last year Nick Sedelnik played football here, it was 1949 and we were playing Visalia. Well, we were down by 6 points and there was less than a minute when Nick . . ." A great bit of recreation for a committee meeting, barbecue or whatever.*

8.   RADIO PLAY. *Why not approach your local radio station about scheduling a weekly program of about ten minutes in length to feature oral history highlights? Some programs could be done live, listeners can be invited to call in to ask questions or supply facts, and announcements of history activities can be aired.*

9.   HISTORY'S GREATEST HITS. *Prepare a twenty minute tape featuring the absolute best stories from all your oral history tapes. Prepare a visual show to go along with it. Make use of this "program package" to get service clubs, schools, even nearby towns tuned in to the nature and the value of your program.*

10.   DRAMA TRUE TO LIFE. *Write a short play based on events which have been rediscovered through oral history tapes. Present the play as a fund raising event for your project.*

HERE'S HOW YOU AND TWO OR THREE FRIENDS CAN START A COMMUNITY ORAL HISTORY PROGRAM.

✦ **People with an interest in gathering local oral history should organize themselves into a committee, and:**

✦ Agree on a list of events to research.

✦ Decide how the program's completed tapes will be used (see FEEDBACK).

✦ Make a public announcement of your program's birth and its initial interests.

✦ Prepare a general information questionnaire to be sent to potential narrators. This should be accompanied by a letter explaining the purpose of the program and the subject of the inquiry.

✦ Personally contact the individual you are to interview. Inform him or her you wish to make a tape, explain where tapes are to be kept, who will have access.

✦ You may want to get together with this person for a preliminary planning session, to pinpoint your interests and give the narrator time to think.

✦ Pre-record a formal introduction to the tape, including the person's name, identity and a brief resume of his or her career.

✦ Let the tape run while you talk about the weather—then play it back to check the recording level.

✦ Begin the recording; ask the person to elaborate upon specific occurrences in which you have an interest.

✦ Take notes—especially of names and places mentioned.

✦ Don't rush along from question to question. Give the narrator a chance to pause and think.

✦ Take breaks during the session. Don't push the endurance of the narrator. (90 minutes is probably the maximum.)

✦ A relaxed, informal session will probably yield more valuable information than a consciously formal one.

✦ As a general rule, avoid yes/no questions.

✦ A negative approach will often yield more information than a positive approach: A question such as, "Although Mayor Felden was generally acknowledged to be kind and wise, he must have had some shortcomings. Can you think of any?" may lead into interesting discussion.

✦ Always establish the speaker's role in the events he or she describes.

✦ Don't challenge what you believe to be inaccuracies in the person's report. You may, however, point out that other points of view exist.

✦ Don't be afraid of wasting tape!

✦ Don't show off your own knowledge.

✦ After the interview is concluded, review the tape and write down a list of subjects covered. Note where each is on the tape, using the counter.

✦ Write a letter of thanks which re-states the intended use of the tape.

✦ Store the tape in a public place (if it is intended for public use). The tape must be protected from extreme temperatures.

---◆◆◆---

Willa K. Baum of the University of California has written a detailed book on how to conduct a sophisticated oral history program. It's called Oral History for the Local Historical Society, *and can be obtained from the American Association for State and Local History, 1315 Eighth Avenue, Nashville, Tennessee 37203. The cost is $2.25.*

1934 ◉ 1935

More new deals: FCC, FHA, SEC, NLRA, WPA, REA established — Social Security starts — Public Utilities, Soil Conservation Acts passed — John L. Lewis founds CIO — Ford restores $5-a-day minimum wage — Nylon developed by DuPont chemist Wallace Carothers — Transpacific air service begins — Philippines gain independence — Puerto Rico requests statehood — FBI shoots John Dillinger — Nebraska adopts unicameral legislature — Drought wipes out Midwest crops — Hitler proclaims himself Fuehrer; rejects Versailles Treaty — Gershwin's "Porgy & Bess" opens.

DOING A HISTORICAL ARCHAEOLOGY DIG IN YOUR OWN BACK YARD

Are you curious about who used to live on the land where you live now? A few days of scratching around in the soil might give you some clues. Digging in your own back yard is a first-rate introduction to Historical Archaeology.

1. Historical Archaeology is the search for objects from relatively recent periods—eras from which we have original written records. Historical Archaeology is an excellent way to taste the challenge of searching for underground history. Objects from historical times are usually fairly easy for a layman to identify; interpretation of soil-layering and object-placement is not of crucial importance; and professional archaeologists normally do not concern themselves with researching historic eras. But some very interesting information can be uncovered (see the Weeksville story, page 105) if you're willing to get down on your hands and knees.

Here are some things to think about when searching for buried history: What occupied the site before its present use? What might have been left to give you clues? Where would these have been left?

Good places to dig: in or around an overgrown house foundation; near a water supply; vacant lot; schoolyard; an old town dump.

Bad places to dig: any private property if you don't have the owner's permission; any public property if you haven't obtained permission from public officials.

After you dig a hole: why not plant a tree in it?

2. Prehistoric Archaeology is a conditional no-no—the search for and analysis of objects left by prehistoric peoples.

CAUTION: If you do find artifacts that suggest an earlier civilization, STOP DIGGING! Notify a professional archaeologist of your discovery. (See our list of addresses.) He will probably ask you to (1) show him the site, or (2) send complete information and photographs of the site's location, and also ask you not to let it be disturbed until such time as a professionally-supervised crew can dig it. It is unwise and unfair for you to dig up a PREHISTORIC site if you have no archaeological training—potentially valuable sites can be rendered unusable and worthless if dug incorrectly.

YOU CAN GET EXPERIENCE IN PREHISTORIC ARCHAEOLOGY

Several states have programs which allow amateurs to participate in digs supervised by professional archaeologists; in most cases you need not be a resident to participate.

The State of Arkansas has a program whereby amateurs can receive official certification for levels of proficiency attained. If you'd like to find out what public archaeology programs are underway in your state, check with either the Anthropology Department of a nearby university, or contact your State Highway Commission or State Parks and Recreation Commission. (Different states have placed

ALTHOUGH DAYS AND YEARS PASS BY AND ARE GONE FOREVER, THE OBJECTS OF THE PAST DON'T NECESSARILY VANISH. ARTIFACTS FROM 50 OR 5000 YEARS AGO MAY LIE JUST UNDER THE TOPSOIL. FINDING THEM LEADS TO KNOWLEDGE OF FORGOTTEN TIMES — HOW PEOPLE ATE, SLEPT, FOUGHT, LOVED, WORSHIPPED, TRAVELED, AND AMUSED THEMSELVES. THIS PROCESS, IS, OF COURSE, WHAT WE CALL ARCHAEOLOGY AND IT IS ONE OF THE MOST EXCITING AND CHALLENGING ADVENTURES OPEN TO YOU.

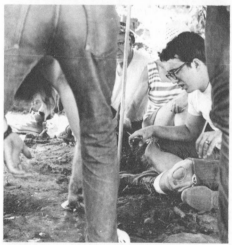

archaeology programs under different jurisdictions.) Or you can send for the free booklet "Stewards of the Past," by writing the Arkansas Archaeology Survey, University of Arkansas, Fayetteville, Arkansas 72701.

Here's what is involved in prehistoric archaeology. You can involve yourself in the process—steps 1 and 2—right now.

1. DISCOVERING A SITE. Man alters natural materials in recognizably different ways than nature does. If you spot even one rock fragment which seems to have been worked by man—or find one shard of pottery—you should realize you may have located a site worth exploring. A careful survey of the surface of the area may give you additional signs of man's work.

2. REPORTING THE SITE. A careful listing of what was found on the surface of a potential site, where on the site each object was found, what the site looks like, and where the site is located should be prepared and brought to the attention of your state's archaeology program. After you send the description of your site to your state program, your site may be assigned an official "state number." And the state organization will probably notify archaeologists of your find.

STOP! From here on, you need professional assistance to do it right.

3. STAKING OUT THE SITE. Before digging commences, a site is normally divided into squares with stakes and twine. This makes it possible for removed artifacts to be precisely identified by position. In archaeology, where something is found is often more important than what it is.

4. DIGGING THE SITE. Or, more precisely, "shaving" the site, because shovels and trowels are used to carefully scrape away layers of soil, and each layer is then carefully sifted for bits of evidence. At first, several spots may be explored; the ones that yield significant objects and information will have the surrounding areas excavated.

5. WASHING AND LABELING ARTIFACTS. Objects uncovered in a dig are normally cleaned, either by washing gently with water using a potato scrubber, or (in the case of pottery scraps and other fragile materials) by dry-brushing. Each object is then identified with a coded designation written on the object, either directly or on a spot of white paint. A corresponding tag is prepared which describes the object and exactly where it was found. Objects from each individual square are washed as a group and kept together as a group.

6. STUDYING AND RESEARCHING ARTIFACTS. The deduction of information from found materials continues long after the physical labor of digging is complete. Slowly a picture of the life of a prior culture (or series of cultures) which once occupied the land takes shape.

7. REPORTING THE FIND. A major part of archaeology is communication. The importance of a dig in the last analysis is how the newly-gained information fits or does not fit with other archaeological information from sites in other areas. Reports of digs completed are submitted to one state office (in most states), so data from one dig may be analyzed in the light of information from other digs.

Here are some projects that are intended for school classes. But they'll work perfectly well for any group with an interest in history.

THIS WEEK WE ARE CELEBRATING . . .

Every day is the anniversary of something. Or several somethings. Some anniversaries are bizarre. Some are very funny. And some are so important the banks and schools close down and everybody stays home. Each week, ask a committee of students to do research in order to find out what we should celebrate next week. On Friday, ask them to read their list to the class. Then select what to do by voting. Also decide how to celebrate (except by staying home from school!).

1936 ⊙ 1937

Hoover Dam completed — WPA theater presents first "Living Newspaper" — Eugene O'Neill awarded Nobel literature prize — Bestseller: Margaret Mitchell's "Gone with the Wind" — Steinbeck publishes "Of Mice and Men" — Amelia Earhart disappears — SS Queen Mary arrives in NY on maiden voyage — Japan sinks US gunboat on Yangtze River — Hindenburg blimp explodes in NJ — Wonder of Wonders: Golden Gate Bridge opens.

The Plainview High School Community Time Capsule

Thinking of the present as history is just as important as any consideration of the past. The history class in your local high or junior high school could organize a community time capsule. Every member of the neighborhood or town should be invited to submit something for consideration. Each entry should be accompanied by a tag which explains its significance. The entries could be exhibited to the whole town at the local library or community center. And a jury consisting of the following kinds of people:

> a first grader
> a fifth grader
> a high school student
> a college student
> a mother
> a professional woman
> a father
> a businessman
> the mayor
> the newspaper editor
> the oldest man
> the oldest lady

. . . should make the choices. The final selection should be printed in the newspaper, along with the explanation for each entry when the capsule is sealed and placed in the basement of the Town Hall.

1938 ⊙ 1939

World War II begins in Europe — Germany invades Czechoslovakia, Poland; Russia invades Finland — U-boat sinks Athenia, 30 Americans die — US ports-waters closed to warring submarines — Igor Sikorsky invents helicopter — Steinbeck publishes "Grapes of Wrath" — Orson Welles "Invasion from Mars" broadcast — Fiberglass, xerography, self-propelled combine invented — CAA established to control non-military flight — First regular transatlantic passenger flights — Ahead of his time: Charles Ives 1915 piano sonata finally performed.

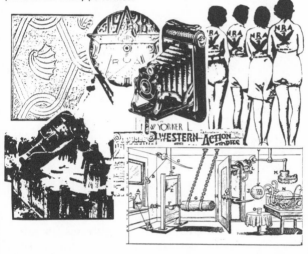

MAKING HISTORY MURALS

There are any number of ways this project could be organized. It could be a contest, sponsored by a local newspaper. The artists who produce the best designs depicting some event or events in neighborhood or town history are given a prize and a wall on which to execute their design, plus materials.

Or it could be a joint project of several local schools. Permission could be obtained from local merchants or property owners to permit a "mural" to be hung on their premises for a period of time. Each separate mural could be painted on a 4 x 8 foot sheet of masonite, either by a single artist or a small group. After the separate paintings have been exhibited around town, they could be assembled into a giant super-mural in one location for the grand finale.

Whichever way it is done, the project should be open to amateur artists, and each should be expected to provide detailed descriptions of the events he has chosen to represent.

The Town "Show Off"

One way to get the people of your town interested in their history and to develop a sense of pride in that history is to show everyone the pieces of history that remain. This function is usually filled by the local museum, but there are many towns which have not established a museum and have no way to collect or exhibit the rich treasure hidden in the houses of the town. The Instant Museum is the answer to that problem. Here is how Cuero, Texas, made one. You can modify theirs to fit your situation.

For their contribution to the Centennial Celebration of their town, the Cuero Historical Society put out a call to the citizens to search their houses for the artifacts and heirlooms that were hidden there. Here's part of a letter received from Sharon Steen of that Society:

"Speaking of 'putting it together'—the Historical Society put together a museum in two weeks in the Reuss Drug Building. Lester Giese organized it and we put out the word that we needed items. We got over 600! We set up room displays (bedroom, living room, kitchen, etc.) plus case exhibits and even a 'granny's attic' for stuff we couldn't find any place else for! The response was so great that we may finally get a decent museum here. I wish you could have seen the lovely old costumes that were worn. Many were original clothing."

A side benefit to the temporary Instant Museum was that it gives the sponsor a chance to inventory the town's heirlooms and collections which would be difficult to arrange in other ways. It also exposed the donors to the experience of having their possessions recognized for their historic value. All in all, it seems like an ideal project with maximum return on effort.

1940 ◉ 1941

Slapstick in Hitler's face: Chaplin's "The Great Dictator" — FDR wins third term; outlines four freedoms — Congress OKs first "peace-time" draft — Smith Act requires fingerprinting of aliens — RCA tests first electron microscope — Hemingway publishes "For Whom the Bell Tolls" — Marines invited to occupy Greenland, Iceland — Federal Wage & Hour Law upheld — Mediation board halts defense industry strikes — Rubber rationed — Atlantic Charter signed — Japan bombs Pearl Harbor — US enters war — Total US pop. 131,669,275; "average" life expectancy 46 years.

SAD SACK

·· the GARAGE SALE/FLEA MARKET SYNDROME ··

America is in a "sell all our stuff to make room for more," frenzy. The fact that Flea Markets are profitable ventures cannot be denied and they could provide needed funds for your preservation projects. I don't think I need to go into the "how to" of Flea Markets. That information is easy to come by and is mostly common sense material anyway. I would suggest that the connection between the Flea Market and the Instant Museum is pretty clear. As long as people are rummaging around in their garages and attics to locate artifacts for your museum, they might as well be looking for artifacts to donate to your flea Market.

HOLD IT!
An Old Time Photo Night

Americans have always loved gadgets, and one of their most beloved gadgets has been the camera . . . fortunate for us, because the record found in old snapshots is unlike any other. People take pictures of everything. The problem is to get them out into the open where we can see them. The Old Time Photo Night is similar to the Instant Museum, but may be easier to arrange. Your group can put out a call for photographs to be used in a history photo exhibit, perhaps as part of a larger function. Be sure to stress that all photographs are fair game. The photos and albums are displayed on tables and walls, and conversation will automatically revolve around the pictures and history. This is a good chance to copy some of the pictures, and make a record of the owners. There will never be a better opportunity to find out who has the pictures in your town.

A more recent gadget (but not *that* recent) is the home movie camera. Home movies make a record which is becoming an important part of our record of history. You could have a Home Movie Festival with Oscars for the funniest, weirdest, best quality, etc., film. It could be an event held as part of Photo Night, too.

HINT: It was discovered very early that watching movies in silence is a drag. Your home movies are no exception. The remedy was and is music. Play music with the movies; you'll love them even more. And *any* music will work surprisingly well.

◆◆◆◆◆◆◆◆◆◆◆◆◆◆◆◆◆◆◆◆
..PHOTOGRAPHY..
Is one of the most interesting, delightful and instructive of pleasures
IT'S EASY
...TO MAKE GOOD PICTURES
◆◆◆◆◆◆◆◆◆◆◆◆◆◆◆◆◆◆◆◆

Another project dealing with photography will produce its own historic record. This would encourage people to bring cameras, especially old cameras, to some function (like the photo show) and take a lot of snapshots. These could be quickly processed and make a part of the event. People should be encouraged to donate their photos to the group sponsoring the show, too.

Dates Are History

If there is any one facet of history in which people will involve themselves, it is that of finding dates for buildings. If we move into an old house, or start research for a town history, the one thing we search for is the date the structures were made. It is that date which seems to mark an important and human involvement with the place. Our interest in dates is well justified. They are vital to a thorough understanding of history. Unfortunately, dates for buildings seem to get misplaced as easily as dates for any other event, and it is often a difficult and complex job to resurrect them. There is no sure method for determining old building dates which works in every case, but here are a few leads to follow:

1. The building may be the best source. Look it over thoroughly (see Buildings Talk on this page).

2. Look for similar buildings in the local area. Are they dated? This can give you a general time period to guide your search.

3. Records. Even though you or the original owner didn't keep records, chances are there's some branch of local government that did or does. County tax records are an excellent source. By examining them year by year, you can determine when improvements were made to the property. Ask the clerk for help in interpreting the records. Also try to locate deeds, grants, plans or any documents pertinent to the property.

4. Another excellent source is the local historical society. They will have a knowledge of the general history of the area and how your building fits into that. Take a photo along and put yourself in their hands.

5. Library work. There are sources in most libraries which could help. Look for county histories and county atlases. These show local buildings and dates. You may be able to date your building by finding one similar to yours in the books. A less reliable source would be architectural handbooks. Good luck!

Two things to remember: First, history and buildings are living processes. There may be no single date for the building in which you are interested, since buildings change to suit changing needs. Additions and remodeling may cover several time periods.

Second, dates are where you find them. One day, after I had spent months trying to track down the date my house was built, a man from the gas company came to install a new line. While I was chatting with him he looked in his record book and said, "I see we first installed this line on the day before the earthquake in 1906." My search was over.

BUILDINGS TALK

Buildings, especially commercial and religious buildings, have been, and still are, encrusted with written and pictorial information which will offer peek holes into history. Plaques, cornerstones, cornice inscriptions, signs and sidewalks will often offer up a variety of facts, including date of erection, builder, owner, architect, contributors, use of the building and many others. The trick is to look everywhere, inside and out, top to bottom. Be sure to record your finds. Photos and rubbings work best for recording.

Some town newspapers have attracted attention to town history by running a photo of an inscription under the question, "Where is this?" The next issue contains the answer, its history, and a new photo question.

· MDCCCLXVIII ·

1942 ◉ 1943

A world at war: Japan occupies Manila, Bataan — US bombs Tokyo, takes Midway, Guadalcanal — Allies win Battle of Bismarck Sea, Bizerte, Attu, Rendova Island, Kiska, Sicily — Rome, Ploesti oil fields bombed — Italy surrenders — Shoes, canned goods, meats, cheese, coffee, sugar, gas rationed — Nevada 6-week divorce upheld — Thornton Wilder writes "Skin of Our Teeth" — Income tax withholding introduced — Race riots in Detroit, Harlem — Penicillin production leaps with cantaloupe mold discovery — Enrico Fermi demonstrates first nuclear chain reaction.

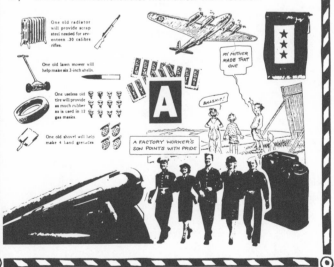

TOMBSTONE TEXTBOOK

If you don't think there is a lot to be learned about the history of a place by spending a few hours reading inscriptions found in its cemeteries, you should just try it. Take someone along with you and talk with them about the things you read. You'll discover: good times and bad, love stories, tragedies, epidemics, the town's early ethnic make up, important families, products of local craftsmen (stone and ironwork), an evolution of taste and much more. Some people collect rubbings of fine tombstone examples. A good way to make a portable copy of the tombstone textbook.

1944 ◉ 1945

World war: Allies take Roi Island, Parry Island, Rome, Normandy (D-Day), Saipan, Brittany, Guam, Paris, Leyte, Aachen, Luzon, Manila, Iwo Jima, Okinawa — Germans surrender at Rheims — The Bomb falls twice: Hiroshima and Nagasaki — Fighting virtually over — Rationing ends — Entertainment bans lifted — UN chartered; US joins — Tennessee Williams' "Glass Menagerie" opens on Broadway.

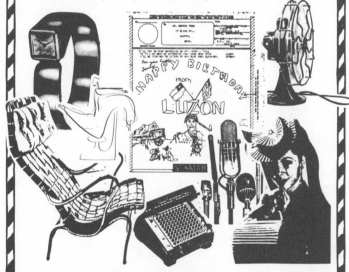

HISTORY ON WHEELS

Some teachers at Baldwinsville High School (New York), members of the Beauchamp Historical Club, are so crazy about old-time crafts that they have built a wagon-shop to haul themselves and their tools around to any place where people will stop and watch (which is almost anywhere). Being thorough craftsmen, they carefully documented the building of their wagon. Being generous, they have given us permission to reprint their plans so that anyone who wants to can copy them. We are particularly grateful to Malcolm MacPherson and Gerald Kranz for their help in making this material available to us.

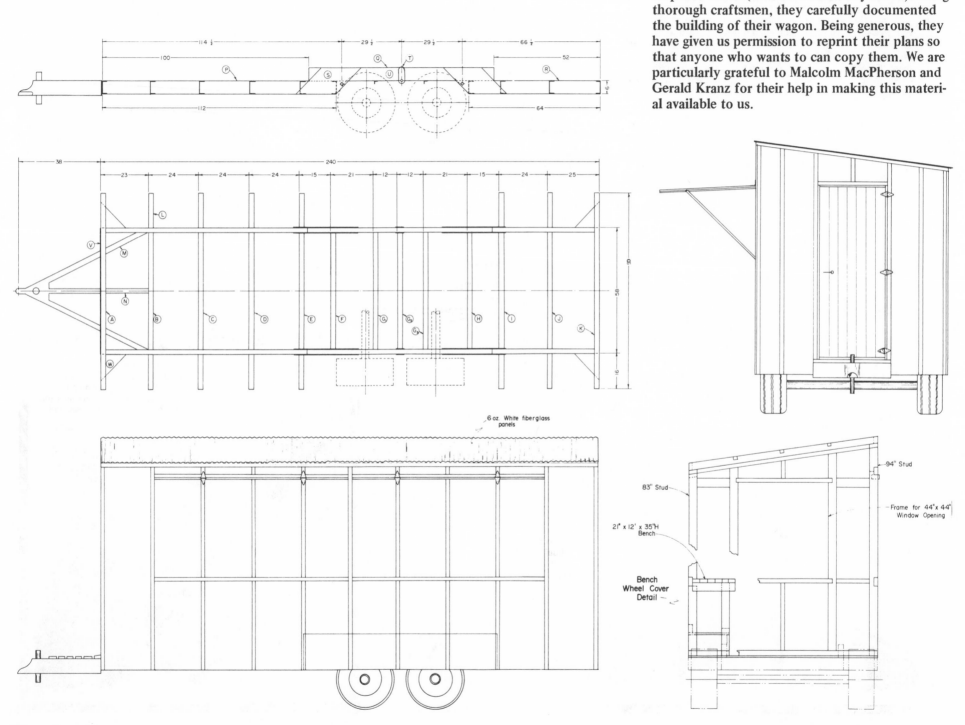

6 oz. White fiberglass panels

94" Stud

83" Stud

Frame for 44" x 44" Window Opening

21" x 12' x 35½"H Bench

Bench Wheel Cover Detail

Framing Materials

Qty	Size	Use
60	2" x 4" x 8'	gen'l framing
6	2" x 4" x 10'	long studs
16	2" x 4" x 12'	bench tops
7	2" x 4" x 20'	side stringers & headers
6	4" x 4" x 8'	corner & center post
2	2" x 6" x 8'	wheel well riser
10	¾" x 4' x 8', ACX fir plywood	step boxes & floor
15	½" x 4' x 8', CDX	siding
450'	1" x 2", pine	batten
3	2" x 4" x 8', pine	steps
20'	1" x 8", No. 1 common pine	trim
50'	5/4" x 8", Nos. 1 & 2 common pine, tongue & groove	door
70'	¼" x 2¼", lattice	step box trim
10	26" x 96"—6 oz., corrugated fiber glass roofing, white	roofing

Chassis (part letter is key to location on chassis drawings)

Qty	Size	Part
2	2" x 6" x 90", 1/8" steel U-channel	A,K
6	2" x 6" x 57¾", steel U-channel	B,C,D, E,I,F
2	2" x 6" x 53¾", steel U-channel	F, H
12	2" x 6" x 16", steel U-channel	L
2	2" x 6" x 112", steel U-channel	P
2	2" x 6" x 88", steel U-channel	Q
2	2" x 6" x 64", steel U-channel	R
2	2" x 6" x 26", steel U-channel	M
1	2" x 6" x 23", steel U-channel	N
2	5¾" x 88", 3/16" steel plate	U (Q box)
2	12" x 96", 3/16" steel plate cut to size for: 8 splice plates / 4 shackel mounts / 4 gussetts	S / T / W
1	7" x 58", ¼" steel plate tongue splice plate	V
3	2" x 2" x 53¾", 1/8" angle iron	G1,G2, G3
1	Tongue—hitch unit with elevating screw from Mobil Home	
2	Mobil home—wheel, tire, axle, spring units with electric brakes	
10 lbs.	Welding rod	

Hardware

Qty	Item	Use
100	1¼" x no. 20 flat head stove bolts with nuts & washers	floor-chassis hinges
60	¼" x 2" lag screws	hinges
11	8" strap hinges	side panels & door
25	¼" x 1½" lag screws	hinges
36	¼" x 2" carriage bolts	hinges
1	4" barrel bolt	door (inside)
1	7¼" hasp	door
2	6" strap hinges	rear panel
10 lb.	No. 10 common nail	gen'l constr.
10 lb.	No. 6 coated box nail	gen'l constr.
12	5/16" x 3½" carriage bolts	sill-chassis
40'	½" black iron pipe	raised panel braces
10'	3/8" hot rolled rod	panel lock pins
20'	1/8" x 1" x 1" angle iron	wheel wells
2 gal.	enamel paint, grey	chassis
1 gal.	roofing tar	wheel wells
2½ gal.	oil stain, walnut	outside
10	caulking tube, latex	all weather seams & joints
4	bumper jacks	corners

Electrical Hardware

Qty	Item	Use
200'	12 gauge, insulated, stranded copper wire	gen'l wiring
4	running lights, red	rear corners
6	running lights, amber	front corners & center
4	4" reflector, red	rear corner
4	4" reflector, amber	front corner
2	combination, tail-brake light and license plate holder	rear
1	6 prong connector	to tow vehicle
1	8 station terminal block	

Note: Detailed dimensions have been omitted from the framing drawings to allow for adaptation to other applications. Generally, 24" O.C. spacing intervals are used to accommodate 4' x 8' construction panels.

NOTE: This trailer was designed to meet New York state highway laws. Anyone living anywhere else should check with their local code before getting started.

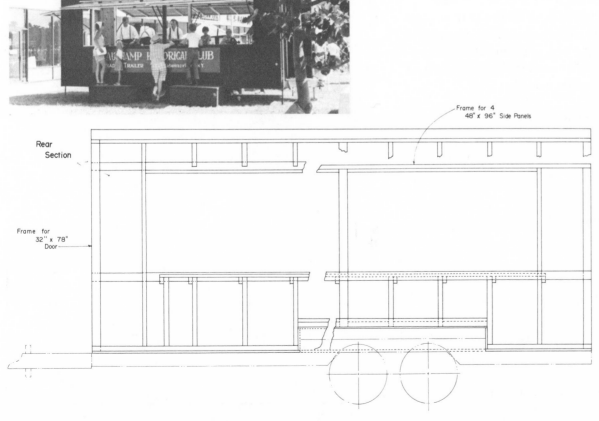

Rear Section

Frame for 32" x 78" Door

Frame for 4 48" x 96" Side Panels

1946 ◉ 1947

UN General Assembly meets — Truman Doctrine outlined — Marshall Plan aids European recovery — Taft-Hartley Law passes over Truman veto — Philippines go independent — Supreme Court bans interstate bus segregation — A-Bomb tests continue in Pacific — 4.6 million out on strike — Dodger Jackie Robinson becomes baseball's first black — New York's deepest snowfall: 25.8 inches — ENIAC electronic computer perfected — First tubeless tires tested — First supersonic flight: Charles Yeager in Bell X-1 — Radar bounced off moon.

DO A
HISTORY ★ PARADE

There was a time (and it wasn't very long ago) when a parade was comprised of men, wagons and animals, and there wasn't a Cadillac convertible in sight. The next time your town has a celebration, consider launching it with a parade in tribute to the community's past. Invite the whole town to join in. Award a prize for the best marching unit, for the best float, for the funniest entry and any other categories that seem right. But leave the internal combustion engine out. Here are some ideas you could consider:

The rickshaw float. Pull it with ten of the strongest young men in town. On foot, or on bicycles.

Mini-floats. Small decorated wagons or carts that are pushed by people or pulled with a single bicycle or horse.

Decorated farm wagons, animals and equipment.

Invite local men's groups or clubs to supply the parade with carpetbaggers, clowns, one-man bands, peddlers, speech-makers and eccentrics.

In addition to bands, invite single musicians to walk in the parade playing their instruments, dressed as historic characters.

Invite the local clubs to participate in the parade as a marching tableau which periodically pauses to re-enact some symbolic town event.

Have the rest of the town throw a picnic for the people in the parade at the town park right after the parade.

History on Two Feet
Making A History Walk

The people in Bethel (Shelby County), Missouri, have hit upon what we think is a mighty fine idea. Someone there came up with an old map of the original town (which was founded back in 1844). They reprinted the old map in the scenes taken around the turn of the century. Then they did a mimeographed version of the same map in a booklet which describes the presently visible historic sites and buildings.

Use a map like this in your town or neighborhood. Make sure it gets to newcomers in the community. Use it as a focus for a centennial celebration, or link it with an old-time progressive dinner (see page 149) as a fund raising idea for your local preservation project.

It works. Ask the people in Bethel.

1 Tour Headquarters--Log Cabin
2 Colony House (Merrill Bower)
3 Colony House (Fannie Bower)
4 Colony House (Herbert Hosmer)
5 Colony House (Don Fisher)
6 Colony House (Wilma Bower)
7 Colony Barn, Restored
8 Colony House (Gus Bower)
9 Colony House (Lloyd Jackson)
10 Colony House (Simon Tungate)
11 Colony School (Dias Bower)
12 Site of Colony Church
13 Colony House (Tom Notley)
14 Colony House (George Dodd)
15 Colony House (Merrill Bower)
16 Oldest House (Don Bower)
   Known as Vandiver House
17 Small Colony Barn
18 Tailor Shop (Nora Bowers)
19 Colony House (Leo Simpson)
20 Colony House (Wes Fuqua)
21 Colony House (Merrill Bower)
22 Carpenter Shop
23 Colony House (Lizzie Latimer)
24 Band Stand--Historical Marker
25 Colony House (Apartments)
26 Colony House (John Tolle)
27 Colony House & Smoke House
   (Evelyn Bailey)
28 Colony House (Funkey Stoneburner)
29 Elim, Dr. Keil's Colony Home
30 Small Colony Barn
31 The Gross House (The Flats)
32 Site of Bread Ovens
33 Colony House (Leona Kilb Bower)
34 Site of Tannery
35 Site of Colony Store
36 Site of Mill
37 Site of Distillery
38 Colony House (Marion Gonnerman)
39 Site of Colony Barn
40 Site of Blacksmith Shop
41 Colony Hotel (Claude Dodd)
42 Site of Carpenter Shop
43 Site of Largest Barn--Oxen
△ Site of Brick Kiln
* Site of Colony Well
MAMRI AREA
44 Colony House (Harold Smith)
45 Colony House (Marie Gume)
HEBRON AREA
46 Colony House (Opal Bower)
47 Colony Log Crib
48 Colony Cemetery
49 Colony Sheep Barn and Deep Well
   (Thelbert Bower)

PAST TIME FAIR

The Craftsman's Village

At the center of the fair is a cluster of tents and booths each of which is occupied by someone who practices an old-time craft. Demonstrations go on continuously. Many of the craftsmen sell their wares. Some also give lessons.

Shepherd.

Chair mender

Hay maker

Old Time Magic Lantern Show

In one old barn, there is a continuous showing of photographs from the town's history (put onto slides) accompanied with old-time songs and spoken commentary.

1948 ◉ 1949

US joins NATO — Tokyo Rose convicted of treason — Nationalist China leaders flee — Acheson's White Paper on China: cut off Chiang aid — USSR tests A-Bomb — Israel proclaimed free state — UN headquarters dedicated in NY — Selective Service Act sets up post-war draft — Displaced Persons Act opens gates beyond the quota — World's largest reflector telescope installed at Palomar — First LP records spin — Cortisone used to treat arthritis — Idlewild International Airport opens.

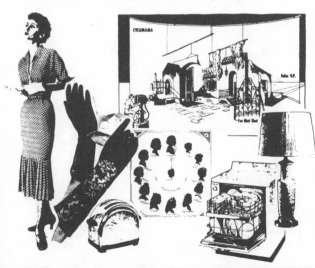

All aspects of the history of the town are represented. Here are a few samples.

Everyone with a collection is encouraged to bring it to the fair and exhibit in the **Great Collection Emporium.** *Prizes will be awarded for the oldest item on display, the most unusual collection, the largest collection, the most valuable collection and the best display. All collectors will be part of the Collector's School which will meet every afternoon for an hour.*

What follows is the description of an imaginary fair entirely based on local history. Perhaps some ambitious community will make it happen for their U. S. Bicentennial celebration.

The Side Street of Spectacle and Scandal

Down an alley, various organizations have contributed peek shows or small tents with tableaus or short acts inside. Each represents some spicy or otherwise exciting event in the history of the town.

In addition, there are:

Animal husbandry, farm produce and home arts displays.

Old auto races. (Entries must be pre-1940 vintage.)

Work animal contests (team oxen, mules, horses).

A small barn raising. (The building and labor is a grand prize.)

A tent circus of old-time acts.

A fortune teller who "predicts" past events.

A vaudeville show.

A patent medicine salesman.

Wood chopping and other field contests.

A cake sale, pie eating contest, pie throwing contest.

Almost Everything You Need to Know About Fund Raising Before You Try It Yourself

If you have, or are planning, a local history project that requires money, here is some friendly advice to consider. First, don't think of it as fund raising. Think of your objective as building support. And support takes many forms.

Make use of local resources. You may get help from out of town, but unless you're better connected than most of us, you'll have to depend on your neighbors.

Think first of volunteer assistance, donated time and materials, rather than cash. If you know how to organize such contributions, they are better than money because they get people directly involved. What you are really doing is building up a constituency, not raising money anyway. No project makes it on money alone. Besides, money is harder to get these days.

Use your imagination. It's important that whatever you do to raise money (or other contributions) also raises hopes and excitement. Think of activities that produce income *and* awareness of history. And make it fun. Remember, local history projects aren't causes. They're the backbone of the community. Being involved is more than digging into your pocket out of a sense of duty. If you ask for money, be sure your giver gets something in return. Fun. Knowledge. Pride. Or all three. And *always* accept non-money contributions in lieu of cash.

Use local merchants. They are busy people with little time to think about how to promote their own businesses. If you go to them with a scheme that (1) doesn't involve extra work for them (your group will do all that); (2) stands a good chance of turning a profit; and (3) results in publicity that makes your merchant look good, you can't, absolutely cannot, get a negative answer. Now think about it: what would your local printer print, your local radio station broadcast, your local nursery grow, that your group could sell for money?

There is no formula for raising money. Keep your objectives in proportion to the size and wealth (and interests) of your community. Keep your budget down, never pay if you can get it donated. Develop good relations with the local newspaper editor, you need him. Return value for value received. And most important:

Be wary of big donors. If you and your neighbors pay for the project, it belongs to the town. If a foundation, government agency or wealthy citizen pays for your project—well, look for strings. And watch for public apathy. That'll kill you.

Making Money

Here are some ideas for projects that can be used either to turn your community on to its past or to raise money for a local history project, or better yet, both.

1. Make a history record of old time music and oral history recollections related to your town. Record companies in Los Angeles, Chicago and New York will do custom pressing from any tape you send them, in 7-, 10- or 12-inch long-playing sizes.

2. Have your local movie house put on an old time Flickers Festival, each Tuesday evening for a month. Show old W.C. Fields, Chaplin, Buster Keaton or other films. Get the nearby soda fountain to come up with an original Flickers soda to go with the movies.

3. Lapel buttons that are colorful and inexpensive can be made on any subject. Message is printed on paper, punched, placed on a metal blank and covered with plastic by an ingenious little machine. Ask your printer to help you locate the nearest maker. Or, make your own using ribbon and cardboard.

4. If you live near the ocean, have an old-fashioned fish fry or clam bake. Be sure it's at the beach and that you include an Old Timers Baseball Game.

5. Get the local school kids to make lots of those swell old time Valentines. The kind that had lots of red paper, paper lace and smelled like library paste. You may have to dredge some out of the attic for samples. Package them in sandwich bags and sell in the local shops.

6. Ask local craftsmen to make two or three handmade toys each. Same with high school are and shop classes. Hold an old time toy show before Christmas. Auction the toys.

7. There are printers who specialize in making huge poster-sized blow-ups of any picture you send them. Do one or two or three of your best old time town photographs and sell in the local book shop, library, gift store.

8. There is always the antique show and flea market. Give it a twist by asking everyone who shows to wear old time clothing. Sell pretzels, beer, Coney Island red hots with kraut and anything else old-fashioned you can get someone to cook up.

9. Give a folk music concert. Invite all the local musicians to show off. Do it outdoors and have a community barbecue going on at the same time.

10. Stage a fashion show and ice cream social. Models have to wear clothes of at least twenty-five years ago.

11. Put on an old-fashioned Fireman's or Policeman's Ball for your local dauntless. Ask everyone to wear old time clothes. Prizes for the best polka, fox trot, Charleston, waltz.

12. Ask the local newspaper editor if he will print a special edition of his paper containing only history "news" if you supply all copy and photos. (He can sell old-timey looking, but real, ads to cover costs. Your group can be ad salesmen.) Ads pay for typesetting, paper, printing. Your group sells the paper for $1 and keeps that money. It's sure-fire.

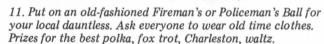

1950 ☉ 1951

Truman authorizes AEC development of H-Bomb — US enters Korea — UN embargoes arms to Communist China — Spy scares: Robert A. Vogler, Judith Coplon, Valentin A. Gubichev, Julius & Ethel Rosenberg, Morton Sobell, David Greenglass caught in the act — Kefauver committee uncovers $20 billion gambling operation — Truman unhooks MacArthur — Air Force C-47 forced down in Hungary — Truman sends Army to seize railroads, avert strike — Transcontinental TV: Truman talks at Japanese Peace Treaty — Total US pop. 150,697,361.

DOING A HISTORY SURVEY

There probably isn't another project we know of that is at one time as useful and as much fun as doing a town history survey. There are two ways to do it—by yourself just for the personal satisfaction, or as part of a group, as a service to your town. Either way is fine, though the latter may take a little politicking. Whichever way you choose to go about it, not only will you enjoy a once-in-a-lifetime discovery experience, you just might start a local preservation movement.

What do town history surveyors look for? *Ivy covered mansions, abandoned railroad sidings, old gardens and garden fences, 300 year old oak trees, forgotten water wells, unspoiled natural areas, old canopied filling stations, lonesome chimneys of burned-out residences, family cemeteries, shady creek beds, Indian burial mounds, legendary sites of buried pirate treasure, old stage coach trails, structures which housed first generation radio stations, zocalos, gazebos, picnic grounds, whipping posts, long-standing grocery stores and brick factories.*

What information does a town history survey include? *A successful town history survey should (1) provide a comprehensive list of all historically-significant properties in or near the town; (2) give an explanation of each property—plus a sketch of its history; (3) provide information as to who owns each property; and (4) mention the owner's plans for the future of the property.*

What do you do with all the priceless information? *First, it's a very good idea to rank your discoveries according to priorities: the* most significant *properties which would give the* most lasting benefit *to the community if saved and which could be saved at the* least cost *(but which are threatened with destruction if not attended to soon) should rank highest on your list. Properties which are beyond repair should be ranked low; properties which are beyond foreseeable financial means also should be ranked low. But* everything *of historic interest should be listed. Second, it will probably be useful to* publicize *the list of properties, emphasizing the need for* action on top-priority items. *(The names of property owners and details of their projected activities should not be included in the publicity—except in special cases.)*

How can a town history survey start a preservation movement rolling? *(1) By getting people directly involved in conducting the survey—taking history into their own hands; (2) By involving more and more people in the survey, as information on old buildings and areas is sought; (3) By showing everyone that historic activity is really underway in your town; (4) By demonstrating a rational, concerned and thorough approach to historic preservation; (5) By making clear the wealth of history that the town still has; (6) By pointing out how close to oblivion many historic properties are; (7) By presenting a rational plan for action; (8) By calling for an immediate move for preservation of the two or three properties at the top of the survey list; (9) By giving owners of historic properties an impetus for cooperating on preservation projects; (10) By giving city government officials the information they need to take actions toward instituting programs to preserve your town's history.*

Does it work? *Fremont, California, says yes.*

That list of how a town history survey can start a preservation movement rolling is drawn from the experiences of Dr Robert Fisher and his fellow Mission Peak Heritage Foundation members. Dr Fisher and friends envisioned the need for an area-wide historic properties survey back in 1960. At that time they were struggling to formulate a solid plan which would protect the vestiges of Fremont's agricultural era from disappearance under approaching waves of suburban expansion. The Fremont survey extended over a two year period, from 1965 to 1967. Members of the survey committee made use of old area maps to determine which buildings shown on those maps were still standing. They also received considerable input from residents. The list they submitted to the Town Council included **360 sites and buildings** *Half of these were rated low-priority and half were rated high-priority. The high-priority items were ranked according to feasibility and value of restoration.*

The Top Ten.

(1) Higuerra Galindo adobe (historic adobe home and surrounding natural land to be a historic park); (2) J.J. Vallejo Adobe and California Nursery; (3) Mission San Jose Plaza Complex; (4) Marshall-Indian Village Site; (5) Irvington Fossil Pits (25 acres); (6) Stanford Winery-Warm Springs Hotel Complex; (7) Ford Home-Nichols Home; (8) Patterson Estate (eucalyptus grove park); (9) Petroglyph Site and Mortar Bed; (10) Washington College. (Note: This list represented properties in need of attention. Other ordered lists, such as a list of properties suitable for historical-recreational parks, were also prepared.)

The Fremont survey was done in conjunction with the City Recreation Commission. Properties were listed as recreational sites and assets—quiet areas of great interest for future generations. That makes perfect sense, because the only large open areas remaining in Fremont are pieces of old agricultural estates. Thus the criteria for the top ten was: A. Prime parcels of land selected before the choice and prices were limited; B. Improved by horticultural amenities which only time can produce; C. Containing man-made structures which survive and remain functional because of the careful construction and materials which were used. (Acquisition of the historic resources is often facilitated by the desire of the heirs to the pioneer estates to perpetuate and protect their heritage by means of City purchase—often accomplished by a very satisfactory financial arrangement to the City with mutual benefit, tax-wise, to the owner.)

The Weight of the Document. *The survey list of 179 primary historic properties was accepted and approved by the City Planning Commission and by the Recreation Commission as a listing of the primary historical resources of the town of Fremont. The list thus became an official part of the Recreational Element of the Fremont General Plan. All primary historic resources were required to be shown on all city planning maps. In addition to legal recognition, the list received excellent publicity. The survey was an excellent first step towards saving some very fragile history.*

Making history economically attractive. *The Fremont people capitalized on the survey—thanks to the generosity of a grand old family and a stroke of genius. The story of how Dr Fisher and the Mission Peak Heritage Foundation received the gift of the Shinn Property and orchestrated different elements of the community on the clean-up and reconstruction appears on pages 78 and 79. That showed* how *and how* cheaply *restoration could be accomplished. The idea of density credits—allowing a builder a density increase in return for sparing historic properties—is also reviewed on those pages; the "density credits" system made protection of historic properties an economically profitable action.*

The Fremont people have proved over the past eight years that historic preservation need not *be a drain on city revenues; in fact, it can be one of the most economical ways to develop properties for community use. This demonstration of fiscal responsibility has added considerable weight to the Fremont historic survey.*

1952 ⊙ 1953

Korean Truce; war without a winner — US drops H-Bomb secretly in Pacific — Britain tests A-Bomb; USSR tries H-Bomb — W. Germany, France, Britain and US sign peace pact — Puerto Rico becomes first US "commonwealth" — Stalin dies in Moscow — Truman seizes steel mills; Supreme Court overrules, strike follows — Soviet troops quell strike-riots in E. Berlin — Tensing Norkay-Edmund Hillary conquer Everest.

DOING A TOWN HISTORY

There is no way anyone but you can decide how to go about producing a history of your community. We *can* tell you, however, that it is something very much worth doing for a couple of good reasons. On this and the next page, we've assembled some general suggestions you could consider while mapping out your own plan for the work.

First, the reasons. There probably isn't any single project that will rivet your community's attention so securely on its past than the preparation of a history, particularly if you can get the whole community involved. What's more, you can, at the same time, identify the things in your town that are worth hanging on to, and in the process, convince others that your town's history is too important to let go by the boards.

1. A Point of View from Eagle Bend. *One of the nicest little local history books we've come across is called* **Self Portrait: Eagle Bend. A Book About and By a Rural Community.** *It was produced by the townspeople of this little Minnesota town, and published by them through the school district. Aside from its design, which is better than average, the book conveys an attitude about the past that is unusual and, we think, very appropriate.*

The book's editor, Patrick Redmond, has incorporated the writing and art work of community members, particularly children, and has asked his contributors to describe their feelings about their town and their hopes for its future. Instead of just another compilation of names, dates and faces out of the past, **Self Portrait: Eagle Bend** *mixes the past with the present, suggesting that history is a continuous fabric, a little of which is woven daily out of the lives of everyone. While the supply lasts, copies may be obtained by sending $1 to Eagle Bend Public School District No. 790, Eagle Bend, Minnesota 56446.*

2. Why a book? *A book may be the least expensive, and possibly the longest-lasting, way to convey information about the history of your town. But it sure isn't the only way. And, depending on your community, it may not even be the best one. Here are some other possibilities to consider:*

> a slide show plus a tape and a talk
>
> an exhibit
>
> a community-made home movie
>
> a special edition of the local paper
>
> a local radio program series

In Cuero, Texas, Reverend Rogers MacLane went around town asking people if he could borrow old photographs for a day or so. He took pictures of all the old photos of Cuero he could get his hands on, and had them made into slides. He mixed some of these old-time pictures with some of his own, wrote a narrative around them, taped some appropriate music and put together the most rousing show you'd ever want to see. Reverend MacLane's show made people in the town realize just how interesting their history is. In fact, it made such an impression that when it came time to collect attic treasure for the Instant Museum or to attract volunteers for the town's restoration project, everyone was ready.

3. Open to the Public. *Whatever it is—book, exhibit, slide show or all three—your project is going to mean a lot more to a lot more people if you let them help. You'll have to set up a method for publicizing the project and attracting willing help. (The Old Time Photo Night idea is perfect for this purpose. See page 172.) You'll need to have some notion of what you need. Encourage everyone to loan you photographs, documents, letters or diaries they have at their disposal. Your project, whatever form it takes, will be better for it.*

4. Categories. *Making up a set of categories will make it easier to look for material. You should consider either one or both of these methods:*

a. *chronological ordering*

b. *topical ordering (lore of commerce, industry or farming; town leaders; scandals, riots or other disturbances; fire, flood or other acts of God; recollections—how it was to live back then; celebrations; parades, circuses and other entertainments; town characters; etc.)*

When asking for help, give examples. Lots of people don't understand how useful their family documents might be. Giving examples will prod their memories.

old letters	poetry
early photos	personal journals
diaries	artwork
old business records	patent drawings
military documents	deeds
maps	etc.
old handcrafted articles	
old art from magazines or newspapers	

5. Research and Organization. *Anyone who has put together a book will tell you that there isn't a perfect formula for gathering information. Material for your project will come from many sources, and for each the formula will be a little different.*

Start with names of sources. People. Long time residents who remember back. Put the names on file cards so that you can keep track of who has been contacted, particularly if you borrow documents or if

more than one person is conducting interviews. It will make keeping track of things much easier.

Make a list of other possible sources: state or local historical societies who have archives; college or university history departments or admissions office records may be helpful; the library may have collections of diaries or letters; the county recorder's office will have information on property transactions; church and business records that go back a long way; newspaper archives.

Have some kind of rough organization in mind as you begin to contact sources, but keep it open. You could consider a chronological presentation, or a topical one, or some combination. Whatever it is, be ready to consider alternatives that are suggested by what you find. It's no good to wreck or omit perfectly good material just to match some preconceived idea of organization.

1954 ⊙ 1955

AFL-CIO merge — Supreme Court orders school integration — ICC bans bus terminal segregation — Montgomery, Ala. blacks boycott buses — Nautilus atomic-sub launched — 5 Congressmen hit in House of Representatives shooting — SEATO formed — Warsaw Pact signed — Summit talks in Geneva — Dr. Jonas Salk demonstrates polio vaccine — Solar battery developed — Dr. Charles Townes invents optical maser.

6. Style. *The physical appearance and style of writing of whatever you produce will be a product of the experience, feelings and knowledge of whoever is involved. And that is the way it should be.*

Factual accuracy and intelligent interpretation of historical evidence are admirable objectives. But don't stop there. They alone won't make your audience enthusiastic. See to it that whatever you produce is at least as interesting and enjoyable as the material you collect.

7. Be Realistic. *At the beginning, it's wise to collect material (or at least locate it) without regard to limits of size or length. But as you begin to formulate a sense of the organization, you should begin to put limits on length, regardless of what form your presentation will take. No one will wade through a 300 page book, or stay awake for a two hour slide show, even if you could afford either one. Start thinking about length. Start thinking about how you're going to pay for it all. And start thinking about how you could make all the material, even including the stuff you don't use, or copies of it, available to everyone as a town historical resource library. (Having gone to all the trouble to locate it, it would be nice to save someone else all that work.)*

8. Money. *Sooner or later (probably sooner), it's going to come up. First, keep the project a labor of love. That alone will impose a natural and healthy limit on magnitude and keep you from creating a monster. Raise money to pay for the printing and binding (if you must), but nothing else. And keep the fund raising effort local. No one from out of town (except perhaps ex-residents) should be expected to contribute. Here are some ideas you would think of yourself eventually:*

1. Sell ads (can be simple name & address).

2. Sell sponsorships. Each donor is named on a list.

3. Sell advance reservations for copies (not recommended).

4. Get local groups to give fund raising events that not only raise money, but also history-consciousness. (Best method because of double benefits.)

5. Borrow necessary money from a local bank against sales of copies (admissions, etc.). It won't be much. It will get the bank involved (good publicity for them). And if they insist, form a committee to co-sign the note.

6. Tell your local newspaper publisher or printer that he can have the printing contract, but he must do it on spec. (All proceeds from sales go to him until his bill is paid.)

7. Offer long-time merchants a chance to advertise their business by publishing its history. Charge by the page. No less. Works like an ad, only makes a more interesting book.

Some advice: You can think of better ideas if you work at it. If you still can't figure out how to raise enough money, then the scheme is too ambitious and you should scale it down. Or, print it yourself. (See diagrams, next page.)

9. Some More Advice. *Don't wait until you've got the whole book done before seeing the printer. If you do, you'll regret it. He can help you save time and money if he's sympathetic and doesn't see just $$ when he looks at you. If you're doing a book, or a slide show (or any other form) for the first time, get yourself some technical help early. For free.*

Don't assume that the world will beat a path to your door when it's all over. You'll have to promote at this end, just as you probably did in the beginning. Think about using local groups to help. Remember, the more people spreading the word, the better.

In the old days, people used to pay to have their family histories included in the town directory. You might include a section on "first families," printing a capsule history of any family that has been in town since its founding. Don't charge. Or, if you do, set up the proceeds in a special fund to be used to restore that old one room school house, or whatever.

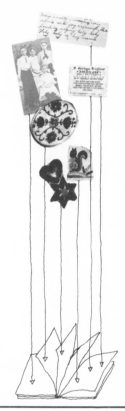

1956 ⊙ 1957

Sputnik I and II put USSR in orbit — US, Russia successfully test ICBMs — British test H-Bomb — First underground nuclear test in Nevada — Shippingport, Pa. site of first nuclear power plant — Montgomery integrates bus system — Race riots in Birmingham, Nashville — National Guard called out at Little Rock Central High — Civil rights act passed — Federal Civil Rights Commission formed — Filibuster record: Strom Thurmond's 24-hr. 18 min. monologue — Egypt seizes Suez — Israel invades Egypt — UN enforces Mideast truce — First transatlantic phone cable opens.

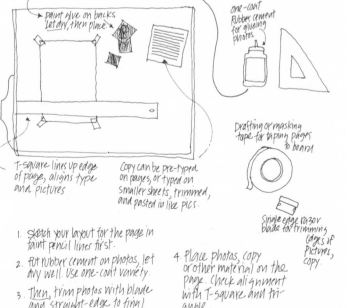

Do It Yourself. *If you own a decent typewriter and want to make the effort, you can do everything but print the book in your own living room. Make each page up on heavy white bond paper (one side only), standard letter size. Use your typewriter as a typesetter. Type copy on one page, put illustrations on the facing page. Then ask your printer to reduce the pages from 8½ x 11 inches to about 6 x 8 inches when your book is printed. This method is only practical when your book is printed by offset lithography, which is a process most printers are equipped for. So check first.*

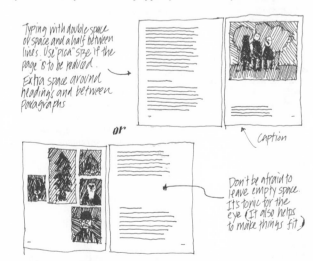

Typing with double space or space and a half between lines. Use "pica" size if the page is to be reduced. Extra space around headings and between paragraphs

or

Caption

Don't be afraid to leave empty space. It's tonic for the eye (It also helps to make things fit)

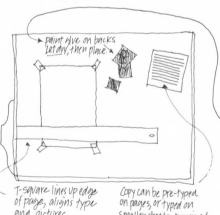

Paint glue on backs let dry, then place.

one-coat Rubber cement for glueing photos

Drafting or masking tape for taping pages to board

T-square lines up edge of page, aligns type and pictures

Copy can be pre-typed on pages, or typed on smaller sheets, trimmed, and pasted in like pics.

Single edge razor blade for trimming edges of pictures, copy.

1. Sketch your layout for the page in faint pencil lines first.

2. Put rubber cement on photos, let dry well. Use one-coat variety.

3. Then, trim photos with blade and straight-edge to final size. (Don't worry about glue, you can lift it after trimming)

4. Place photos, copy or other material on the page. Check alignment with T-square and triangle. Once in position, rub firmly to adhere.

THE WHERE TO GO FOR HELP GUIDE

This brief guide contains names and addresses of organizations which potentially can help your grass roots history project. It also lists several books, pamphlets and magazines we think may be useful.

Before you dive in too deeply, consider this maxim that many project leaders have found to be true: The further away from your community a source of assistance is, the less likely it is to yield substantial help.

People's history projects are of greatest importance to the *community*: they involve the saving of a part of community life by the people of the community. Local people normally understand the importance of a history project in their own town and will help willingly if the project is well-presented. But it often takes great time and energy to convince state or federal personnel that your project needs and deserves help of any kind. Financial aid from state or national organizations may be worth going after, but if you depend on it you may be headed for trouble.

The same general principle holds true for information: The best place to find out about life in your town yesterday is your town today. Not all of the information is written down. Some of it is buried underground, some of it is pasted in old albums, quite a bit is in the memories of elderly residents. This goes for technological know-how *and* historic data (not to mention creative ideas). Searching within your town is often a much more rewarding information-gathering process than poring through nationally-oriented publications.

We realize that this list is not absolutely complete, so although we have tried to be as accurate as possible, it would be a good idea for each individual or group to check into the areas which pertain to him or her.

Look Locally First

Your Local Library *has considerably more than just hard-backed books, slick magazines and encyclopedias. Ask your librarian about original manuscripts written by townspeople; about books and booklets describing your local history; about genealogies which may list some of your relatives; about old local newspaper issues and local periodicals. In fact, ask the librarian herself. She probably has better than passing knowledge of your town's history, and she may be quite willing to involve herself in your project.*

Your Town Clerk *is the keeper of records—and he doesn't do it just for his health. Old town records are there to be used; otherwise there's no point in keeping them. The town clerk should have vital statistics (listings of births, deaths and marriages) and land records going well back into the nineteenth century. Especially interesting are Sanborn Maps; these are large-scale maps which are prepared for most towns. They show every building in town and denote what material (wood, brick, concrete) comprises each.*

The County Recorder, *who probably has an office in or near your county courthouse, has county land records which may pre-date those of your town. He may also have early vital statistics for your area.*

The Probate Office, *which is also probably in or near the county courthouse, has records of wills, probate settlements and lawsuits. These are useful for genealogical research and also for details on your town's epic legal conflicts.*

Schools and Universities *should be involved in any project you undertake. Students have made major contributions in many town-wide history projects—actually, they have organized and provided leadership in several. Teachers and school administrators will undoubtedly*

be interested in preservation projects because of their value as vehicles for making history meaningful.

Local Industries, Church Groups, Service Clubs and Groups of Professionals *are good places to take your campaign. Each is a potential source of good advice . . . of information . . . of building materials . . . of meeting space . . . of funds . . . of publicity . . . and most important, of skilled and influential volunteers.*

Your Town Government *will probably be interested to hear about your project, and may give you considerable support. But it should not be looked to as a major source of funds: a thousand dollars taken from the city treasury to shore up an old schoolhouse sometimes causes controversy and ill will; a thousand dollars raised through private donations and at community events always is cause for civic pride.*

Your Town Newspaper *may have been reporting news longer than anyone alive remembers. Many papers keep complete files of back issues, plus clipped articles from past issues kept by subject in the "morgue." The "morgue" is a far more convenient source of data than bound issues, except when you know an exact date. The newspaper editor himself quite possibly knows more about your town—yesterday and today—than anyone else, and also probably has a high sense of the importance of civic involvement. And he's a good man to have on your side. Don't leave him out of your project.*

The Small Towns Institute

The Small Towns Institute *(Box 517, Ellensburg, Washington 98926)* is the only organization we know about which is working actively to solve the social and economic problems peculiar to American small towns. They serve as a source of information and a referral agency. Concerned citizens of small towns experiencing economic and/or social difficulties might do well to correspond with co-directors Clayton C. Denman and Anne Smith Denman.

In their article called, "About the Small Towns Institute and the Future of Small Town America," they say: *"The Small Towns Institute is a national organization whose members are dedicated to making small town America a viable alternative to congested cities and the sprawl of suburbs. In order to make small towns vital communities of the future, we must develop new methods to bring economic prosperity, to save the rural environment, and to increase opportunities for young people to use their skills in the countryside.*

"As environmental pollution and social disorders spread across metropolitan America, many citizens have come to realize that small towns offer a contrasting way of life that combines the beauty and serenity of the countryside with greater opportunities for participation in a true human community. For it is here in the countryside that small towns, family farms, small businesses, and local government all contribute to a sense of community. It is here that the enthusiasm and energy of the young, and the tempered wisdom of older generations can come to develop common interests.

"S T I was founded in 1969 as a non-profit, tax deductible organization to focus political, business, and academic studies on the real needs of small towns. Institute programs include the publication of the newsjournal Small Town; *the development of educational and library resources, lectures, conferences, workshops, and a scholarship program; and research on technical, economic, and social problems. We strongly believe that these new efforts must go far beyond research to produce practical programs for revitalization of the countryside."*

The newsjournal publishes articles which are thought-provoking and also of great practical value. Topics of previously-published articles include "Rural Poverty and Land Ownership," "Art in the Small Community," "Administration Policies Aimed at Small Farmers," "Education Serving Rural Youth" and "The Town Government as a Community Development Corporation."

A new feature of the S T I newsjournal is a review of all Congressional legislation introduced which relates to small towns. Information carried in the newsjournal can help residents interested in preserving traditional ways of life in their town; the newsjournal is sent regularly to individuals and organizations who become members of the Small Towns Institute. Membership may be obtained by writing the Institute; annual dues are $10 for individuals.

The Oral History Association

The Oral History Association is an international society of organizations and individuals interested in advancing the practice and use of oral history. They say:

"To further liaison among its members, the Association publishes quarterly the Oral History Newsletter, which announces oral history projects, describes new developments, and provides a forum for exchange of views on practical and intellectual problems in this growing field. In addition the Association holds a colloquium each fall and publishes the proceedings.

"Oral history was established in 1948 as a modern technique for historical documentation when Columbia University historian Allan Nevins began recording the memoirs of persons significant in American life. Gradually similar projects developed at other institutions. The technique has come into use increasingly as a tool for historical research in such fields as politics, science, the arts, agriculture, natural resources, industry, labor, and ethnic and local history."

Everyone is invited to participate in the activities of the Oral History Association. Information about membership may be obtained from The Oral History Association, Box 20, Butler Library, Columbia University, New York, New York 10027.

The Smithsonian Institution

The Smithsonian Institution (Washington, D. C. 20560) has several departments which are interested in preservation projects. The Laconia, New Hampshire, project has been helped considerably by correspondence from Smithsonian officials expressing support for their project.

Records of your Ancestors' Arrival

The Immigration and Naturalization Service
119 "D" Street, N. E.
Washington, D. C. 20536

The Immigration and Naturalization Service keeps copies of the naturalization petitions of all immigrants. This record of an ancestor's arrival includes much family information, and should be especially useful to anyone working on a family tree.

In order to obtain a copy of the naturalization petition of your ancestor, you need to send a copy of the passenger list from the voyage on which your ancestor arrived. (See page 141, step 19, for details on how to get this.) The copy of the complete naturalization petition costs $3.75.

The American Association for State and Local History

This organization is a well-established national organization dedicated to serving the interests of local historical societies. They do this primarily by offering a large variety of rather inexpensive informational books and pamphlets on such subjects as: *School Loan Exhibits for the Local Historical Society; Nail Chronology as an Aid to Dating Old Buildings; Leather: Its Understanding and Care; Industrial and Organizational Sponsorship of Museum Exhibits.*

The AASLH pamphlets should be quite helpful to people responsible for small museums or antique collections. They are strong on specific preservation techniques.

They also publish a monthly magazine entitled *History News.* It is sent free to Association members, and contains such timely information as where grants are available, what's changing in national museums, and what new historical books are being published.

Membership in the Association is $12.50 annually, and members receive a discount on all AASLH publications. To join, write to The American Association for State and Local History, 1315 Eighth Avenue South, Nashville, Tennessee 37203.

Library of Congress

The Library of Congress (Washington, D. C. 20540) serves a dual function: it provides research and reference services for the Federal Government and it also functions as a National Library. As of 30 June 1971, the Library of Congress had over 64 million items in its collections.

The general reference and bibliography division has a local history and genealogy room which contains more than 200,000 volumes of U. S. and European genealogy, heraldry and local history—including city directories, published vital statistics, military records and church registers—and such items as a 155,000 card index to biographical histories from fifteen midwestern states.

There are several divisions of the Library of Congress which the history-seeker may find useful, such as the law library, the manuscript division, the music division (which has an extensive collection of American folk music), the prints and photographs division, the rare book division, the geography and map division (which holds copies of old maps of most American towns) and the science and technology division.

The Library of Congress staff will respond to brief inquiries and will make photostat or microfilm copies of items in the collection which you need. There is a fee for the service.

For advice on preservation techniques:
Specialists of the Library of Congress Preservation Office will answer without charge brief technical inquiries on matters relating to the preservation, restoration, protection and physical custody of library materials. Write to the Assistant Director for Preservation, Administrative Department, Library of Congress, Washington, D. C. 20540.

Government Printing Office

The United States Government Printing Office can provide a lot of information. You may either write to the Superintendent of Documents, Government Printing Office, Washington, D. C. 20402, or visit one of their regional offices to find out about available resources. Regional offices are located in many major cities. Price lists are free.

If you're involved in a large-scale project which seems to require outside financial aid, you would do well to order the *Catalogue of Federal Domestic Assistance.* This publication contains official information about every

Federal program which provides goods or services to either individuals or organizations. It is issued by the Office of Management and Budget (under the Executive Office of the President) and is revised annually. The cost is $7.00, and it may be ordered from the U. S. Government Printing Office, Washington, D. C. 20402. Each entry explains the program's objectives, uses and restrictions, eligibility requirements, literature available and information contacts.

The National Archives

The National Archives hold permanently valuable records of the three branches of America's government. In past years, they have tended to function like a giant safe-deposit box; just sitting behind locked doors for the day they would be needed (which seldom came for most of the records).

But during the past few years, the General Services Administration (which oversees the Archives) has been at work trying to put all the accumulated documents to good use.

1958 ⊙ 1959

Explorer I: first successful US satellite — Atlas ICBM developed — NASA born — Russia's Luniks: first man-made "planets" reach the moon — Nautilus subnavigates North Pole — Transatlantic jet passenger service begins — Little Rock integration delay blocked — Castro takes control of Cuba — Alaska, Hawaii join union — St. Lawrence Seaway opens — Nixon, Khruschev exchange visits — TV quiz scandals uncovered — Oklahoma goes wet, prohibition finally dries up — One continent without boundaries: Antarctica preserved for science.

What you'll probably find in your regional archives:

What they've done is to open eleven regional archives, and stock them with records interesting to the local community. They have also inaugurated a fantastic microfilming program—and these rolls of microfilms which tell so many true stories of America's younger days are available to *you* through your local library (thanks to the Archives' inter-library loan program). Staffers at the regional centers also put together traveling exhibits about events in regional history.

Records of District Courts of the United States—including criminal, civil, admiralty and bankruptcy dockets and case files. Records of the United States Courts of Appeals. Records of the Bureau of Indian Affairs. Records of the Office of the Chief of Engineers.

The decentralization is still in progress. The following are scheduled to be available in Regional Centers soon: Bureau of Land Management; National Park Service; Department of the Interior; Forest Service; Department of Agriculture; Bureau of Customs.

And some very fascinating special records groups—such as the records of the National Recovery Administration, the records of the territorial government of Alaska, and the records of American Samoa—are kept in the appropriate regional center.

Here is a list of the Regional Archives Branches and the areas they serve. For each of the following, address inquiries to: Chief, Archives Branch, Federal Records Center.

Boston

380 Trapelo Road
Waltham, MA 02154
(617) 223-2657
Serves Maine, Vermont, New Hampshire, Massachusetts, Connecticut and Rhode Island.

Seattle

6125 Sand Point Way
Seattle, WA 98115
(206) 442-4500
Serves Washington, Oregon, Idaho and Alaska.

New York

641 Washington Street
New York, NY 10014
(212) 620-5837
Serves New York, New Jersey, Puerto Rico and the Virgin Islands.

Philadelphia

5000 Wissahickon Avenue
Philadelphia, PA 19144
(215) GE8-5200, ext. 588
Serves Pennsylvania, Delaware, Maryland, Virginia, West Virginia and the District of Columbia.

Atlanta

1557 St. Joseph Avenue
East Point, GA 30344
(404) 526-7477
Serves North Carolina, South Carolina, Tennessee, Mississippi, Georgia, Alabama, Kentucky and Florida.

Chicago

7201 South Leamington Avenue
Chicago, IL 60638
(312) 353-5720
Serves Minnesota, Illinois, Wisconsin, Michigan, Indiana and Ohio.

Kansas City

2306 East Bannister Road
Kansas City, MO 64131
(816) 361-0860, ext 7271
Serves Kansas, Iowa, Nebraska and Missouri.

Fort Worth

4900 Hemphill Street
P. O. Box 6216
Fort Worth, TX 76115
(817) 334-5515
Serves Texas, New Mexico, Oklahoma, Arkansas and Louisiana.

Denver

Bldg. 48, Denver Federal Center
Denver, CO 80225
(303) 234-3187
Serves Colorado, Montana, Wyoming, Utah, North Dakota and South Dakota.

San Francisco

Bldg. 1, 100 Harrison Street
San Francisco, CA 94105
(415) 556-8452
Serves Nevada except Clark County, California except southern California, Hawaii and the Pacific Ocean area.

Los Angeles

4747 Eastern Avenue
Bell, CA 90201
(213) 268-2548
Serves Arizona, the southern California counties of San Luis Obispo, Kern, San Bernadino, Santa Barbara, Ventura, Los Angeles, Riverside, Orange, Imperial, Inyo and San Diego, and Clark County, Nevada.

Further information on the National Archives is available free. Write to the National Archives, GSA, Washington, D. C. 20408, and ask for general information leaflets 1 and 22. Free information about collections held in a particular regional center can be obtained by writing to the director of that regional center. There is also a list of 200 publications available from the Archives—"Publications of the National Archives and Records Service." It's free—write the Publications Sales Branch, National Archives, GSA, Washington, D. C. 20408.

Society for the Preservation of Old Mills

This organization will help with preservation when it can, and honors individuals whose work in this area is outstanding, or who made the mills possible originally. The Society acts as a clearing house on mill information. It publishes a quarterly newsletter called *Old Mill News* which is filled with information and stories "to promote interest in old mills and other Americana now passing from the present scene." Membership (which includes the newsletter) is $5 annually. Write to the Society for the Preservation of Old Mills, P.O. Box 435, Wiscasset, Maine 04578.

Association for Living Historical Farms and Agricultural Museums

This Association was started by people interested in preserving historical farms and other aspects of agricultural history. Its publication, *Living Historical Farms Handbook*, is a high-quality, comprehensive book which should be of great interest to any group considering starting (or saving) a historical farm. Besides specific operational suggestions, the book includes a twenty page list of people all across the United States who are particularly interested in historic farms. Information about the Association and the Handbook is available from the Smithsonian Institution Press, Washington, D. C. The Handbook was written by John T. Shlebecker and Gale E. Peterson (1972).

The Pioneer America Society

The journal of the Pioneer America Society, Inc., carries short articles about historic events and places, and also features preservation projects. Subscriptions to *Pioneer America*, published twice yearly, are $2.50 to members, $3.00 to non-members. (Membership dues for the Pioneer America Society are $5.00 per year.) An article reprinted from the Pioneer America Journal appears on page 124 of this book. The Society's address is 626 South Washington Street, Falls Church, Virginia 22046.

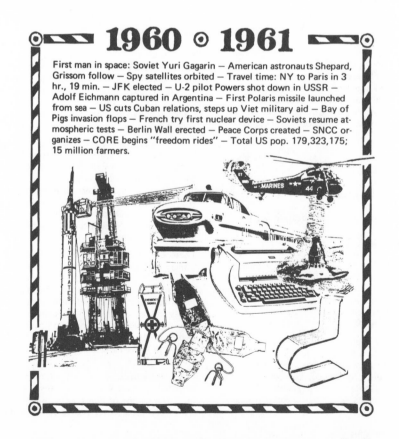

1960 ◉ 1961

First man in space: Soviet Yuri Gagarin — American astronauts Shepard, Grissom follow — Spy satellites orbited — Travel time: NY to Paris in 3 hr., 19 min. — JFK elected — U-2 pilot Powers shot down in USSR — Adolf Eichmann captured in Argentina — First Polaris missile launched from sea — US cuts Cuban relations, steps up Viet military aid — Bay of Pigs invasion flops — French try first nuclear device — Soviets resume atmospheric tests — Berlin Wall erected — Peace Corps created — SNCC organizes — CORE begins "freedom rides" — Total US pop. 179,323,175; 15 million farmers.

Archaeology

On page 170 are some hints for readers who hanker to dig for their history. Also on that page is a prominent caution against digging up prehistoric artifacts willy-nilly without adequate professional assistance. If you find something in the ground that you believe is a bona fide prehistoric artifact, contact the group on this list in your state.

Alabama
Department of Anthropology, Box 6136, University of Alabama, University, Alabama 35486

Alaska
Department of Anthropology, Alaska Methodist University, Anchorage, Alaska 99504

Arizona
State Archeologist, Arizona State Museum, University of Arizona, Tucson, Arizona 85721

Arkansas
State Archeologist, Arkansas Archeological Survey, University of Arkansas Museum, Fayetteville, Arkansas 72701

California
State Park Archeologist, Department of Parks & Recreation, P.O. Box 2390, Sacramento, California 95811

Colorado
Department of Anthropology, University of Colorado, Boulder, Colorado 80302

Connecticut
State Archaeologist, Jorgensen Avlitorium, University of Connecticut, Storrs, Connecticut 06268

Delaware
Delaware Archaeological Board, RD 2, Box 166A, Chestnut Grove Road, Dover, Delaware 19901

Florida
State Archeologist, Bureau of Historic Sites & Properties, Department of State, The Capitol, Tallahassee, Florida 32304

Georgia
Department of Sociology & Anthropology, University of Georgia, Atlanta, Georgia 30601

Hawaii
State Archeologist, Department of Land & Natural Resources, P.O. Box 621, Honolulu, Hawaii 96809

Idaho
Department of Anthropology, Idaho State University, Pocatello, Idaho 83201

Illinois
Illinois Archaeological Survey, Department of Anthropology, Davenport Hall, University of Illinois, Urbana, Illinois 61801

Indiana
Department of Anthropology, Rawles Hall 108, Indiana University, Bloomington, Indiana 47401

Iowa
Office of State Archeologist, 129 S. Capitol, State University of Iowa, Iowa City, Iowa 52240

Kansas
State Archeologist, Kansas State Historical Society, Topeka, Kansas 66603

Kentucky
Kentucky Archeological Survey, Department of Anthropology, University of Kentucky, Lexington, Kentucky 40506

Louisiana
Department of Geography and Anthropology, Louisiana State University, Baton Rouge, Louisiana 70803

Maine
Department of Anthropology, University of Maine, Orono, Maine 04473

Maryland
State Archeologist, Maryland Geological Survey, Latrobe Hall, Johns Hopkins University, Baltimore, Maryland 21218

Massachusetts
Bronson Museum, 8 N. Maine Street, Attleboro, Massachusetts 02708

Michigan
Museum of Anthropology, 4011 Museums Building, University of Michigan, Ann Arbor, Michigan 48104

Minnesota
State Archeologist, Department of Anthropology, 200 Ford Hall, University of Minnesota, Minneapolis, Minnesota 55455

Mississippi
State Archeologist, Mississippi Archaeological Survey, Department of Archives & History, Jackson, Mississippi 39201

Missouri
Director, Archaeological Survey, 15 Switzler Hall, University of Missouri—Columbia, Columbia, Missouri 65201

Montana
Montana Statewide Archeological Survey, Department of Anthropology, University of Montana, Missoula, Montana 59801

Nebraska
Nebraska State Historical Society, Lincoln, Nebraska 68501

Nevada
Nevada Archeological Survey, University of Nevada, Reno, Nevada 89507

New Hampshire
Department of Sociology—Anthropology, Franklin Pierce College, Rindge, New Hampshire 03461

New Jersey
Bureau of Research—Archeology, New Jersey State Museum, Trenton, New Jersey 08625

New Mexico
Division of Anthropology, Museum of New Mexico, P.O. Box 2087, Santa Fe, New Mexico 87501

New York
State Archeologist, Social Science 369, New York State Museum, Albany, New York 12203

North Carolina
State Archeologist, Department of Anthropology, University of North Carolina, Chapel Hill, North Carolina 27514

North Dakota
State Historical Society of North Dakota, Liberty Memorial Building, Bismarck, North Dakota 58501

Ohio
Division of Archaeology, The Ohio Historical Society, Columbus, Ohio 43210

Oklahoma
State Archaeologist, Oklahoma Archaeological Survey, 1335 South Asp, University of Oklahoma, Norman, Oklahoma 73069

Oregon
Museum of Natural History, University of Oregon, Eugene, Oregon 97403

Pennsylvania
State Archeologist, William Penn Memorial Museum, Box 232, Harrisburg, Pennsylvania 17108

Rhode Island
Department of Sociology & Anthropology, Brown University, Providence, Rhode Island 02912

South Carolina
Institute of Archeology & Anthropology, University of South Carolina, Columbia, South Carolina 29208

South Dakota
W.H. Over-Dakota Museum, University of South Dakota, Vermillion, South Dakota 57069

Tennessee
The McClung Museum, University of Tennessee, Knoxville, Tennessee 37916

Texas
State Archeologist, State Building Commission, P.O. Box 12172, Austin, Texas 78711

Utah
Statewide Archeological Survey, University of Utah, Salt Lake City, Utah 84112

Vermont
Department of Sociology & Anthropology, University of Vermont, Burlington, Vermont 05401

Virginia
Archeologist, Virginia State Library, Richmond, Virginia 23219

Washington
Department of Anthropology, Washington State University, Pullman, Washington 99163

1962 ⊙ 1963

JFK assassinated — Medger Evers killed in Mississippi — 210,000 march for equal rights in Washington — Martin Luther King has a dream — 4 black girls die in Birmingham church bombing — Diem regime overthrown in Viet coup — Britain, USSR, US sign nuclear test ban — Supreme Court rules out required school prayers — Soviet Missile crisis in Cuba — 200 millionth auto rolls from Detroit — First woman in space: USSR's Valatina Tereshkova — Glenn first American in orbit — Carpenter, Schirra, Cooper follow in Mercury missions — Soviets rendezvous in space.

West Virginia
Section of Archeology, West Virginia Geological Survey, Box 879, Morgantown, West Virginia 26505

Wisconsin
State Archeologist, State Historical Society of Wisc., Madison, Wisconsin 53706

Wyoming
State Archeologist, Department of Anthropology, University of Wyoming, University Station Box 3431, Laramie, Wyoming 82070

Archaeology and the Historical Society, by J. C. Harrington, is available for $2.00 from the American Association for State and Local History, 1315 Eighth Avenue South, Nashville, Tennessee 37203. This extensive pamphlet has useful general information for would-be diggers, and is slanted towards historic archaeology.

Stewards of the Past. A 24-page pamphlet which is worth handing out to friends and acquaintances. It tells of the need for increased prehistoric archaeological research. Just $5.50 buys you *fifty* copies. (Arkansas Archaeological Society, University of Arkansas Museum, Fayetteville, Arkansas 72701.)

Roland Robbins, RFD 2, Lincoln, Massachusetts 01773. Mr Robbins has published several booklets on Historic Archaeology and on specific projects he has completed. These give procedural tips on how to conduct a thorough historic dig.

Public Archaeology, by Dr. C. R. McGimsey III, published by Seminar Press, 111 Fifth Avenue, New York, New York 10003. Price $9.50. Dr. McGimsey is a co-organizer of Arkansas' excellent public-participation archaeology project. This book is especially useful for those interested in setting up a state-wide program of participatory archaeological research.

Federal Archaeological Salvage Program

If an archaeological site in your area is in danger of being disturbed by a federally-funded project such as a highway or a dam, the National Park Service may be able to make money available for a survey to be done before the project gets underway. Applications must be made by a qualified educational or scientific institution (such as a State archaeological survey group). Offices are as follows:

Headquarters Office: Director, Office of Archeology and Historic Preservation, National Park Service, U. S. Department of the Interior, Washington, D. C. 20240, (202) 343-2573.

Regional or Local Office: Southeast Region: Southeast Archeological Center, National Park Service, P. O. Box 4547, Macon, Georgia 31208, (912) 745-2243; *Northeast Region: Division of Archeology, National Park Service, 801 19th Street, N. W., Washington, D. C. 20006, (202) 343-8932;* Midwest Region: Midwest Archeological Center, National Park Service, 2605 North 27th Street, Lincoln, Nebraska 68504, (402) 475-3666; *Southwest and Western Regions: Southwest Archeological Center, National Park Service, University of Arizona, P. O. Box 49008, Tucson, Arizona 85717, (602) 792-6501;* Pacific Northwest Region: Pacific Northwest Regional Office, 4th and Pike Building, 1424 Fourth Avenue, Seattle, Washington 98101, (206) 583-5565.

Sanborn Maps

The Sanborn Map Company (629 Fifth Avenue, Pelham, New York 10803) produces the large scale land use maps that towns use for planning and tax purposes. These maps are bound into books for ease of use; photostatic reproductions of current Sanborn maps may be obtained from the Sanborn Company at a cost of from $5 to $10 per page. Many towns save their old Sanborn Maps, but some do not. If you want to find out what sort of buildings once occupied a section of your town, but your town clerk's office doesn't have the old Sanborn Maps, you can contact the Map Reference Department in the Library of Congress and obtain a copy of the map or maps of your city with this information. Copies are fairly expensive but quite interesting and useful for history projects.

Department of Housing and Urban Development

Historic Preservation in Urban Renewal Areas is a pamphlet (designated HUD-84-R) available free from the Department of Housing and Urban Development. It outlines steps necessary to apply for funds to save and restore historic properties within an urban renewal area.

Another free pamphlet available from the Department of Housing and Urban Development is entitled *The Historic Preservation Program* (HUD-139-MD). If you have a preservation project in an urban area, you may be eligible for financial assistance from HUD, and probably should read this pamphlet.

Write: Department of Housing and Urban Development, Washington, D. C. 20410.

Historic American Buildings Survey

The Historic American Buildings Survey records and photographs important examples of American architecture, and deposits those in the Library of Congress. Inclusion does not guarantee preservation—in fact, one half of the 12,000 buildings recorded since 1933 have been destroyed.

The Survey is conducted by the National Park Service in cooperation with the American Institute of Architects and the Library of Congress. The Headquarters' address is: Historic American Buildings Survey, National Park Service, 801 Nineteenth Street, N. W., Washington, D. C. 10006.

Public Land for Recreation, Public Purposes and Historic Monuments

Available public lands may be used for historic, educational or recreational purposes. States, counties, municipalities and non-profit organizations may apply for transfer of land to their control. For historic monuments there is no monetary consideration involved; for other uses a minimum fee must be paid. The national office administering this program is the Division of Lands and Realty, Bureau of Land Management, U. S. Department of the Interior, Washington, D. C. 20240.

Disposal of Federal Surplus Real Property

State and local agencies are eligible to apply to the General Services Administration for transfer of surplus federal property which has value as a historic park or a historic monument. The transfer can either be free or at a discount of actual value. The Regional Director of Property Management and Disposal Service—General Services Administration—is the man to contact first. The program is headed by the Assistant Commissioner, Office of Real Property, Property Management and Disposal Service, General Services Administration, Washington, D. C. 20405.

The American Museum of Folk Art

The American Museum of Folk Art, 49 West 53rd Street, New York City 10019, focuses on the beauty of the works of art made by self-taught artists of America's past and present. Each year the museum produces a series of folk art shows. Several of these travel across the country and are shown in regional museums, schools and libraries. Museum membership is $15 annually.

1964 ⊙ 1965

Gulf of Tonkin: Viet war escalates — Communist China explodes first A-Bomb — US steps up Viet bombing after Pleiku attacks — OAS troops quiet Dominican turmoil — KKK charged in Mississippi civil rights slayings — 35 die in LA Watts riot — King leads first Selma march — Viola Liuzzo shot and killed — Voting Rights Act signed — Warren Commission pins Oswald — Great NE Blackout: 30 million in dark for a night — Ranger 7 takes first lunar close-up photos — Gemini 6-7 rendezvous — Soviet Aleksei Leonov, US Ed White take first space walks.

The organizations here may be able to assist you with money for your project, but don't count on it. You are much more likely to get help from these groups if they think you're going to get the money one way or another on your own. Like we said before: Keep your money needs small and you can almost always accomplish a reasonable objective without outside help.

The National Register of Historic Places

The National Register of Historic Places *is an inventory of properties deserving of preservation. It includes historical areas in the National Park System, and also properties of state or local significance nominated by the state and approved by the National Park Service. An entry must have significance in American history, architecture, archaeology or culture, but need not be associated with historically important events.*

The National Register of Historic Places is administered by the National Park Service, which is a part of the Department of the Interior. Offices are in Washington, D. C. A brochure explaining the program is available FREE from the U. S. Government Printing Office, Division of Public Documents, Washington, D. C. 20402.

Historic Preservation Project Grants

The National Park Service (under the Department of the Interior) makes funds available to help finance state surveys and plans for historic preservation, staff salaries and equipment and materials. Funds can also be used directly for acquiring historic property and preparation of restoration plans. Only properties listed on the National Register of Historic Places are eligible. All applications are handled through the National Trust for Historic Preservation. The main administrative office is the Office of Archeology and Historic Preservation, National Park Service, U. S. Department of the Interior, 801 Nineteenth Street, N. W. Washington, D. C. 20006. Phone: (202) 343-2573.

The America the Beautiful Fund

The Fund is a national, non-profit foundation which is supported by public contributions and which gives assistance to local preservation and other environmental projects. Small "seed" grants are available to qualifying groups for launching projects. Field assistance is available in some states. See the Reader Response form at the end of this book for information on how to contact the Fund.

1966 ◉ 1967

Pentagon protest: 647 marchers arrested — 6-Day war in Middle East — First heart transplanted — LBJ, Kosygin meet in NJ — Medicare goes into effect — Adam Clayton Powell loses House seat; Thomas Dodd censured in Senate — US, Russians soft-land probes on moon — Surveyor 3 digs first lunar soil sample — Gemini 11-Agena D make first space dock — Apollo fire: first astronauts die on board — Edward Brooke (R. Mass.) first black Senator in 85 years — Race riots in Newark, Detroit — Thurgood Marshall first black Supreme Court Justice.

Grants for Preservation

The National Trust for Historic Preservation
740-748 Jackson Place, N. W.
Washington, D. C. 20006

The National Trust for Historic Preservation is a private non-profit organization chartered in 1949 by an Act of Congress to encourage participation in the preservation of districts, sites, buildings, structures and objects significant in American culture. The Trust is involved in local preservation projects through the *Consultant Services Program*, which provides matching grants to be used to obtain the advice of professional consultants on preservation projects; and through the *National Historic Preservation Fund*, which makes available to private preservation groups low-interest loans and matching grants for actual project costs. Check with your state Historical Society for information about the location of the National Trust's regional offices.

Open Space Land Programs

Local communities may apply to the Department of Housing and Urban Development for funds to purchase open space land in urban areas. Such space can include historic buildings listed on the National Register of Historic Places—and the funding can include money for restoration. Acquisition and development of the open space land must be in accord with a unified and officially coordinated program for development of open space land as part of local and area-wide comprehensive planning. Inquiries should be directed to your Area Office Director of the Department of Housing and Urban Development or to the Headquarters Office, Community Development, Washington, D. C. 20410. (202) 755-5435.

Historic American Engineering Record

Funding is available for projects which seek to document significant structures in the history of American engineering; most projects involve the employment of university architectural students and professors. If you have such a building in your area, bring it to the attention of either your local government, your local historical society or the university in your area. They then can apply for funding to: Historic American Engineering Record, National Park Service, 801 Nineteenth Street, N. W., Washington D. C. 20006.

Acknowledgments

We would like to thank the following for their help in providing photographs or other material on the pages listed.

Page 12 *Cuero Historical Society;* **Page 17** *Joel F. Overholser;* **Page 19** *Ben Hendricks;* **Page 20** *Last Indian Raid Museum;* **Page 23** *Hellen Caldwell, Virginia Cavalcade (Winter 1971), Roanoke World News (12/16/70);* **Page 24-25** *Susan Pelham;* **Page 26-27** *Wayne Wright;* **Page 28** *Charles La Forge;* **Page 30** *Laconia News (Krug), Save the Mills Society;* **Page 32** *Jack Reineck, San Luis Obispo Telegram-Tribune;* **Page 35** *The Canaltowner (May 1972);* **Page 37** *Arizona Historical Society;* **Page 40-41** *Historic Annapolis, Inc.;* **Page 45** *Decatur Messenger, Wise County Historical Society;* **Page 46-47** *Albany Historical Society;* **Page 48** *Dixie Schoolhouse Foundation;* **Page 49** *Dave Greenlee (Beloit Daily News), Mrs Evlyn Beck, Norm Hofstrom (Yagla's);* **Page 51** *Boone News-Republican, Mr Edward Meyers;* **Page 52** *Mr and Mrs Frederick M. Winkler;* **Page 53** *Nancy Burrows;* **Page 54** *Littleton Courier, Mrs Greta Poulsen;* **Page 55** *Woodland Democrat, Don Denison;* **Page 56** *Mrs Sewall C. Brown, Rockport Garden Club;* **Page 57** *Arthur Baird, Mrs Russell Derby;* **Page 59** *Dr. John Schott;* **Page 60** *Georgia S. Robertson;* **Page 62** *Marion Gonnerman;* **Page 66** *Earl Muehlenbach;* **Page 67** *Alfred M. Hottes (California Horticultural Journal, October 1971);* **Page 71** *Free Press Standard;* **Page 73** *Mary Sienkiewicz;* **Page 74** *Minnesota Valley River Project, Mrs Ginger Timmons;* **Page 75** *Harry V. Leida;* **Page 77** *Ernst Henes;* **Page 78-79** *Dr Robert B. Fisher, Hayward Area Recreation and Parks District;* **Page 82** *Spencer-Owen Civic League;* **Page 83** *Mike Gill;* **Page 84-85** *Herbert Redhead;* **Page 86** *Mrs Robert Hotz;* **Page 87** *The Granger Homestead Society, Inc.;* **Page 88** *Little Beaver Historical Society;* **Page 89** *Molalla Area Historical Society;* **Page 90** *America the Beautiful Fund;* **Page 92** *Keith Richard;* **Page 95** *Davis photo of Joan van den Hende;* **Page 98** *John Bussman;* **Page 99** *J. Sheldon Fisher;* **Page 101** *Thorne Gray;* **Page 104** *Gerald Boucher;* **Page 105** *James Hurley;* **Page 107** *June Knaack, Ohio Historical Society;* **Page 108** *Morristown Foundation;* **Page 109** *Malcolm MacPherson;* **Page 113** *Perron Studio, Charles Thompson;* **Page 118** *Weare Junior Historical Society;* **Page 119** *Debbie and Mike Gill, Hoosick Falls Area Senior Center;* **Page 123** *APPALSHOP;* **Page 124** *Pioneer America Society;* **Page 125** *Suzanne Raikin Mintz;* **Page 126** *Mrs Sandra Weinberg;* **Page 127** *Joe Liles;* **Page 158** *Cassell's Book of Sports and Pastimes;* **Page 159** *A. DeCosmos Daguerrean Studio;* **Page 163** *California Historical Society;* **Page 169** *Sure Shot Photo Archives, Berkeley;* **Page 172** *Jamie Jobb.*

DIRECTORY OF HOMETOWN HISTORY PROJECTS

This is a list of all the hometown history projects we knew about at the time this book was sent to the publisher. It is by no means complete. Projects marked with an asterisk (*) are the ones that are included in the first part of the book. (See the Table of Contents.)

ALABAMA

Ashland
Library in wood community hut building

***Bucksville**
Tannehill State Park

Tuscaloosa
Saving "The Dismals"

Tuscumbia
Restoration of Ivy Green, Helen Keller's Birthplace

ALASKA

Anchorage
State arts program

ARIZONA

Douglas
Mexico-America Two Flags Festival

Tolleson
19th century railroad station

***Tucson**
Preservation of Barrio district

ARKANSAS

Alleene
100 year old log house

***Emmett**
Public Archaeology

Fayetteville
Mountain View Cultural Center

Helena
Restoration of landmarks

Little Rock
Historic Preservation Program

CALIFORNIA

Anaheim
Converting abandoned school building into cultural center

Arroyo Grande
Renovation of historic "hoosegow"

Benicia
Southern Pacific Depot

***Carmichael**
School house

Cazadero
Fort Ross Elementary School

Cucamonga
Alta Loma (Ioamosa) railroad station

***Cucamonga**
John Rains House

Dutch Flat
Mining town preservation

***Fremont**
Shinn House and grounds

Freshwater
1884 Schoolhouse

Fullerton
50 year old Muckenthaler mansion and grounds

Garden Grove
Stanley House Museum

Hanford
Hanford-Carnegie Museum

Hayfork
Schoolhouse

***Hayward**
Meek House

***Huntington Beach**
Oral History project

***Kenwood**
Railroad station

***La Grange**
Gold dredge museum

Livermore
Old artillery armory re-use; Art-In-Action festival

Los Banos
Railroad station

Madera
Court House and clock

Mariposa County
Fremont's Fort in Bear Valley

Martinez
Los Californianos Society

National City
Granger Music Hall

Newark
First school building

Oakland
Cameron-Stanford House

Oakland
Hellman Park-Dunsmuir House

Pleasanton
St. Raymond's Church

Pomona
First brick house

Redding
Eureka schoolhouse in Shasta County

Reedley
Oldest redwood tree park

Rialto
Adobe building; museum in old church

Riverside
Mission Inn (1878)

San Carlos
1929 first church in area

San Francisco
Western Addition oral history project

San Jose
Oldest mining community in California

San Luis Obispo
Agricultural Education building at Cal Poly (1906)

***San Luis Obispo**
Construction of Mission Plaza

***San Rafael**
Dixie Schoolhouse

San Rafael
People's Archaeology—Miwok Indian Preserve of Marin

Santa Cruz
City buildings re-use; Cooper House

***Santa Susana**
Mountain Park Development

Saratoga
Community garden/farm

Sonoma
Town plaza beautification

***Sun Valley**
Native plant garden/nursery

Torrance
Torrance Craftsmen's Guild

Tujunga
1913 Bolton Hall

Upland
Foothill Symphony Chorale

Winterland
Preservation of historic stone dance hall

***Woodland**
Opera House restoration

Yreka
Historical district

COLORADO

***Buena Vista**
Park Chapel

Colorado Springs
Van Briggle Pond

Crested Butte
Photo search and tape oral history program

Fairplay
1860 buildings

Ignacio
Huck Finn Pond

Springfield
Santa Fe Trail museum

Strasburg
Museum to celebrate "first truly continuous chain of railroads across the country from the Atlantic to the Pacific."

CONNECTICUT

***Gaylordsville**
Merwinsville Hotel

Harwinton
First district schoolhouse

Hebron
Methodist Meeting House on town green

Waterford
Schoolhouse

Windsor
Nature preserve

DISTRICT OF COLUMBIA

Washington
Charles Town spring house

FLORIDA

Coral Gables
Landmark preservation

Gainesville
Stephen Foster Memorial Gardens at White Springs

GEORGIA

***Blakely**
Traditional crafts program

***Lumpkin**
Westville Historic Handcrafts

***Social Circle**
Town development program

Sylvania
Refurbish old building for county museum

IDAHO

Jones County
"Uncle Frank's" Living Historical Peach Farm

ILLINOIS

Carbondale
Southern Illinois Folk Festival

Downers Grove
Downtown revitalization

Downs
100 year old log cabin

Elmhurst
Landmark preservation

Enfield
Enfield Acadamy restoration

Galena
Save Turner Hall Society

***Mound City**
Restoration of railroad depot, Naval hospital & Navy yard

Oakland
Landmarks, Inc., restoring old Pennsylvania Railroad depot

Quincy
Adams Landing Pioneer Village; Quincy Indian Museum

Rossville
Chapel restoration

Rushville
PRIDE: Promote Rushville's Image, Design & Environment

Schaumburg
125 year old Lutheran Church

Shabbona
1899 Railroad depot

Shawneetown
Landmarks in Old Shawneetown

St. Charles
1851 Catholic Church

***Warren**
Die Alte Kaserei Cheese Wagon

INDIANA

Athens
95 year old brick schoolhouse

Battle Ground
Hand-operated blacksmith equipment operation

Clinton
Preservation of town character; "Coal Museum" in depot

Fort Wayne
Art Museum

Gosport
Civic League

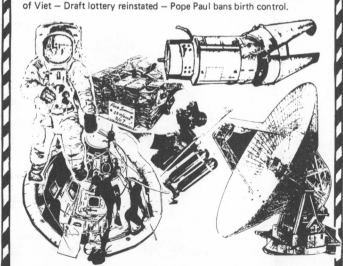

1968 ⊙ 1969

Men on the moon: Armstrong, Aldrin establish Tranquility Base — Turmoil on earth: Tet offensive heats up Viet war — King, RFK assassinated — North Koreans sieze Pueblo — 99 lost in nuclear sub Scorpion mishap — LBJ refuses to run for reelection — 250,000 march in Moratorium Day war protest in DC — Student riots at Columbia; France — SALT talks begin in Helsinki — Viet talks begin in Paris — First 25,000 troops pulled out of Viet — Draft lottery reinstated — Pope Paul bans birth control.

Lafayette
Tippecanoe Battlefield Area study

*Madison
Historic Hoosier Hills Handcraft & Antique Guild

New Albany
1814 house repaired for school children tours

North Manchester
100 year old covered bridge

*Spencer
Robinson House

Tippecanoe County
Fort Quiatenon and grounds

IOWA

*Bentonsport
House Museum

*Bonaparte
Town restoration

*Boone
Hickory Grove schoolhouse; Kate Shelley homesite

Creston
Burlington Northern train building

Decorah
Stone schoolhouse

Laurens
Theater group using old Rock Island Depot as theater

Sioux City
Old Central High School

Swea City
Celebration of Swedish heritage

Van Wert
Brick church

KANSAS

Colwich
Train depot

Dodge City
Crafts Center: Western Kansas Community Services Consortium

Newton
Victorian Warkentin House

*Oberlin
Last Indian Raid in Kansas Museum; Sappa Valley Arts Club

*Paxico
Snokomo Schoolhouse

*Russell Springs
Court House preservation

*Sabetha
Schoolhouse

Summerfield
1862 St. Bridget's Church

KENTUCKY

Covington
1902 Carnegie-built library

1970 ○ 1971

Earth Day: thousands demonstrate against pollution — "Chicago 7" innocent in conspiracy case — Medina acquitted, Calley guilty in My Lai trials — Vote OKd for 18 year olds — Alcatraz Indians ousted — Angela Davis charged in Marin Courthouse shootout — Nixon sends troops to Cambodia — National Guard kills four students at Kent State — Pentagon Papers released — Amtrak: federal passenger rail system in operation — Apollo 14-15: four more men on moon — 43 die in prison riot at Attica, NY.

Harrodsburg
"Old Mud Meeting House" (Dutch Reformed Church); 19th century graveyard.

Jackson
Grassroots Craftsmen of the Appalachian Mountains, Inc.

*Knox County
Oral history program; crafts program

Middletown
Landscaping & historic homes

Pikeville
Pike County Museum

*Whitesburg
Appalachian Film Workshop

LOUISIANA

Baton Rouge
Port Hudson Battlefield site

Elton
Coushatta Tribe center

*New Orleans
U.S. Mint restoration

MAINE

*Buckfield
Old Church on the Hill

Dresden
Planning central Village Green

North Jay
House restoration

North Windham
Bodge House

Portland
Waterfront restoration; living 19th cent. maritime museum

*Rockport
Opera House

Wiscasset
Society for Preservation of Old Mills

MARYLAND

*Annapolis
Town preservation

*Frederick
Children's Museum

*Wye Mills
Grist mill restoration

MASSACHUSETTS

*Arlington
Picture frame manufactory

Boston
"Grandma's Attic" children's museum

Boston
Preservation of Crown & Eagle mills in Uxbridge

Brookline
Crafts teaching program

Lanesborough
1836 St. Luke's stone church

*Lincoln
People's Archaeology

Nabnasset
Town program

New Bedford
1861 Civil War Fort Taber

North Attleboro
1850 Adamsdale Schoolhouse

Norton
Historic schoolhouse

Petersham
1830 A. Brooks law office

Plymouth
1799 Court House Museum

Plymouth
Town Brook Project

South Dartmouth
Colonel Green's Estate; stone Gobell Building

Stockbridge
Citizen's Hall

Wayland
Judge Mellon law office

Wrentham
Tricentennial celebration

MICHIGAN

Grand Haven
100 year old Grand Trunk depot

Lake City
Celebration of July 4th and Military Muster

Manton
Transformation of old water works building into museum

Ortonville
Grist mill

Pelkie
Small town beautification

Sault Ste Marie
County Landmarks

Waterford
Expansion of Timberland Nature Sanctuary

MINNESOTA

Annandale
Soo Line depot renovation

Edina
Schoolhouse

*Prairie Island
Pipestone carving; preservation of Dakota Indian traditions

*Shakopee
Minnesota Valley River Project

St. Peter
Victorian gothic 1871 cottage

Winona
Church museum

MISSISSIPPI

Canton
1850 Jail

Natchez
"King's Tavern"—the oldest house in Mississippi

MISSOURI

*Bethel
Bethel Colony restoration

Callao
County Museum

Mexico
Civil War cemetery

North Kansas City
Town festival

*Warrensburg
Court House restoration

MONTANA

Butte
65 acre Columbia Gardens

Butte
Replica of old open street car

*Fort Benton
Community Improvement Program

Missoula
Western Montana Ghost Town Preservation Society

Sidney
Moving & restoring 1880 log cabin stage coach stop

Sidney
Museum and library

Stevensville
Mission Church & drug store

NEBRASKA

Beaver City
George Norris home

Brownville
Old home preservation

Gering
Gering Museum

Omaha
Community development work—Northern Natural Gas

Rulo
Landmark preservation & town improvement

NEW HAMPSHIRE

*Canterbury
Shaker Museum

Concord
Franklin Pierce's home; The Pierce Brigade

Dorchester
Bicentennial celebration

*Francestown
Old Meeting House

Harrisville
Town crafts program

*Laconia
Saving Belknap and Seeburg-Busiel Mills

Lake Winnipesaukee
"Postmaster of the Lake"

*Littleton
Opera House

*Mt. Washington
Cog railway restoration

*Weare
Junior Historical Society

NEW JERSEY

*Burlington
Gingerbread house

Camden
1726 Pomona Hall

Camden
Griffith Morgan House

Matawan
Schoolhouse museum

NEW MEXICO

*Mesilla
Fountain Theater

Tierra Amarilla
La Cooperative y La Clinica

NEW YORK

*Baldwinsville
Trade Guild Craft Trailer

Barneveld
1809 Unitarian Church

Big Flats
Town history program

Brewerton
People's Archaeology

*Brooklyn
People's Archaeology—Weeksville program

*Busti
Mill restoration by 4-H Club

*Canandaigua
Granger Homestead

*Cazenovia
Railroad station

Cold Spring on Hudson
People's Archaeology

Crown Point
Family Museum & Recreational area

*Delhi
Rural Craft Guild

Earlville
Opera House Restoration

*East Durham
Schoolhouse museum

East Islip
Taped oral history

*Fishers
Valentown Museum

Florida
Synechia Arts Center

Greenwich
Mill preservation

189

Groton
Graveyard preservation

*High Falls
DePuy Canal Tavern

Holmes
People's Archaeology—old
cemetery restoration

*Hoosick Falls
"Tapes Tell Traditions"

Ironville
Heritage Day pageant

Ithaca
Historical cable TV shows

Letchworth
State park summer program

*Little Falls
Bank restoration

*Morristown
Craft program

Naples
Renovation of grain storage mill

Ogdensburg
Documentary filmmaking

Olean
Bolivar Oil Museum

Oneonta
Upper Catskill Community
Council of the Arts

Ontario
Slide documentary of town

Oyster Bay
Oral history project

Penn Yan
Greek Revival mansion restoration on Keuka Lake

Port Henry
Community Development

*Pultneyville
Gates Hall restoration; Burnt
Over District Society for the
Performing Arts

Rensselaerville
Mill restoration

*Rhinebeck
Town preservation; Beekman
Arms Hotel

*Rockland County
Crafts program

Syracuse
Arts Workshop

*Tivoli
Preservation of old crafts, skills
and traditions

Warrensburg
North Country Cultural Center

Watkins Glen
Community cultural center

Westchester County
Collecting underground railroad
stories—oral history project

Williamson
Wayne County Choral Society;
1825 Gates Hall preservation

*Williamsville
Senior Citizens history projects

Wyoming
Pioneer crafts classes in converted carriage house

Yonkers
1789 church restoration

NORTH CAROLINA

Albemarle
Conversion of old library

Hudson
Landscaping and painting
old depot

Salisbury
Carson House

*Wadesboro
Lumbee and Friends, traditional
singing group

NORTH DAKOTA

Fort Mandan
Lewis and Clark landmarks
and Fort preservation

Inkster
Log cabin project

OHIO

Alliance
Re-use of wagon trains

*Carrolton
Algonquin Mill

Chesterland
Schoolhouse on 5 acres of land;
120 year old Methodist Church

Gambier
Mid-1800s stone chapel

Greenfield
Town project

Hillsboro
Opera House

Hiram
Identification and restoration
of pre-Civil War houses

Lebanon
Freight station

Lisbon
Grist mill; covered bridge, log
schoolhouse & log cabin

Mantua
1840 Church

Martins Ferry
Pioneer artifacts museum

Millersburg
Community park; restoration
of old covered bridge

Mt. Hope
Amish traditional buggymaker

North Lima
Church and park project

Novelty
1818 church and cemetery

Portsmouth
Boneyfiddle historic district

*Wellington
Community Museum

*Zoar
Researching old crafts

OKLAHOMA

Heavener
Artesian well restoration

OREGON

Klamath Falls
Improvement festival

*Molalla
Dibble & Von der Ahe Houses

Springfield
Walterville Museum

Union
Town restoration starting
with 1898 First National Bank

PENNSYLVANIA

Bangor
Schoolhouse restoration

*Beaver County
Spring house

Camp Hill
Landmark preservation—Friends
of Peace Church

Chambersburg
Jail complex restoration

*Delaware County
Caleb Pusey House

Greenville
Riverside Park Amphitheater

*Indiana
People's Archaeology

Menges Mills
Colonial Valley Park; mill
restoration

Middletown
Preservation of old homes

Monaca
Blacksmith shop

Oley
Preservation of early American
architecture

Saltsburg
1840 farmhouse

*Stroudsburg
Living Farm operation

Titusville
200 year old schoolhouse

Waterford
Old Eagle Hotel

Waynesburg
Greene Academy of Art

Windber
Town museum

RHODE ISLAND

Pawtucket
The Ferry Art Center

Providence
Middle House, the 1819 addition to Moses Brown School

SOUTH CAROLINA

Charleston
Ansonborough residential area

Jamestown
Birthplace of Congressman
Rivers; Hell Hole Swamp festival

Summerville
Town gardens

SOUTH DAKOTA

Colome
Historical sites

TENNESSEE

Knoxville
Preservation of Jonesboro,
oldest town in Tennessee

Richard
Wyman County Choral Society

TEXAS

*Cuero
Town renovation

Dallas
Early settlers' homesites at
Ivanhoe

*Decatur
Junior College Restoration

*Fredericksburg
Traditional foods and crafts

Galveston
Arts academy

*Luckenbach
Old town preservation

Panhandle
Building restoration; Savar
House Museum

Roma
"Old town Roma," architectural restoration

San Antonio
Belgian convent restoration

Schulenberg
1800 iron bridge

Taylor
Independence Days Arts &
Crafts Show

*Ysleta
Mission restoration; Tigua
Indian cultural center

VERMONT

Barre
Thwing Mill

Hardwick
Town park, bridge restoration

Wells River
Historical village

VIRGINIA

Accomac
1819 building

Bacova
Bacova Chapel

*Falls Church
Pioneer America Society

*Fincastle
Town architecture preservation

Fredericksburg
John Paul Jones' home

Hopewell
18th century Weston Manor

Lynchburg
1905 Opera House

*Millford
Grist mill restoration

*Pocahontas
Town restoration

*Roland
Bull Run Mountain acreage
preservation & central house

WASHINGTON

Black Diamond
1800s confectionary

Port Angeles
Senior citizens group activities
in oral history

Sedro Wolley
Schoolhouse restoration

Spokane
Fort Wright Museum; "Spokane
Falls Patchwork Factory"

Vancouver
Marshall House

WEST VIRGINIA

Harper's Ferry
Historic town & national park

Omar
Boy Schout Hall re-use

Pipestem
Appalachian South Folklife
Center

Salem
Log cabin reconstruction

WISCONSIN

*Beloit
Daisy W. Chapin Schoolhouse

Eau Claire
Building a museum

Green Bay
Rural country church

Lake Geneva
Webster Home

Menomonie
Mabel Tainter Memorial
Building

Oak Creek
Crafts center in City Hall

1972 ⊙ 1973

U.S. backs out of Vietnam War—Nixon visits Red China, Russia; re-elected in landslide to "four more years"—J. Edgar Hoover, Truman, LBJ pass away—George Wallace crippled in assassination attempt—Chaplin returns to Hollywood—Apollo 17 closes U.S. manned moon walk series—Skylab space station points NASA back toward earth—Mariner 9 unlocks surface secrets of Mars—Black Mesa power dispute heats up—Indians raid BIA headquarters—DDT banned—Congress OKs 10-year phase-in of metric system.

Warning: The Surgeon General Has Determined That Cigarette Smoking Is Dangerous to Your Health.

POSTSCRIPT

History, it turns out, is what we make it. Perhaps that is the principal message of this book -- as seen in the actions of all the people whose work is represented on the preceeding pages. Each of them has found a way to become personally responsible for a small piece of the history of America. And though this is seldom put into words, each has reclaimed his own roots in the bargain.

The strength and power of many people at work to save the history of the land is beginning to make itself felt. It is both a social process, and at the same time, a deeply personal one. That is the secret of its strength. Its significance, on a large scale, can't be tested. But its importance in the lives of individuals and communities is unquestionable.

If you would like to help, turn the page.

SUPPORT THE AMERICA THE BEAUTIFUL FUND

As the number of hometown history projects grows, the demand for recognition and assistance increases. The America the Beautiful Fund needs your support in order to give the national recognition that helps local projects on their way. If this book has personal meaning for you, send $5, or whatever you can afford, to help the Fund help your neighbors. Do it now. All contributions are tax-deductible.

START A PROJECT

of your own, or join one that's already going. There isn't a community in America that is without its share of history. Look around.

SEND US INFORMATION

If your project isn't in this book, it may be because we don't know about it yet. We're planning a second book--to celebrate the Bicentennial of the American Revolution. Send us the story of your project, with as much visual information (photos, drawings, publicity samples) as possible. We'll see that it is considered for the next book.

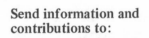

Send information and contributions to:

The America the Beautiful Fund
Shoreham Building
Washington, D. C. 20005